Writing the Apocalypse

Writing the Apocalypse

Historical Vision
in Contemporary U.S. and
Latin American Fiction

LOIS PARKINSON ZAMORA

University of Houston

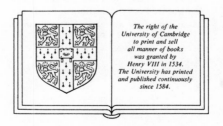

The right of the
University of Cambridge
to print and sell
all manner of books
was granted by
Henry VIII in 1534.
The University has printed
and published continuously
since 1584.

CAMBRIDGE UNIVERSITY PRESS

Cambridge

New York   Port Chester   Melbourne   Sydney

Published by the Press Syndicate of the University of Cambridge
The Pitt Building, Trumpington Street, Cambridge CB2 1RP
40 West 20th Street, New York, NY 10011, USA
10 Stamford Road, Oakleigh, Melbourne 3166, Australia

First published 1989
Reprinted 1990

Printed in the United States of America

Library of Congress Cataloging-in-Publication Data
Zamora, Lois Parkinson.
Writing the apocalypse: historical vision in contemporary U.S.
and Latin American fiction / Lois Parkinson Zamora.
p.   cm.
Bibliography: p.
Includes index.
ISBN 0-521-36223-7
1. Spanish American fiction – 20th century – History and criticism.
2. American fiction – 20th century – History and criticism.
3. Historical fiction, Spanish American – History and criticism.
4. Historical fiction. American – History and criticism.   I. Title.
PQ7082.N7236 1988
863 – DC19   88 – 10947   CIP

British Library Cataloguing in Publication Data
Zamora, Lois Parkinson
Writing the apocalypse: historical vision
in contemporary U.S. and Latin American fiction.
1. Fiction in English.   American writers,
1945 – Critical studies   2. Fiction in
Spanish. Latin American writers. 1945 –
Critical studies.   3. Fiction in Portuguese.
Brazilian writers, 1922 – Critical studies
I. Title
813'.54'.09

ISBN 0-521-36223-7 hardback

For Steve, of course

And besides, the last word is not said – probably shall never be said. Are not our lives too short for that full utterance which through all our stammerings is of course our only and abiding intention? I have given up expecting those last words, whose ring, if they could only be pronounced, would shake both heaven and earth.

Lord Jim, Joseph Conrad

CONTENTS

ACKNOWLEDGMENTS

I WANT TO THANK a number of friends, colleagues, relatives, and students for their help and encouragement: Robert Alter, Donald Barthelme, John D. Bernard, Susan Bielstein, Richard and Janet Caldwell, Lee Dowling, Ted L. Estess, Carlos Fuentes, Dan Garver, Richard Howard, William B. Hunter, Karen Kovacs, David Lazar, Quealy Lewis, Cynthia Macdonald, Guillermo Margadant, Robert and Amy Parkinson, Emilio Rabasa, José Saldívar, and Camille and Peter Zamora. To Wendy B. Faris and Stephen Zamora, for their careful critical reading of my manuscript and for their insights, I am especially grateful. The National Endowment for the Humanities and the American Council of Learned Societies provided me with grants to advance the work of this study, and the University of Houston paid for the preparation of the manuscript. This institutional encouragement came at just the right moments.

I would also like to thank the following journals for permission to reprint, in revised form, portions of my previously published articles: "Voyeur/Voyant: Julio Cortázar's Spatial Esthetic," *Mosaic,* 14, iv(1981), 45–68; "The End of Innocence: Myth and Narrative Structure in Faulkner's *Absalom, Absalom!* and García Márquez's *Cien años de soledad,*" *Hispanic Journal,* 4, i(1982), 23–40; "Movement and Stasis, Film and Photo: Temporal Structures in the Recent Fiction of Julio Cortázar, *The Review of Contemporary Fiction,* 3, iii(1983), 51–71; "Carlos Fuentes's *Terra Nostra* and Giambattista Vico's *The New Science,*" forthcoming in *The Review of Contemporary Fiction.*

1

INTRODUCTION:
THE APOCALYPTIC VISION
AND FICTIONS OF HISTORICAL DESIRE

We are designed to want: with nothing to want, we are like windmills in a world without wind.

The Aristos, John Fowles

A S THE YEAR 2000 APPROACHES and we become accustomed to thinking of crisis in global terms, references to apocalypse seem to be increasing steadily, both in frequency and volume. Our modern sense of apocalypse is less religious than historical: The word is used again and again to refer to the events of recent history, whether nuclear or ecological or demographic, which suggest all too clearly our ample capacities for self-destruction. The end of this millennium has displaced 1984 as a focus of speculation, and apocalypse is in vogue. However, we should remind ourselves that visions of apocalypse have in fact long been a significant source of inspiration for literary and visual art.

Since its establishment as a literary genre in the century or so preceding the birth of Christ, apocalypse has held a special fascination for artists, in part because of its arresting imagery and powerful poetry, in part because of pride of place. It is, after all, ostensibly God's last word on his creation. The Revelation of St. John, by many judgments the most complete and the finest of traditional apocalyptic texts, occupies the final place in the Christian canon, as if to reinforce by position the authority of its summarizing intent. Apocalyptic visions, particularly John's, began to inspire a significant body of imaginative literature and visual art in the later Middle Ages, and have continued to do so, variously and abundantly. (There is some irony in this, given the difficulties and delays which testamentary apocalypse generally encountered before being accepted into the canon – integrated belatedly, as if grudgingly, because of its subversive nature.[1]) Though Revelation announces itself as the definitive reading of history, its innumerable literary and pictorial interpretations seem to mock the very notion of a definitive reading.[2] It is, in short, a text which has directly or indirectly engendered and enriched other texts, including the novels I will be discussing here.

In the second part of my introduction, I will review in some detail the conventions of biblical apocalypse and their implications for contemporary novelistic narration. Here at the outset, a brief summary of apocalyptic elements will suffice to suggest the historical and narrative concerns of this mythic mode. In both the canonic Hebrew apocalyptic texts (Ezekiel, Daniel, Zechariah) and the Christian apocalypses (the thirteenth chapter of Mark, the twenty-fourth chapter of Matthew, the Second Epistle of Peter, the Revelation of John), the end of the world is described from the point of view of a narrator who is radically opposed to existing spiritual and political practices. Whether Jew or early Christian, his narrative reflects not only his opposition to existing practices but also his political powerlessness to change them. His is a subversive vision: He is outside the cultural and political mainstream (in John's case, literally in exile on the Greek island of Patmos), awaiting God's intervention in human history, when the corrupt world of the present will be supplanted by a new and transcendent realm. From a point ostensibly beyond the end of time, the apocalyptist surveys the whole of human history, focusing on its cataclysmic end. For him, the future is past: He states God's plan for the completion of history, alternately in the prophetic future, then as accomplished fact.

Preceding the end, there will be upheavals which in the Book of Revelation include the turbulent reign of the Antichrist, the Second Coming of Christ, the consequent cosmic battle of Armageddon, a thousand-year earthly reign of Christ, a last loosing of Satan, the Last Judgment, and the appearance of "the holy city, the new Jerusalem, coming down from God out of heaven, prepared as a bride for her husband" (Rev. 21:2). So catastrophe is balanced against millennium, desolation against fecundity, God's wrath against his mercy. Because the readers of apocalyptic texts associate themselves with those who will be saved by God at the end of time, the plagues and torments which the apocalyptist describes are a source of consolation rather than dismay. The series of historical disasters projected by the fantastical images of the apocalyptist represent God's vengeance on his (and his people's) enemies. Thus, apocalypse is not merely a vision of doom: For its original audience it was, on the contrary, a luminous vision of the fulfillment of God's promise of justice and communal salvation.

My subject is not biblical apocalypse per se but rather the literary uses of apocalypse in selected works of fiction by contemporary U.S. and Latin American writers. I will be discussing the historical consciousness and the mythic vision of six writers and, more particularly, the relationship of their visions of historical ends to their narrative endings. I will argue that their self-conscious use of the imagery and narrative forms of biblical apocalypse affects this relationship between ends and endings, and I will be comparing their work in terms of their various uses of that biblical mode. These writers do not always use apocalyptic modes without question or criticism: If Gabriel García Márquez, Julio Cortázar, and Walker Percy accept and incorporate the forms of biblical apocalypse into their fiction, Thomas Pynchon, John Barth, and Carlos Fuentes invoke those forms in order to modify or reject them. Thus the fiction I will discuss may define its historical and narrative perspectives by explicitly departing from the forms of apocalypse, as well as by integrating them into its structure. In either case, the work of these writers embodies the suspicions of apocalypse that pervade our times.

Most of us do not conceive of time as it is presented in biblical apocalyptic narrative, nor do the novelists whose work I will discuss take literally its metaphoric history. Nevertheless, biblical formulae and images are woven into the fabric of the cultures and languages of the United States and Latin America, and control in essential ways the articulation of our thinking. The Americas have inherited from Judeo-Christian thought its philosophy of history, and though modern secular conceptions of history do not posit a finite beginning or end to time (in fact, quite the opposite), we share the need of the apocalyptist to interpret and assign significance to our experience of history.[3] In Latin America, the reception and assimilation of this European biblical heritage has no doubt been conditioned by instances of indigenous apocalyptic historicism: Historians and anthropologists have identified points of congruence in the apocalyptic expectations of European and indigenous historical thinking, especially among groups in Brazil and Peru, despite otherwise vastly different conceptions of temporal movement.[4] As research continues, more extensive literary critical discussions of the multiple sources of apocalypticism in Latin American fiction will certainly be called for. In this study, I will discuss non-European strains of apocalypticism in Carlos Fuentes's work but, in general, my critical concern is with the biblical sources of apocalyptic mythology in contemporary fiction.

The use of apocalyptic structures and images in contemporary U.S. and Latin American fiction is likely to place the literary discussion of human time somewhere between myth and history, an observation that I will develop in my discussion of *One Hundred Years of Solitude* and *Absalom, Absalom!* in the next chapter. The apocalyptist describes the broad strokes of history by which human beings are moved. Novelists who employ the images and narrative perspectives of apocalypse are likely, therefore, to focus less on the psychological interaction of their characters than on the complex historical and/or cosmic forces in whose cross-currents those characters are caught. Their awareness of the historical forces conditioning and constraining individual existence suggests a dissenting perspective: Novelists who use apocalyptic elements, like the biblical apocalyptists, are often critical of present political, social, spiritual practices, and their fiction entertains the means to oppose and overcome them. They are also concerned to create comprehensive fictions of historical order, universal dramas that moralize judgments of isolated events and individual behavior. And they will often address, in their own narrative structures, the means by which to narrate history, a question as essential to apocalypse as the nature of history itself.

The writers whom I will discuss here correspond in a variety of ways to these generalizations. They use the historical vision and narrative forms of apocalypse to explore the relationship of the individual, the community, and the novel itself to the processes of history. In some cases, they are less explicitly interested in biblical apocalypse than in their own visions of the end of the world. But generally, there is a strong metaphoric association in their novels between their own apocalyptic visions and the conventions of the biblical mode. I will, therefore, be proposing implicitly throughout my study that apocalypse functions in these novels as what Mikhail Bakhtin has called the chronotope, that "élément privilegié" of the literary work which is "la condensation et la concrétisation des indices du temps – temps de la vie humaine, temps historique, dans différents secteurs de l'espace."[5] I will argue that apocalypse is the chronotope of these novels, their organizing principle and their figurative center. It is what makes time visible in them and determines their relation to historical reality.

I.

I will begin to make these generalizations specific and relevant with a discussion of the fiction of Gabriel García Márquez in the chapter which follows. García Márquez employs the dissenting perspective of apocalypse to criticize political and social structures, and the eschatological perspective of apocalypse to comment upon the structure of time. Though his novels differ markedly from one another, they are all meditations on the nature of duration, and the ways in which duration ends. In this chapter, I will propose *Absalom, Absalom!*, by William Faulkner, as a model of this apocalyptic narrative stance. Because Faulkner is universally acknowledged as an important precursor of contemporary Latin American fiction, this initial discussion will provide substantial grounds for my subsequent comparative conclusions.

My third chapter is on the fiction of Thomas Pynchon. Like the biblical apocalyptists, Pynchon is concerned with death – of individuals, society, the universe. However, his vision is not of a cataclysmic end, but of gradual loss and disintegration. Pynchon is related to the apocalyptic tradition not by his use of the conventional sense and structure of apocalypse, but by his reaction against them: He explicitly rejects an apocalyptic narrative perspective for one based on the thermodynamic concept of entropy. I juxtapose this chapter on Pynchon's fiction to my discussion of García Márquez's novels because of the striking contrast between these authors. Whereas García Márquez's view of time is organic, Pynchon's is mechanical; if García Márquez's precursors are Faulkner and, through Faulkner, the "vitalist" Henri Bergson, Pynchon's are Henry Adams and, through Adams, the physicists and mathematicians Clausius, Kelvin, Bolzmann, Gibbs, Heisenberg. Although both entropy and apocalypse are metaphors, and only metaphors, by which these novelists describe their characters' relationships to the reality of temporal ends, they are nonetheless important metaphors which convey their novelistic conception of human beings in the world. The promise inherent in the apocalyptic vision, the radical transformation of old worlds into new, is absent in the entropic vision: The apocalyptic tension between the anthropomorphic symbols of good and evil collapses in Pynchon's fiction into a formula for the statistical measurement of molecular probability.

Chapters 4 and 5 are also conceived in relation to each other. Julio Cortázar is concerned with the visionary experience of the artist in his early fiction; and with the visionary experience of the political activist in his later work. In both instances, he depicts the inspired transcendence of the ordinary, invoking the myth of apocalypse as a metaphor for his characters' privileged perspective. In contrast, John Barth's fiction does not embody apocalyptic experience, political or artistic, but rather employs what I call an apocalyptic style. Barth says of this style that it "deliberately exhausts (or tries to exhaust) its possibilities and borders upon its own caricature."[6] Barth displays – like Jorge Luis Borges, but for different reasons, which I will explore briefly – an almost obsessive fascination with narrative endings. Paradoxically, this fascination with endings often manifests itself in elaborate strategies for their subversion or negation. Apocalypse thus becomes for Barth a formal question rather than a philosophical one: Confronted with the baroque realities of the present moment, it is, according to Barth, the "virtuoso," the master of technique, the craftsperson who will be "the chosen remnant of the literary apocalypse." If Barth creates closed narrative endings which send the reader back in circular fashion into the narration, Cortázar creates open narrative structures which multiply potential endings. Both writers present dilemmas which they cannot, and do not want to resolve: They believe neither in answers nor in endings. In their very different ways, each uses the mythic vision and narrative structures of apocalypse to embody this postmodern skepticism about the very possibility of conclusion.

My sixth and seventh chapters discuss the fiction of Walker Percy and Carlos Fuentes. Of the writers whose work I treat in detail in this book,

Percy and Fuentes are the most profoundly versed in philosophies of history, without reference to which no serious discussion of their fiction is possible. For both, a knowledge of mind and a knowledge of culture are based on an understanding of the nature of history.

The avowedly Catholic eschatological point of view in Walker Percy's fiction reflects this author's belief in the original intent of apocalypse as divine revelation. To his orthodox Catholic understanding of apocalypse, Percy adds an existential interpretation based on a number of modern philosophers of history, among them Romano Guardini, Eric Voegelin, and Martin Heidegger. In an essay entitled "Notes for a Novel about the End of the World," Percy expresses his sense of postmodern culture, and the relation of the novel to that culture. The subject of the postmodern novel is a man who has "very nearly come to the end of the line," and the function of this fiction is to avert that end by writing about it.[7] Apocalypse is explicitly invoked in all of Percy's novels, but I will argue that in the Christian existential context of his fiction, the end becomes something present and potential in every moment of his characters' lives. Apocalypse is the symbol and the means of renewal in the present, and the novel, according to Percy, must be the vehicle for this renewal.

Like Percy, Carlos Fuentes is concerned less with an actual end than with an "eternal present" which integrates the past and the future, and which he announces as the subject of his fiction. In *Terra Nostra,* Fuentes's context and concerns are less psychological and metaphysical than Percy's. The larger historical and political patterns of nations are invoked in this monumental investigation of the origins and identities of Mexico, and it is Giambattista Vico whose work provides a complementary structure to apocalyptic historicism. The novel begins in 1999, in the midst of global revolution, but after some thirty pages leaps back into the sixteenth century to what Fuentes calls "the least realized, the most abortive, the most latent and desiring of all histories: that of Spain and Spanish America."[8] Fuentes's novel is a sustained critique of many modes of historical desire. For this reason and others, the title of my chapter on *Terra Nostra* is "Beyond Apocalypse."

My comparative approach will lead me to propose lines running north to south and south to north which may suggest affinity, influence, or the conditions of literary reception. Above all, however, my discussion depends upon the similarities and differences which become apparent when novels from different national and linguistic contexts are juxtaposed, opposed, superimposed. I have chosen to discuss these six novelists in detail because they use the historical vision and narrative forms of apocalypse throughout their work. I will also refer tangentially to a number of other writers who employ apocalyptic imagery or structures in a single novel or story, but I will focus on writers for whom an apocalyptic vision coincides

6

with and repeatedly expresses their most persistent esthetic and philosophical concerns. I will therefore be referring to the evolution of apocalyptic attitudes in each author's work, a critical perspective which may itself approximate the apocalyptic desire for a comprehensive view of history, in this case, the history of the myth in these writers' work.

The virtual absence of women writers from my study would seem to suggest that apocalyptic modes of conceiving history and narration are less attractive to women than to men. Though such a generalization is problematic, it is undeniable that by far the largest part of contemporary apocalyptic fiction is written by men. There are exceptions, among them Flannery O'Connor and possibly Joan Didion. And although Latin American women writers like Elena Poniatowska, Isabel Allende, Luisa Valenzuela write pointed political fictions, their work is not generally characterized by the use of specifically apocalyptic devices. Is it that the militantly destructive elements of the myth of apocalypse contradict what we traditionally consider to be the female impulse to create, nurture, regenerate? Or is it a question of scale? Perhaps the macrocosmic and totalizing political intent of apocalyptic visions is less compelling for most women writers than psychological relations on a more intimate scale? Such hypotheses are easily assailable because they are based on sexual stereotyping, but I entertain them because they may provide at least a partial explanation for the lack of apocalyptic fiction by women. Furthermore, such antiapocalyptic stereotypes are in fact explicitly dramatized by female characters in *One Hundred Years of Solitude* and *The Second Coming*. Carlos Fuentes also engages the decidedly masculine orientation of apocalypse in *Terra Nostra,* not by opposing male and female characters' attitudes toward apocalypse as do García Márquez and Percy, but by integrating apocalyptic visions from mythological sources other than the Judeo-Christian. We will see that these other traditions contain radically different attitudes toward the female role in the cosmic drama of apocalypse, and hence serve to highlight the masculine nature of the Judeo-Christian version of the myth.

My comparative discussion is based on a historical awareness of the shared origins of the United States and Latin America in the mind of Europe, and particularly on an awareness of the apocalyptic aspirations imposed upon the New World by Europeans, beginning with Christopher Columbus. To convey to his royal patrons his conviction that his mission represented the fulfillment of apocalyptic prophecy, Columbus referred in letters and in his diary to passages from Revelation and Isaiah which describe the new heaven and new earth.[9] So he immediately initiated what was to become a perennial imaginative association of America with the promise of apocalyptic historical renewal. It is an association which continues to make itself felt, though often ironically, in the apocalyptic perspectives of the contemporary fiction I will discuss here.

7

In *The Millennial Kingdom of the Franciscans in the New World,* John Leddy Phelan writes that apocalyptic optimism pervaded the Age of Discovery in Spain. Explorers, statesmen, and clergy alike viewed the events of geographical exploration and colonization of America as the fulfillment of the prophecies of Revelation – that is, as necessary prerequisites to the end of the world.[10] Phelan discusses Spain's sense of its messianic historical mission, and the essential role of the New World's territory and inhabitants in that mission. No colonial empire has ever been built upon such an extensive philosophical and theological foundation as that empire the Spaniards created for themselves in the New World, although Phelan notes that a century later, the Puritans settling North America were also impelled by theological visions of a new heaven and new earth. If the Messiah–Emperor myth of the Middle Ages was embraced by Spain and imposed upon the Spanish New World in the sixteenth century, it was Martin Luther's apocalyptic interpretation of the Reformation that was accepted by the Puritans in England and the English New World in the seventeenth century. The possibility of achieving in the future the primal unity that was lost in the past, when Adam and Eve sinned and were separated from God, seemed to inhere in the virgin territory of America.[11]

Not only could the geographical plenitude necessary to the world's end be achieved thanks to the New World, but also the demographic plenitude. The native inhabitants of America were generally understood to be the lost tribes described in Rev. 7:4–9, who were prophesied to reappear before the Last Judgment. Linked to this prophecy was another, found throughout the apocalyptic literature of the time, that the Jews would be converted as the end of the world approached. If the Indians were the lost tribes of Israel, and if they were converted, both prophecies would be fulfilled at once and the kingdom of God might be initiated. Arguments forwarded in support of the Jewish identity of the Indians were that the Indians knew of the universal deluge as well as of a promised savior, ideas both considered to be of Hebraic origin. It was reasoned that Quezalcoatl, the awaited Aztec god, was actually the Messiah that the Jews expected when they rebelled against Roman rule in 66–70 of the Christian era.[12] So the conquest of the Aztec empire immediately began to accrue levels of apocalyptic significance. Phelan notes that the idea of the Jewish descent of the Indians also appealed to the Puritans settling North America: In fact, he asserts, it is on this very point that the theology of Protestantism meets that of Spanish Catholicism during the "Age of Discovery."

For the Puritans in New England in the seventeenth century, the literal interpretation of Revelation located the site of the new heaven and earth in America. The earliest Puritan texts attest to constant attempts to unite apocalyptic theology and American history: The New World is directly associated with the culmination of history.[13] It is, however, a Spanish Franciscan, Gerónimo de Mendieta, who provides perhaps the most articulate expression of the mystical interpretation of America as the necessary prerequisite for God's apocalyptic plan. Mendieta arrived in what is now Mexico in the middle of the sixteenth century, and became one of the great chroniclers of the age. He wrote long interpretations such as those I have mentioned on the role of the Native Americans in bringing history to its culmination, and he, like the Puritans, applied the symbolic historical scheme of Revelation to the specific history of the New World. Referring to the work of conversion, he writes, "God has been calling all the peoples of the earth to hasten to prepare themselves to enter and to enjoy that everlasting feast that will be endless. This vocation of God shall not cease until the number of predestined is reached, which according to the vision of St. John must include all nations, all languages and all peoples."[14] In Mendieta's redundancy – "the everlasting feast that will be endless" – we sense the apocalyptic ardor invested in the colonization and conversion of the New World. And we will see, particularly in Carlos Fuentes's fiction, the dramatized extension of that ardor, an irony set in the very foundations of America: It is humanity's fate to dream of heaven and create hell.

The initial attractions of America were hardly singular, and the apocalyptic potential of the New World was seen not only in spiritual terms but also in material ones. The New Jerusalem envisioned by the Franciscans had its physical analogue in Hispanic America in the golden city of El Dorado. For the majority of laypersons who came to New Spain and for many of the clerics as well, America represented the illusion, almost always false, of wealth. And the Puritans were attracted to North America 100 years later not only by the promise of spiritual renewal but also by the promise of political and institutional freedom. We are reminded to this day of these various attractions and their continuing allure in the motto printed on every dollar bill – *Novus Ordo Seclorum,* A New World Order.

I will explicitly address these early apocalyptic interpretations of America only in Carlos Fuentes's *Terra Nostra* and Walker Percy's *The Second Coming;* however, I consider them to be the implicit point of departure and the basis for my comparative discussion generally, as they are for many of the novelistic attitudes and perspectives that I will explore. I do not attempt here to survey historically the apocalyptic tradition in U.S. and Latin American literature, but rather to suggest the ways in which selected contemporary novels may recognize and perpetuate that tradition.[15] These novels remind us that Americans on both continents have inherited a sense of the eschatological significance of their historical and national destiny.[16] They make us conscious that it is against the initial apocalyptic promise of America that we often measure our present and assess our future.

II.

Before I pursue the apocalyptic elements in particular works of fiction, I want to trace the myth back to its historical and scriptural origins. I will begin by reiterating what apocalypse is *not,* so as to dispense quickly with a simplistic but common usage of the word. Apocalypse is *not* merely a synonym for disaster or cataclysm or chaos. It is, in fact, a synonym for "revelation," and if the Judeo-Christian revelation of the end of history includes – indeed, catalogues – disasters, it also envisions a millennial order which represents the potential antithesis to the undeniable abuses of human history. While it is true that an acute sense of temporal disruption and disequilibrium is the source of, and is always integral to, apocalyptic thinking and narration, so is the conviction that historical crisis will have the cleansing effect of radical renewal. In Revelation, John, exiled by the authority of the Roman Empire, responds to God's injunction to "Write the things which thou hast seen, the things which are, and the things which shall be hereafter" (Rev. 1:19). "The things which are" require of the disenfranchised narrator a lurid description of evil in the world; however, his description of "the things which shall be hereafter" is quite something else. It is John's purpose, as it is the purpose of the Hebrew apocalyptists in Isaiah and Daniel and numerous other pseudepigraphic apocalyptic texts, [17] to convey God's promise that justice will shortly prevail and that those suffering persecution for their religious beliefs will be vindicated. We sense the universal and perennial appeal of that promise: "And God shall wipe away all tears from their eyes; and there shall be no more death, neither sorrow, nor crying, neither shall there be any more pain: for the former things are passed away. And he that sat on the throne said, 'Behold, I make all things new'" (Rev. 21:4–5). Apocalypse sets tribulation against triumph and defines suffering in terms of transcendence.

The word itself originally derives from the Greek word *apokálypsis,* to uncover, reveal, disclose (the root is *kalypto,* to cover or conceal, and is familiar to us in the name of the nymph Calypso, who hides Odysseus for seven years.) Apocalypse is eschatological in nature (the root in this case is *eschatos,* furthest or uttermost); it is concerned with final things, with the end of the present age and with the age to follow. (Like apocalypse, the Greek word for truth, *aletheia,* begins with the negative particle: The etymology of both words suggests that essences must be unveiled and deciphered by the perceiving, narrating consciousness.) As a mode of historical thought and a literary form, apocalypse developed out of the Hebrew prophetic tradition in response to a worsening political situation. [18] With the growth of the great empires of Persia, Greece, Rome, and the consequent political powerlessness of the Hebrew people, the contradiction between prophetic ideals and the actual experience of the nation became more and more apparent. The prophet sees the future as arising out of the present and exhorts his listeners to action on the basis of an ideal to be realized in this world; the apocalyptist, on the contrary, sees the future breaking into the present, and this world being replaced by a new world under God's aegis. The apocalyptic vision began increasingly to replace the prophetic vision in the century preceding Christ. Indeed, Christ's immediate appeal may be partially understood in terms of the development of the apocalyptic vision-ary medium: Christ assures first his disciples, then all of his followers, that the end of this world and the beginning of his messianic kingdom are near. That the appeal of this promise continues – literally in fundamentalist Christianity, and figuratively in art and literature – 2,000 years after it was made and despite innumerable falsified predictions of the end, suggests the deep psychological needs to which it responds, as well as the flexibility of interpretation allowed by the form. My point here is that in the historical development of apocalyptic thought one sees the direct relation of the myth of apocalypse to its sociological and political context. The resurgence of apocalyptic modes of thought and expression is a predictable reaction to social disruption and temporal uncertainty, and explains in part its currency in our own popular vocabulary.[19]

The biblical apocalyptist feels himself both inspired and compelled to reveal to his audience what has been revealed to him by God: the divinely predetermined totality of history. He is convinced that the end of time will soon overtake the present; God's Last Judgment will give significance to all that has gone before and justify the suffering of those who have remained faithful to God's word. John's description provides us with some of the most familiar of all biblical images: the seven seals on the book of destiny, broken by Christ for John to witness and describe, including the four horse-men of the apocalypse (war, oppression, famine, and death); the whore of Babylon; the grapes of wrath; the plagues of locusts like horses prepared for battle; the monstrous embodiments of evil, Gog and Magog; the bottomless pit and the lake of fire and brimstone. Space becomes the index of time: The physical world mirrors the historical drama. Earthquakes, floods, falling stars, extinguished sun and moon add to the description of a world swept up in the headlong current of history. These images are of course part of a rich mosaic of allusions to previous apocalyptic texts – to Ezekial, Zechariah, Isaiah. Revelation proposes not only to summarize and encom-pass the total meaning of history but also the total meaning of the sacred scriptures.

The lurid immediacy of apocalyptic imagery, both in Christian and Hebrew texts, is meant by the apocalyptist to convey the power of God's retributive justice. It also conveys, less intentionally but no less clearly, the desperate longing of the narrator for vengeance on his oppressors. This ambivalence of motives, both conscious and unconscious, explains the odd mixture of tones that characterizes apocalyptic description: The apocalyptist is both appalled and enthralled by God's wrath. He catalogues its signs to reassure his audience and himself of God's power to save them from their oppression, and to exhort his audience to maintain their faith even if they must suffer martyrdom. Martyrdom, his readers are meant to understand, is a fate preferable to apostasy, the consequences of which are enthusiastically enumerated by the apocalyptist.

The apocalyptist's description of the punishments to be wreaked on the faithless is balanced by his description of the rewards that await the faithful. The moral dualism of apocalypse is embodied in the metaphoric contraries of Christ and Antichrist, whore and bride, Babylon and the New Jerusalem, this world and the next. Even the numbers which pervade Revelation represent either good or evil. Its arithmythic symbols (as Carlos Fuentes calls his own apocalyptic numerology in *Terra Nostra*) include 666, the number of the beast and symbol of political evil; and three, seven, twelve, 144,000, symbols of wholeness which figure God's intervention in and completion of history.[20] At the end of time, God will judge all people and the faithful will enter a timeless realm of perfection, described metaphorically in Revelation as the New Jerusalem. Here again, this densely coded text reaches back into the visionary scriptural tradition, combining in its culminating description images of human artifice and natural, Edenic perfection. As if in response to God's demand for quantitative definition from Job ("Where wast thou when I laid the foundations of the earth? Who hath laid the measures thereof, if thou knowest? Or who hath stretched the line upon it?"); or Ecclesiasticus's lyrical plaint in the *Apocrypha,* ("The sand of the seas, and the drops of rain, and the days of eternity, who shall number them? The height of the heavens and the breadth of the earth, and the deep, and wisdom, who shall search them out?"); the holy city is described and measured – its pearly gates, its golden streets and walls of jasper, sapphire, amethyst, and more, all laid out in perfect proportion by its divine architect. After beholding the magnificent city, we are ushered into the garden which is at its center. There we discover the river and the tree of life, the original elements of creation described in the second chapter of Genesis. This final complex of symbols from both nature and culture pertains to various important sets of beliefs about ideal times and spaces, promise and fulfillment, immanence and transcendence. So Northrop Frye's definition of myth as "an imitation of actions near or at the conceivable limits of desire" seems particularly apposite.[21] Apocalypse purports to measure and transfigure human longings into matters of eternal value.

The myth of apocalypse is, then, both a model of the conflictual nature of human history and a model of historical desire. This tension between transformation and completion, desire and its satisfaction, has as much to do with fictional form as it does with historical vision. Though a given work of literature may emphasize one side of the myth or the other, when the tension disappears, when the vision is merely optimistic *or* pessimistic, we do not have apocalyptic literature but fantasy. Hence my distinction between mere visions of doom, to which the word apocalypse is commonly misapplied, and the more complex history envisioned in the myth itself. Apocalyptic literature is fundamentally concerned with our human relation to the changing forms of temporal reality, not with static simplifications.

The spiritual realities described by the biblical apocalyptist are given a historical embodiment which is essentially linear. Time becomes the vehicle of divine purpose: It moves teleologically (here the root is *telos,* goal) toward a specified end. The apocalyptist assigns to event after event a place in a pattern of historical relationships that will not repeat itself in the cyclical manner of oriental myth, but that presses steadily toward culmination. The repeated, numbered series of events in Revelation underline this sense of the inexorable movement of history and give to the narration an urgent, even obsessive quality. The seven seals are broken to reveal, one after another, the calamities which God will visit upon the earth; the seventh seal reveals seven angels who are given seven trumpets, which sound forth seven more plagues, after which yet another set of seven, the seven vials of God's wrath, are enumerated. These narrative patterns, when added to the specific temporal and spatial calculations of apocalypse, indicate and also symbolically satisfy the desire of the apocalyptist and his audience for control over the otherwise intractable movement and meaning of history. Apocalyptic narration is offered as the account of how divine word becomes historical fact and, conversely, how historical fact reveals God's eschatological design. We may, therefore, also apply Roland Barthes's definition of myth as a type of speech chosen by history, for biblical apocalypse grows out of, responds to, and describes metaphorically the historical context that surrounds it.[22] The contemporary apocalyptic fictions of García Márquez and Cortázar and Fuentes reflect the political realities of Latin America, as those of Pynchon and Barth and Percy reflect the malaise of contemporary U.S. culture.

The directedness of apocalyptic narration is closely related to narrative plot. Like apocalypse, most plots may be described as a teleology of words and episodes, as comprehensible structures of action that are interrelated in a legible whole.[23] Indeed, with its series of events in metonymic relation and its metaphoric, totalizing ending, apocalypse gives to history a coherence which can only be told, not experienced. It might thus be proposed as the very model of narrative plot, though as we will see in the work of Julio Cortázar and Carlos Fuentes, it does not always inspire novelistic structures that move from beginning to end according to chronological or causal sequence. But of course not all plotted fictions are apocalyptic: Fictions based on the movement of individual consciousness without respect to historical or communal consciousness are *not* apocalyptic in the sense that I intend here. Nor are fictions apocalyptic in my definition which do not self-consciously consider the implications of ends and endings: Apocalyptic fictions address the very nature of finality – historical and narrative – more explicitly and emphatically than most plotted narratives. The biblical apocalyptist proposes nothing less than God's own plot for history – the only plot, he insists, in which by definition end and ending coincide. Contemporary fiction that is informed by an apocalyptic vision will reiterate this emphasis in a variety of ways, and for a variety of reasons, as we will see. Thus, while any narrative text may be said to disclose its full meaning only at its point of closure, apocalyptic narrative makes the conjunction of meaning and ending its theme, both in its expressed understanding of history and in its own narrative procedures. Apocalyptic narrative moves toward an *ending* that contains a particular attitude toward the goals of the narration, and toward an *end* that implies an ideology. Among the novels I will discuss, *One Hundred Years of Solitude* is the most explicit example of this movement, but by no means the only one.

The insistence on the connection between narrative closure and historical disclosure is another source of tension in apocalyptic narrative. The pace and tone of the narration become increasingly urgent as time bears down upon the apocalyptist. In Revelation 10:10, John describes the moment when he eats his own book, as if to symbolize the consuming quality of his text. This desperate eating of the book which he is also attempting to read and write suggests both his need for divine sustenance and his desire to comprehend (literally to incorporate) the terrible finality of his vision. Because in apocalypse the death of the individual and the end of the world by definition coincide, personal and communal social goals become inextricably bound: For the apocalyptist, there is no distinction between history and biography. So he must balance the individual's need to reform against his vision of the communal end, and the finality of God's historical plan against the choices that the individual may yet make within that plan. He literally works against time to assure that it does not end before his vision of history is fully disclosed and digested. In *One Hundred Years of Solitude* and *Absalom, Absalom!*, in *Lancelot* and *Terra Nostra,* we sense the vatic intensity of this rush of time toward its end, and we sense as well the narrative ambivalence toward the end which the text both describes and forestalls.

Biblical apocalypse, it is clear by now, embodies two parallel quests, one for an understanding of history, the other for the means to narrate that understanding. It bequeaths to contemporary fiction a wonderful complex of images of historical process, and also of the act of writing itself. We may speculate that apocalyptic imagery has been perennially suggestive to artists and writers not only because it can be endlessly interpreted but also because it addresses the problem of interpretation itself. The hermeneutic and scribal concerns of the Book of Revelation are suggested by the recurrent images of the power of language: Christ's repeated self-characterization as Alpha and Omega, the beginning and end of the Greek alphabet, conveys the encompassing power of God's word (and the apocalyptic text); the two-edged sword which is alternately held in and issues from Christ's mouth figures the retributive power of God's word (and again, of the apocalyptic text). Indeed, Christ's sword *pre*figures John's stylus as a symbolic instrument of destruction, for it is the authority of language – God's word and its narrative embodiment in the apocalyptic text – that will change the world.

The biblical apocalyptist self-consciously presents himself as both reader and writer, as the narrative medium between God's projection of truth and his reader's reception of that truth. He must decipher the signs of history even as he struggles to create his own encoded version of that history. The conflict between self-promotion and self-deprecation is inherent in this task. He is God's vehicle, disavowing omniscience, yet he often repeats God's wisdom without attribution and presents his own narrative vision from God's point of view beyond the end of time. Hence the narrative tone fluctuates between authority and uncertainty, assertiveness and awe. It would seem that the apocalyptist, by means of his narration, aims alternately to understand and to escape historical reality. Overriding these fluctuations, however, is the sense of community created by the narrator and his audience. The apocalyptist consoles his readers by letting them see, beyond the landscape of catastrophe, the small elect community of those who write and those who read. Again, the power of language is at issue: The shared secrets of the apocalyptic text itself, perhaps as much as what it explicitly describes, afford the means to rise above the banality of evil. In the discussion that follows, Melquiades's coded parchments in *One Hundred Years of Solitude* will provide our clearest novelistic embodiment of this aspect of apocalyptic discourse, but again, not our only one.

Revelation is, then, as much about the capacity of language to conceal as to reveal. John's cryptic imagery and numerology are a response to political necessity. Even as he announces the breaking of God's seven seals, he creates his own metaphoric seals to obscure his seditious predictions and protect himself and his readers. This ambivalence between concealing and revealing is apparent in Revelation, when John is commanded first to seal his text, then to unseal it. [Although John issues the order, "Seal not the sayings of the prophecy of this book: For the time is at hand" (Rev. 22:10), he also warns against tampering with the unsealed book; in any case, his order hardly makes his text less hermetic, if less prescriptively closed.] The apocalyptist's strategies of concealment attest to the sanctified status conceded to the narrative by both author and audience. The tendency to make texts obscure when an elevated degree of truth is desired is familiar in religious ceremonial language, oracular and poetic utterance, specialized academic and professional discourse. In such contexts as these, the perceived significance of the text may grow as the text's accessible linguistic meaning is suppressed, as translation or interpretation is required. As the coded images and numerical patterns of apocalyptic narration proliferate, so does the weight of their significance for those who are initiated into their secrets. Apocalypse thus presents not only a model of historical desire but also of linguistic desire: The apocalyptist's language strains to embody his fiction of historical fulfillment. As we will see, Walker Percy's characters use the erotic imagery of Revelation to express their radical rejection of their cultural and historical situations; it is only in terms of the coincidence of historical and linguistic desire in apocalyptic utterance that their sexual statements may be fully understood.[24]

I have said that apocalyptic narration presents itself as the most conclusive of plots and is, at the same time, the narrative embodiment of ongoing historical yearning after an imagined ideal. In biblical apocalypse, as well as in the contemporary fiction I will discuss, the narrator's eye may be *caught* by the static, ideal realm at the end of the historical upheaval, but it is *held* by the dynamism of the upheaval itself. John's description of the chaotic turmoil of the present is much longer and more compelling than the set piece, the description of the New Jerusalem, which concludes his Revelation. Of course the biblical apocalyptist's nightmare vision of hordes and swarms and blood and beasts may be understood, like the final vision of the jeweled city, to represent an unattainable ideal – that of complete retribution, of wholly satisfying vengeance. But more importantly, the plagues and cataclysms also represent the apocalyptist's metaphoric expression of God's actual engagement in the present time, and suggest the ways in which historical renewal may proceed from historical disaster. Thus, along with the culminating ideal when, according to John, time will cease (Rev. 10:6), we are asked to entertain the endless transformative potential of historical process. At the heart of apocalypse lies the contradictory proposition that we will never be satisfied, that historical transformation will never be definitively resolved.

In fact, this contradiction also inheres in the ending of Revelation. Although the narrative structure of Revelation is decidedly teleological, and its ending appears to express achieved historical desire, there is also the suggestion of continuing transformation in the final image of the New Jerusalem. In *The Great Code: The Bible and Literature,* Northrop Frye discusses this "second or participating apocalypse" of Revelation, saying that in its proposed beginning of a new world beyond the text, the divine–human antithesis will cease to exist, the split of subject and object will no longer limit human vision. This second apocalypse suggests to Frye the way the world will look after ego has disappeared. He concludes that the apocalyptic promise of a new heaven and new earth leads to "the antitype of all antitypes, the real beginning the light and sound of which the first word of the Bible is the type."[25] Again we sense that apocalypse mocks the notion of conclusive ends and endings even as it proposes just that – the conclusive narration of history's end.

Frye's observation suggests the contradiction between the deterministic finality of the apocalyptic agenda and the resistence of apocalyptic narration to such finality. This contradiction may be said to exist in most narrative texts, the endings of which often suggest other events beyond the determined world of the text itself, as in the archetypal fictional conclusion, "And they lived happily ever after." Applying this formulation to apocalyptic narration, we may say that though the apocalyptic narrator's psychological investment is in the "happily ever after," his narrative emphasis is on the "lived" – that is, on time rather than eternity. Revelation builds toward the closure the narrator advertises from the beginning, but his text is not fully or finally determined by it. Despite his desire to intuit (or impose) ultimate patterns of order, the apocalyptic narrator yields to the historical processes of this world, chaotic and inconclusive.

It is on this point that an apocalyptic vision may be distinguished from a utopian vision. Whereas apocalypse is impelled by the historical dialectic between evil and good, and confronts the violence of the present, utopia focuses on a future, perfect world.[26] The utopian ideal is envisioned as an external moral and political regime, whereas the kingdom of God proposed by Christian apocalyptists came to be understood, by the end of the first century, when the Second Coming of Christ failed to occur, as interior and spiritual and hence potentially present, despite its metaphoric spatial projection in the future New Jerusalem. In response to the official acceptance of Christianity by the Roman Empire, Augustine insisted early in the fifth century that Revelation be considered a spiritual allegory; the Catholic Church, by then an official and powerful institution, could hardly hold to earlier subversive dreams of supplanting the existing order with a new earthly paradise. Apocalypse thus came to be read as the outer events of sacred history and also as the inner events that may occur within the soul of every person. This parallel construction of communal and individual destinies is always present in the apocalyptic fiction I will discuss, though greater narrative focus and emphasis on one or the other will suggest important differences in Latin American and U.S. novelistic attitudes and intentions.

Apocalypse must also be distinguished from fictions of desire that envision a return to Eden or a past golden age. Northrop Frye's comment that the ending of Revelation is the "real beginning" of the world described by the first words of Genesis does not imply that it represents a return to Eden, but that it responds to it, encompasses it, supplants it metaphorically. Nostalgia for an idealized past is related to a longing for an idealized future, but the former is based on the undoing of historical experience, the latter on the completing of it. If *innocence* inhabits Eden, it is *virtue* which gains the New Jerusalem. The final image of the New Jerusalem in fact combines innocence and experience: The Edenic river and the tree of life reappear in Revelation, but they are not the same as they were in Genesis, before time began. The tree literally reflects human history, its twelve fruits representing the twelve months of the year, its leaves the healing of the discord which accompanied man's fall into time (Rev. 22:2). There is no question here of returning to prehistory: The ideal is to be realized, not recaptured, at the end of the history. Like the literary plots to which we commit our imaginings, the myth of apocalypse is deeply rooted in the imperfection of historical being.

We arrive, then, at what seems yet another contradictory formulation: Apocalypse is historicized myth, a myth about history.[27] It is both synchronic and diachronic, mediating and resolving the conflicting claims of real historical anguish and the imaginative transcendence of that anguish. This dual character of apocalyptic temporality has particular significance with regard to its Judaic historical and cultural origins. Herbert N. Schneidau, in *Sacred Discontent: The Bible and Western Tradition* (1976), speaks of the Bible as *historicized* prose fiction, arguing that biblical narration self-consciously departs from legend and myth as it strives to suggest the unfathomable quality of historical existence under an inscrutable God. Robert Alter, in *The Art of Biblical Narrative* (1981), observes that among ancient peoples, only Israel chose to cast its sacred national traditions in prose. The rejection of the epic mode in favor of prose fiction was, Alter shows, bound up with the rejection of the polytheistic cults which used the epic; the new narrative form was fashioned by the ancient Hebrew writers for their monotheistic purposes, not the least of which was to express their God's plan for history. In *The Great Code,* Northrop Frye also discusses the Hebrews' departure from the pagan sense of cyclical time to a teleological vision of time, a departure reflected in the large proportion of stories in the Bible. Each of these scholarly treatments of biblical literature thus begins with the essential relation of the Judeo-Christian historical vision to the principal mode of biblical discourse, prose narration.

For the purpose of my own discussion of contemporary fiction, we may think of biblical apocalyptic narration as situated at the crossroads of myth and history. It is mythic in Lévi-Strauss's terms, linking the present with both past and future, presenting an "explanation" of the world that is transhistorical and transcultural.[28] And yet it is also historical by virtue of the biblical tradition of historicized prose and by its subject matter, which is of course the substance and form and meaning of history itself. The contemporary fiction I will discuss negotiates the distance between history and myth in a variety of ways; in the case of the novels of Gabriel García

Márquez and Carlos Fuentes, the collapse of any clear distinction between history and myth may be their most characteristic feature.

III.

I began this introduction by observing that references to apocalyptic imagery have consistently figured in the Western literary tradition since the later Middle Ages. What has *increased* over the past two decades or so is the literary critical attention being paid to apocalypse – to the historical attitudes and narrative strategies it implies. Although myth has always provided images and structural patterns with which to regulate the flux of time, few myths are so explicit in this regard as apocalypse. In his book, *The Sense of an Ending* (1967), Frank Kermode was perhaps the first literary critic to explore this terrain. He argues compellingly that the esthetic and historical order – the wholeness – of the apocalyptic vision is a model of the order created by fictional narration. Considerably before Kermode, however, the philosopher Henri Bergson observed our human desire for fictional endings despite (and also because of) our modern disbelief in the end of history. [29] The historiographer Hayden White has elaborated this paradox in his discussion of "narrativity," arguing for the indispensability of narrative endings to comprehensible historical discourse, and to a moral understanding of culture. [30] And Meyer H. Abrams, in his discussion of the esthetic and philosophical bases of Romantic poetry in *Natural Supernaturalism* (1971), explored a related aspect of apocalypse, the simultaneous reference to the communal history of mankind and the spiritual history of the individual – what he calls the "spiritual eschatology" of the single believer.

Frank Kermode's discussion of apocalypse as an archetypal model of narrative closure established a rich conceptual framework for subsequent ciritical discussion. [31] My contribution to this discussion will lie in my choice of fictional works, and also in my comparative approach. Comparative literary studies involving American literature have tended to run east to west, between Europe and either North or South America. [32] The reasons for the relatively few comparative studies of the literature of the Americas is suggested in the inadequacies of the very terms *North* and *South America*. Though *America* does, after all, apply to the whole hemisphere, the term is rarely used in the United States to refer to anything beyond its own borders. To call Gabriel García Márquez and Julio Cortázar and Carlos Fuentes American writers, while correct, may be confusing. Nor will North American be a useful term in this study, because I do not deal with Canadian fiction at all, and Mexican fiction is not, culturally speaking, North American, but rather Central American. *Inter-American* suggests my comparative intent, but this term may also be misleading, since it is sometimes applied to relations among countries within North or South America, as well as to relations between North and South America. In the following chapters, I will use *Latin American* to refer to the fiction of both Central and South America, but at the risk of being too inclusive, because I do not deal specifically with fiction from all of the countries implied by that term. Even my use of the term *U.S. fiction* is ambiguous in this comparative context, because Mexico is also a "United States" – "Los Estados Unidos de México."

Yet another crucial question of denomination (hence definition) remains. Is there such a thing as "Latin American literature"? Latin America is by no means a cultural unit, and to speak of Latin American literature may convey a misleading sense of an integrated geographical and literary entity. The countries of Latin America differ greatly one from another. Ethnically, some national populations are preponderantly descended from indigenous civilizations, whereas others are almost wholly the product of European settlement. In yet other Latin American countries (Brazil, Colombia, and Cuba, for instance), the African heritage is essential, or (again in Brazil, notably in the region around São Paulo, and in Peru) there are significant populations from the Far East. Beyond these differences of ethnic heritage and composition, there are vast differences in economic and educational and political systems, not to mention differences in language. (Even when the language in question is Spanish, there are significant national and local variations in idiom, accent, syntax.) When we contrast the relative cultural homogeneity of the United States and its status as a single political entity to the many countries and cultures of Latin America, we might conclude that these areas are too asymmetrical for useful literary comparison.

But Latin American countries also *do* share cultural and political features, in both the past and present, and much contemporary Latin American fiction *can* be said to exhibit features that are increasingly recognized as "Latin American" by readers in Latin America and the rest of the world. Pablo Neruda was perhaps the first to give unconditional primacy to the project of defining a Latin American commonality, though the project had existed since the previous century.[33] Each of the writers I discuss here recognizes and participates in this tradition in various ways. García Márquez frequently refers to the role that literature is currently playing in the articulation of a Latin American cultural identity; after the Cuban Revolution, Cortázar explicitly aligned his literary activity with revolutionary politics in all of Latin America; Fuentes refers to himself as "a citizen of Mexico, and a writer from Latin America."[34] Furthermore, contemporary Latin American writers are engaged in an unprecedented literary conversation, reading each other's work with an imaginative energy and responding to it with a narrative continuity that can only emphasize the communal nature of their literary project. In short, these writers are self-consciously engaging, and in some sense also creating, a reality shared by the many countries and cultures of their region.

The reader or critic interested in evolving a comprehensive American literary context must also deal with obvious political and economic and cultural differences between the United States and Latin America. If, as I have argued, contemporary Latin American writers are together defining a shared Latin American reality, then a primary fact of that reality is colonization, first by Europe, then by the United States. The colonization has been both political and cultural, of course. At no time in a long history of intervention in Latin America has the political and military presence of the United States been more damaging than during the past two decades. And the material presence of the United States continues to increase as markets are expanded and exploited in Latin America. How does the U.S. comparatist effectively address this political and cultural appropriation, when her very project – the creation of an integral American literary critical context – may itself seem an appropriation? How can she cite García Márquez's comment about the Hispanization of the United States without seeming to trivialize or justify U.S. cultural and commercial opportunism in Latin America?[35] Indeed, is it valid at all to compare Pynchon and Barth and Percy, writing in the context of late capitalism, to García Márquez, Cortázar, and Fuentes, writing in economic and social situations very different from those of U.S. writers, and for very different reading publics?

There is no simple response to what is understandable (and necessary) skepticism about the plausibility of a hemispheric American comparative context. But the existence of this comparative study obviously implies my own conviction that there are not only differences between the United States and Latin America, but also fundamental similarities (suggested most broadly, perhaps, in our common denomination of *New World*) which are imaginatively recuperated in the fiction I will discuss here. As I refer to both convergent and divergent literary traditions and practices in the Americas, I will be aware of the danger of oversimplifying for the sake of establishing literary parallels; and also of the opposite risk, of oversimplifying for the sake of creating archetypes of otherness. My aim is not to define contemporary U.S. literature in terms of the contemporary Latin American literature or vice versa; nor is it to posit a consistent set of influences, though I will point to instances where writers have explicitly acknowledged influences running in one direction or the other. Rather, I will be moving between assumptions of basic cultural differences on the one hand, and literary examples of shared apocalyptic historical attitudes and modes of narration on the other. To recognize *only* the differences between the United States and Latin America (admittedly great), *only* the abuses of the political past and present (also enormous), is to deter or defer comparative literary study and resign ourselves to further mutual misunderstanding. Latin American literature is currently providing U.S. readers with insights into Latin American culture, and with broad perspectives on the hegemonic policies of the United States in this hemisphere. The comparatist can hope to encourage these critical insights by working to create an American literary context that, as Fuentes has put it, extends not from sea to shining sea, but from pole to pole.

As is clear in my introductory comments, my approach is essentially a thematic one, and my overarching concern is with the literary cultures reflected in the novels I discuss. My study does not systematically compare the material contexts of literary production and reception in the Americas. Such comparative studies will be of vital interest when they appear, but are as yet virtually nonexistent. Nonetheles, in my conclusion, I *do* compare (and contrast) cultural attitudes toward writers, literature, and language. Furthermore, the theme I have chosen directly addresses the relation of the narrator and audience to historical process, and therefore *does* raise pointed questions about the context of the literary text. The myth of apocalypse repeatedly leads me to issues of authority, autonomy, and action – issues which are, of course, grounded in the existing material and social realities of the countries and cultures of the novels under discussion. Because apocalypse integrates memory and anticipation, it leads me to the actual historical circumstances of those countries and cultures, not just to their philosophical conceptions of history. Contemporary apocalyptic narratives are often re-creations of the past, and that part of ourselves already present in the past, as well as projections of alternative futures. Apocalyptic discourse also engages gender issues in culturally specific ways which I identify in the course of my discussion, but which await systematic treatment in future comparative studies of American literature.

Because comparative literary studies deal with works in different languages, there is always the question of whether, and how, the various languages are to be cited in the critical text. This question, of course, involves the critic's conception of her audience, as well as the language in which she herself is writing. Obviously, all of my readers will read English, and some will also read Spanish. In my initial typescript, I therefore cited passages from Latin American fiction both in the original Spanish and in the English translation, because I wanted to speak directly to both of these groups. However, within the context of my own English sentences, this policy of dual citation often, and ultimately, proved cumbersome and intrusive; readers of the typescript (specialists in both Latin American and U.S. literature) strongly advised me to settle for one language or the other. Since citing passages in Spanish would exclude some of my readers, whereas citing in English will not, I have opted for English. Latin American fiction in English translation has a wide and committed audience outside of academia, as well as inside: It seems to me essential that this audience – potential readers of my own text – have access to the literary passages upon which I will be basing my discussion. Contemporary Latin American writers, and their readers in English translation, are fortunate in having had excellent literary translators, and I avail myself gratefully of their labors. I will, of course, cite the original Spanish text where I feel that the English translation might obscure meaning, or create extraneous issues of interpretation. I will also be referring to many secondary works of literary and cultural criticism written in Spanish, but unavailable in English translation.

I have said that I will move between assumptions of cultural difference and works of literature that transform those differences imaginatively via a shared apocalyptic understanding of history. Some of the points of difference and similarity I will be pursuing have been incisively addressed by the Mexican poet and essayist, Octavio Paz. Paz's comparative essays on Anglo-American and Hispanic-American culture and literature often treat the same general topic as mine: the origins and contemporary versions of American time. In *The Labyrinth of Solitude* (1950), Paz seems at first to propose more differences in these versions than similarities: in our attitudes toward work (that is, toward progress, and hence toward the future); play (communal self-forgetfulness or individual self-fulfillment, hence our attitudes toward the present); cultural traditions (preservation or not, hence our attitudes toward the past); and death (as a part of the present or as its negation). Paz's intellect is, however, a synthesizing one, and he moves naturally from observations about the differences between Mexican and U.S. cultures to observations about the shared aspects of "modern" or "Western" culture, and beyond, to humanity itself.

At the end of the essay entitled "The Mexican Intelligentsia," Paz makes an observation that is particularly relevant to my discussion of recent literary visions of apocalypse. Referring to Mexico, he states:

> Despite our national differences – historical superimpositions, an ambiguous tradition, semicolonialism, etc. – our situation is now no different from that of other countries. Our cultural crisis, for perhaps the first time in history, is the same as the crisis of our species. We are no longer moved by Valéry's melancholy reflections on vanished civilization, because it is not Western culture that is in danger of being destroyed tomorrow, as the cultures of the Greeks and the Arabs, the Aztecs and the Egyptians were destroyed in the past: it is man himself. . . . Each man's fate is that of man himself. . . . World history has become everyone's task, and our own labyrinth is the labyrinth of all mankind.[36]

23

The literature I will discuss acknowledges the danger that Paz describes — and also the opportunity. Apocalypse asks us, and the novelists who employ it, to consider profoundly important questions about human history and destiny, about the relation of the individual to the human community, about suffering and the transcendence of suffering, about the end of life and after. Apocalyptic modes of apprehending reality appeal to us in our secular times because they rest on the desire that history possess structure and meaning, if only the structure and meaning we attribute to it in our literary forms and fictions. It is by dealing seriously with this fundamental human desire that novelists create fictions of enduring relevance, an assertion I will attempt to illustrate in the following chapters.

2

APOCALYPSE AND HUMAN TIME IN THE FICTION OF GABRIEL GARCÍA MÁRQUEZ

For all our days are passed away in Thy wrath: we spend our years as a tale that is told.

Psalms 90:9

THE FICTION OF GABRIEL GARCÍA MÁRQUEZ presents an extended consideration of temporal reality, of the beginnings and ends of individual human beings and humanity as a whole. García Márquez's perspective is mythical and eschatological: Temporal movement in his novels is neither aimless nor endless but successive and purposeful, advancing on an end to which significance can be assigned, if not by the characters in the novel, then by the novelist and the reader. The history of Macondo, presented whole by García Márquez in *One Hundred Years of Solitude* (1967), is a monumental fiction of succession and ending, of communal and narrative fulfillment. Much of the rest of García Márquez's fiction is also impelled by a powerful eschatological impulse. In *The Autumn of the Patriarch* (1975), the apocalypse is political. Moral and social degeneration become a function of the political travesties of the general in this novel, his dictatorship an image of the last loosing of Satan, his prolonged domination suggestive of the reign of the Beast which in Revelation signals the end of time. In *Chronicle of a Death Foretold* (1981), the end is neither social nor political but individual, and wholly inevitable. Alfred J. MacAdam has asserted quite correctly that "the essential problem of [*One Hundred Years of Solitude*] structurally and in its attitude toward history is duration."[1] My discussion here will amplify that observation to include the proposition that in much of García Márquez's fiction, the essential problem is how duration ends.

García Márquez uses the patterns of apocalypse to structure and direct his temporal fictions, and to relate human time to the time of the universe. Frank Kermode observes in *The Sense of an Ending* that the relationship between the individual human span and the span of history has become increasingly problematic with the modern lengthening of the scale of perceived history, an observation immediately applicable to García Márquez's

25

fiction, as is Hannah Arendt's discussion of the absence of a beginning and end in our modern conception of history.[2] If the individual's relation to the beginning and end of time now seems impossible to imagine, it is precisely the temporal patterns of apocalypse which provide for García Márquez the mythological and narrative means to do so. Though the author bases his novels on the specific historical and cultural conditions of Colombia and Latin America, events of the actual past repeatedly adhere to the mythic shape of apocalyptic history. In accordance with much contemporary Latin American narrative, García Márquez engages historical fact the better to assert the primacy of historical fable.[3] Gregory Rabassa, translator of García Márquez, has commented with regard to *One Hundred Years of Solitude,* "The broadest tale of a people, and therefore of an individual, is more often than not elegiac or apocalyptic. Beowulf's funeral pyre is also sensed to be that of all the Geats. . . ."[4] Whether individual and collective ends coincide, as at the end of *One Hundred Years of Solitude,* or whether the end is a measure of individual solitude, as in *Chronicle of a Death Foretold,* García Márquez's vision of history is like a tale that is told, a tale that presses steadily toward conclusion.

I.

The title of *One Hundred Years of Solitude* suggests its central concern with the nature – and the limits – of human time. In 100 years, the history of the Buendía family and their town is chronicled from beginning to end. Like a biblical apocalyptist, García Márquez's narrator, Melquíades, recounts the past, present, and future of Macondo from a point beyond the future. He constantly relates past events to subsequent events in a retrospective future tense, because the fates which await the characters are already known to him: For Melquíades, the future is past. He also relates past events to an even more remote past, revealing the lifespan of Macondo and its inhabitants with sweeping totality. Thus, in a room of the Buendía house where it is always March and always Monday, Melquíades unifies past, present, and future by means of his narrative art. Melquíades is linked early in the novel with Nostradamus, the sixteenth-century French astrologer and mystic whose books of apocalyptic predictions were divided into 100 rhymed quatrains called centuries. We learn at the end of the novel that what Melquíades has been writing is another kind of apocalyptic century: Macondo's history is "written by Melquíades, down to the most trivial details, one hundred years ahead of time"; in it, he concentrates "a century of daily episodes in such a way that they coexisted in one instant."[5]

The temporal structure of *One Hundred Years of Solitude,* like apocalypse, is rectilinear rather than cyclical. Of course, human temporal reality can never be described as merely flat or linear: García Márquez manages to convey the temporal vagaries that make moments seem endless and ages like moments, and that make Macondo's history seem to double back upon itself and describe circles in time. Several critics have commented on the cyclical movement inherent in Macondo's structure. Ricardo Gullón and G. D. Carillo emphasize the repetition of the Buendías' names and personalities, the recurring events and activities from one generation to another, the seemingly endless series of futile civil wars that involve one character after another; Carmen Arnau describes Macondo as cyclical in the Spenglerian sense that the town participates in birth, growth, maturity, decline, death, and rebirth.[6] This is certainly so during the course of Macondo's 100-year history, but those 100 years do come to an end, and a rebirth ultimately fails to occur. García Márquez concludes his novel on this very point: "races condemned to one hundred years of solitude did not have a second opportunity on earth" (384).

Mikhail Bakhtin, in his *Esthétique et théorie du roman,* raises the interesting question of whether cyclical temporal patterns can ever provide the structural principle of the novel. Discussing *Madame Bovary,* he contrasts "la vie quotidienne" to progressive temporal structures, recognizing that the life of the "petite ville de province" seems nothing but repetition. Time appears bereft of any historic movement: In its repetitive sameness, one day is never only one day but every day, all days, and one life is by definition endlessly multiplied in the undistinguished sameness of all of the lives in the town. Despite the enormous distance of Yonville from Macondo, Bakhtin's comments about the temporal stasis of daily routine in *Madame Bovary* may nonetheless be applied to *One Hundred Years of Solitude:* "Time here is without event and therefore, seems almost to stand still. Here there are no meetings, no partings! It is a viscous and sticky time that drags itself slowly through space."[7] For this reason, continues Bahktin, repeating cycles cannot sustain a novelistic structure, though the novelist may use such cycles as the contrasting background for "energetic and eventful temporal series" – as do both Flaubert and García Márquez. The seemingly endless generational cycles of the Buendías and the recurring sequences of events in Macondo are set against the progressive temporal structure of the myth of apocalypse. They do eventually reach their end: "the family was a machine with unavoidable repetitions, a turning wheel that would have gone on spilling into eternity were it not for the progressive and irremediable wearing of the axle" (364). José Arcadio Buendía's city of mirrors, with its seemingly infinite self-reflections, proves in fact an unrepeatable mirage: "It was foreseen that the city of mirrors (or mirages) would be wiped out by the wind and exiled from the memory of men . . ." (383). The end of the Buendía line is anticipated from its beginning.

Eschatological pressure is inherent in the temporal organization of the narrative. The phrase "many years later" begins the novel and is repeated frequently by Melquíades. As the narrative progresses, "many years later" becomes "some years later," "a few years later," and then "a few months later": The end of the history of Macondo approaches relentlessly. The decline of Macondo, which begins with the banana boom, is filled with reminders that the "banana company hurricane" is an anticipation of "the prophetic wind that years later would wipe Macondo off the face of the earth" (305). The events that destroy Macondo – the oppression of the banana company, the strike and massacre of the banana company workers, the ensuing flood – lead to the inevitable moment when Macondo will be blown away, and the tropics will reclaim its territory. The cataclysm occurs at the same moment that the last surviving Buendía, Aureliano *Babilonia,* completes the deciphering of Melquíades's coded history of his family. He understands that the family's history has been fulfilled, that the child with a pig's tail, long predicted, has arrived. The end of the apocalyptic manuscript and the end of time coincide.

Just as the whole history of Macondo is revealed, so is the whole history of the characters, their beginnings constantly related to their ends by Melquíades from his point of view beyond the end. Colonel Aureliano Buendía's career is summarized before it is dramatized, and long before his death is described, Melquíades tells us that all that remains of his illustrious life is a street bearing his name. Meme, one of the ill-fated Buendías, experiences a tragic love affair as a young girl, and the rest of her life is quickly recapitulated in terms of that tragic love. She enters a convent, thinking about her lover, "and she would keep on thinking about him for all the days of her life until the remote autumn morning when she died of old age, with her name changed and her head shaved and without ever having spoken a word, in a gloomy hospital in Cracow" (275). Meme's individual span is related to the collective span as she leaves Macondo: From the train window, she glimpses the carbonized skeleton of the Spanish galleon which José Arcadio had encountered as he entered the pristine world of Macondo almost a century earlier.

All of the characters in *One Hundred Years of Solitude* feel the pressure of time from two directions: Past and future, memories and premonitions burden their present and separate them from one another. Unlike many modern fictional characters who, in existential (and archetypically American) fashion, leave their pasts behind in order to remake themselves according to their own design, García Márquez's characters are inextricably bound to their pasts and, at the same time, long for the future. Georges Poulet, in *Studies in Human Time,* discusses "romantic nostalgia," which seems to describe the situation of the inhabitants of Macondo. "It is as if duration had been broken in the middle and man felt his life torn from him, ahead and behind. The romantic effort to form itself a being out of presentiment and memory ends in the experience of a double tearing of the self."[8] The characters in *One Hundred Years of Solitude* constantly search on both sides of the moment for an escape from their solitude. Their futile search for release in the passionate present of sex only emphasizes the compelling necessity of this process.

Memories are important to the Buendías because they offer the illusory possibility of transcending the momentary, or as Poulet puts it, the possibility of participating in duration. It is thus poignantly ironic that throughout the novel memories are associated not with duration but with death. The characters' most vivid memories are recounted as they realize that they are about to die. The novel begins with Colonel Aureliano Buendía's first memory as he awaits death before a firing squad. The memories of Arcadio, Aureliano Segundo, Meme also irrupt as they face death. José Arcadio Segundo sees a man shot – the only memory he retains of his childhood. Memories become an especial source of isolation for José Arcadio Segundo, who later remembers with painful clarity the slaughter of the workers by the forces of the banana company, a fact which everyone else has been induced by those very forces to forget. Facing death, the characters' memories only serve to heighten their realization that the past is irretrievable and incommunicable. The wise Catalan bookstore owner speaks for most of the Buendías when he insists that "the past was a lie, that memory has no return, that every spring gone by could never be recovered, and that the wildest and most tenacious love was an ephemeral truth in the end" (370). Memory accentuates, rather than mitigates, each Buendía's isolation in the time capsule of his or her own history.

Premonition, like memory, leads the characters to the inevitable fact of death. Amaranta has a premonition of her own end; she sees death, a woman dressed in blue with long hair and an antiquated look: "Death did not tell her when she was going to die or whether her hour was assigned . . . but ordered her to begin sewing her own shroud on the next sixth of April" (260). Like Penelope in *The Odyssey,* Amaranta devises ways to prolong her task and thus her life, but her resignation to the truth of her presentiment of death is absolute. As she painstakingly stitches her shroud, she understands why Colonel Aureliano spent his last years making little gold fishes, melting them down, and making them again. She knows that the vicious circle of little gold fishes, like her intricate embroidery, reduces the world to a surface and temporarily denies annihilation. Úrsula, the matriarch of the Buendías, also knows with certainty when she will die. After the banana company massacre, it rains for four years, eleven months and two days: When the rain stops, she expects death. In the "clairvoyance of her decrepitude," she perceives a progressive breakdown in time itself. She knows that "the world is slowly coming to an end" (176), and there is nothing in the future to assuage her solitude.

García Márquez provides an anterior comic version of Úrsula's death, as he has of several of the apocalyptic elements in *One Hundred Years of Solitude*.[9] In his short story, "Big Mama's Funeral" (1962), García Márquez parodies the hyperbole of apocalyptic description and the magnitude of its terminal vision with his own fantastically exaggerated account of the end of Big Mama; she and Macondo are coterminous, but her funeral is a comic saturnalia rather than a *dies irae*. The carnival atmosphere surrounding the death of Big Mama is replaced in the novel by the monotonous sound of rain as the end approaches. Not only Úrsula but the whole town of Macondo as well is waiting for the rain to stop in order to die. One of the Buendías observes that Macondo's inhabitants no longer divide the years into months, or the days into hours. This sense of endless, hence meaningless, duration is the subject of another of García Márquez's early stories about Macondo, "Monologue of Isabel Watching It Rain in Macondo" (1955). In this story, García Márquez's geographical and historical cipher of the world – Macondo – is already visible: the intolerable heat, the relentless rains, the tropical ennui of habit and unpunctuated time. Isabel describes time as viscous (also Bakhtin's word), as a physical, jellylike thing, and the people as paralyzed, waiting for the rain to stop. Waiting is also the subject of *No One Writes to the Colonel* (1961), the account of an aged colonel who fought with Aureliano Buendía on the losing side of the civil wars, and who has waited decades for the pension promised him by the victorious generals. The colonel's hope turns to self-delusion as nothing happens, nothing concludes. His expectations are never realized: They serve only to delineate the shape of human impotence in a realm of fated history. These last two stories describe the violence with which the apocalypse fails to occur; as in the epoch of the flood in *One Hundred Years of Solitude,* undifferentiated time stretches before the characters. In García Márquez's tropics, temporal resolution, even cataclysmic resolution, comes to seem welcome. In accordance with apocalyptic convention, all that can be anticipated is the end of time itself.

Waiting is inherent in apocalypse, and the biblical apocalyptists conceived the need to wait in terms of eschatological conviction. The goal of time was understood to be God's perfect realm, and waiting implied the realization of history and the fulfillment of providential plan. The Book of Daniel presents patience as an apocalyptic policy. Rejecting political involvement, Daniel argues that waiting itself represents an ideological commitment, that refusal to wait represents a failure of faith and a repudiation of the divine plan for history.[10] This policy is based on an understanding of secular history as separated from sacred history, an understanding that was institutionalized by Augustine; it is not until the twelfth century, with Joachim of Fiore and the subsequent growth of popular millenarian movements, that apocalyptic visions began to inspire *im*patience, and hence revolutionary ideologies (an eventuality dramatized by Carlos Fuentes in *Terra Nostra*).

García Márquez does not, of course, reject political involvement, but his character in *No One Writes to the Colonel* does. In this story, all of García Márquez's characters are caught in webs of circumstance they cannot influence. So are most of the inhabitants of postdiluvian Macondo, in *One Hundred Years of Solitude*. Only the inheritors of Melquíades's manuscripts, particularly Aureliano Babilonia, are capable of doing anything other than waiting, arms folded, for the end. The apocalyptic narrators' textual deciphering is the sole activity of import in the drenched and dying Macondo.

But time was not always an unbearable and seemingly endless burden in Macondo, nor did memory and premonition always reinforce the solitude of the characters' present. In prelapsarian Macondo, the past and the future were scarcely distinguished from the present, for time was unified in innocence. Then, memory and premonition enhanced the present, and allowed the earliest Buendías to participate in duration. José Arcadio Buendía finds in the original Macondo a paradise which calls up ancient memories of archetypal realms. For him, the most intriguing of the gypsies' inventions are the apparatus to make a person forget his bad memories, and a poultice to assuage the effects of time; indeed, suggests the narrator, José Arcadio must have wanted to invent a memory machine in order not to forget all of the things brought by the gypsies to Macondo. In fact, the young and innocent town survives the plague of forgetfulness by labeling everything and describing its use. José Arcadio's premonitions are not about death but, on the contrary, about the existence of the Buendías *per omnia saecula saeculorum:* He is a prophet who guides his people to the promised land which, like Israel, represents the fulfillment of their history.

It is not long after the founding of Macondo that José Arcadio's prophetic vision is replaced by the apocalyptic vision of his heirs, as I have already suggested. This shift from prophetic to apocalyptic eschatology reiterates that of Hebrew history. The biblical prophets' vision of their history as moving toward the establishment of a blessed community seemed less and less likely in view of their contemporary historical situation of exile and oppression. By the second century before Christ, their prophetic vision began to be replaced by an apocalyptic vision which insisted on a radical change or break in history as the only possible remedy for existing evils.[11] Early in Macondo's history, José Arcadio prophesies an eternal city with great glass houses, a luminous new community separated physically and morally from the old world of temporal decay. After all, he has left the old world behind, arriving full of insight into the possibilities of moral freedom in a new world. In him, we recognize initially the Latin American counterpart to what Earl Rovit calls the "seminal image" of U.S. literature, "man against the sky, the lone figure in an infinite cosmos, trying either to come to terms with the cosmos or force the cosmos to come to terms with him."[12] For a brief moment, Macondo remains balanced between the terms of the cosmos and those of José Arcadio, but death, war, pestilence, and the banana company intrude upon his arcadia, tainting the future he has conjured. His dream of history becomes a nightmare of politics, a progression that makes the novel's critical perspective inevitable.

It is the breakdown of the patriarch's perpetual motion machine that heralds the shift, early in the novel, from prophetic to apocalyptic eschatology. Its failure forces José Arcadio to recognize that time is discontinuous, that Macondo is no longer paradise. Clocks appear, and so does an old man with white hair. He is Prudencio Aguilar, whom José Arcadio has killed years before, and who signals the irruption of the past, and death, into Macondo. Prudencio's appearance initiates Macondo's apocalyptic history, just as the appearance of a man whose "hairs were white like wool" (Rev. 1:14) initiates the apocalyptic events recounted in Revelation. It is José Arcadio's realizations about time that drive him crazy. He is tied to a chestnut tree and there he remains, insensible to the apocalyptic decline and destruction of the city that he prophesied would endure forever.

If, as I have said, memory is the source and confirmation of the Buendías' solitude, it is above all one particular memory, that of the paradisal Macondo, which isolates José Arcadio and alienates the rest of the characters from their present time and place. In *The Labyrinth of Solitude,* Octavio Paz proposes that the Latin American sense of solitude originates as a longing for the idealized time and place in the mythical past – whether a paradise or a holy center, an omphalos of the universe. To this longing, Paz relates a nostalgia for the divine body from which, he argues, humanity senses itself separated. He points to the idealized history which all mythologies describe, "a time when time was not succession and transition, but rather the perpetual source of a fixed present in which all times, past and future, were contained. . . . As soon as reality was divided up into yesterday, today, and tomorrow, into hours, minutes, and seconds, man ceased to be one with time, ceased to coincide with the flow of reality."[13] With clocks in Macondo, the rhythms of nature are replaced by those of empire: rise and fall, beginning and end, institution and catastrophe. Like the Latin American history which it epitomizes, Macondo's history begins as an idyll, degenerates into an imperial epic, until – we understand at the end of the novel – it is reconstituted by the mythic vision of Melquíades's text.

II.

If *One Hundred Years of Solitude* is about the cataclysmic history of the Buendías and Macondo, it is also about the deciphering of the manuscript that records and preserves their history, and about the narrative equivocations inherent in the process. It is this aspect of the novel that most clearly connects García Márquez to his "maestro," William Faulkner. García Márquez has repeatedly acknowledged his great appreciation of Faulkner's fiction, most recently in his speech accepting the 1982 Nobel Prize for literature; for García Márquez, Faulkner is the most influential of Latin America's literary predecessors. He describes his own affinity for Faulkner's fiction in terms of shared worlds and world views, saying that "Yoknopatawpha County has Caribbean shores; thus, in some sense Faulkner is a Caribbean writer, in some sense a Latin American writer."[14] It is tempting to stop and explore this expanded map of the Caribbean, and if we did, we would find that it has been charted in similar ways by the Cuban writer, Alejo Carpentier.[15] In Carpentier's special understanding of the idea of America, in his development of the concept and techniques of magical realism, even in the green wind that sweeps Haiti away at the end of his apocalyptically titled novel, *The Kingdom of This World* (1949), we would find important sources of the contemporary Latin American fiction I discuss here. However, my own comparative aims will be more broadly served by relating Macondo to Mississippi, rather than to Cuba; in fact, I will return to the issue of the affinities between Southern U.S. fiction and Latin American fiction in my discussion of the fiction of Walker Percy. Here, I only begin to trace the lines of intersection.

Carlos Fuentes describes one point where the lines converge in these terms: "Until recently, American writers never had the chance to deal with a national failure. The American ideal of success has done a great deal to standardize American art forms. That's why I think that for many years the most original American writing has come from the South, where there had been a real sense of regional tragedy and where there was a need to re-examine the things that had been taken for granted."[16] Fuentes singles out Faulkner to exemplify his contentions: "Suddenly there is the spectre of failure facing a country based on success. Then you can write *Absalom, Absalom!* and all the other great novels of Faulkner."[17] Fuentes overstates his case here. There have of course always been U.S. writers (and not just Southerners) who have known that one can suffer from the past: Consider Saul Bellow or Bernard Malamud or, perhaps the greatest example of the type, a New Englander – Nathaniel Hawthorne. But this does not obviate Fuentes's assertion that contemporary Latin American writers have found in the literature of the U.S. South, and especially in Faulkner's work, elements kindred to their own national experience: the guilt of the colonist who had profaned his pristine land, the decadence of an irrelevant aristocracy, the injustice and racial cruelty of the white-skinned usurper.[18] I will not explore the provocative question of Faulkner's influence on Latin American literature. Rather I want to juxtapose novels by Faulkner and García Márquez, and point to similar apocalyptic thematic and narrative structures which illuminate a shared comprehension of America and a shared mode of narrating its history.

It is in *Absalom, Absalom!* (1936) and *One Hundred Years of Solitude* that Faulkner and García Márquez are most closely aligned.[19] The history of the Sutpens, like that of the Buendías, reiterates the archetypal American experience of leaving the past behind and striking out to create an innocent new world in the timeless wilderness; it reiterates, furthermore, the equally American experience of discovering that virgin territory can be the site of evil as well as innocence. And because it is the memory of the narrators, however fallible, upon which these stories rest, they are not only about the Sutpens and the Buendías but also about the nature of historical truth, about how we remember and how we create the past with our words and our literary forms. Faulkner, like García Márquez, depends for the elaboration of his essentially American tale upon an apocalyptic perspective from which his narrators view the beginnings and ends of the world that they describe. Their accounts of the disparity between the original potential of America and its imminent ruin combine nostalgia and violence in an apocalyptic tone which both Faulkner and García Márquez recognize as altogether appropriate for telling secular tales of paradise lost.

As I have said in my introduction, apocalypse is an emphatically inclusive mythical history: Christ's statement, "I am Alpha and Omega, the beginning and the end, the first and the last" echoes throughout Revelation. Speaking from a point beyond the future, the narrator of Revelation senses himself compelled to write his history, for God has ordered him: "Write the things which thou hast seen, the things which are, and the things which shall be hereafter" (Rev. 1:19). Addressed to early Christians at a time of political persecution, John's apocalyptic narrative attempts to make sense of present suffering by seeking a design in history, by ascribing teleological significance to events. Of course, such paradigmatic history has more to do with fictional narration than with experience, for temporal progression is not intrinsically coherent or significant, nor can we relate cause to effect, origin to ending, so readily in our own worlds. Historiographer Hayden White has written about the process of creating explanatory history out of experienced data, of "fashioning human experience into a form assimilable to structures of meaning."[20] In order to comprehend reality, White argues, it is necessary "to narrativize" it, to impose the form of a story, with its well-marked beginning, middle, and end, upon experience: "The events must be not only registered within the chronological framework of their original occurrence but narrated as well, that is to say, revealed as possessing a structure, an order of meaning, which they do not possess as mere sequence" (9). This narrativizing impulse is present in the explanatory histories of individuals as well as larger political and social groups. In his discussion of Freud's case history of the Wolfman, Peter Brooks shows that narrative ordering, the constitution of a coherent order of events with an intelligible beginning and end from inchoate psychological data, is basic to Freud's achievement.[21] The narrativizing of history, the emplotting of the raw material of experience, is relevant here because *Absalom, Absalom!* and *One Hundred Years of Solitude* dramatize this very activity in their narrative techniques. The narrators of these novels use the explanatory structures of apocalypse to give comprehensible – and comprehensive – shape to the histories they survey.

Like José Arcadio Buendía, Thomas Sutpen dreams the peculiarly American dream of creating out of primal territory a world which he may endow with his own stamp and image. For that purpose alone, he rides into Yoknapatowpha County, Mississippi, in the shape of "man–horse–demon" with his "dream of castlelike magnificence," a band of "wild niggers" and a French architect.[22] José Arcadio Buendía also leads an expeditionary force into a new world, and he too dreams an urban dream oddly out of keeping with the surrounding wilderness, a foreshadowing of the inevitable gap between nature's promise and man's fulfillment. Seeing a dazzling city with houses having mirror walls, and hearing the name of the city spoken with a supernatural echo, he orders his men to make a clearing beside the river at the coolest spot on the bank, and there to found Macondo. Both Sutpen and José Arcadio foresee the establishment of a line that will continue forever; both are oblivious to the fact that their histories press steadily toward apocalypse.

Whereas José Arcadio immediately evokes the Judaic patriarch who leads his people into a promised land, Sutpen's aims seem purely selfish. Despite appearances, however, their motives are remarkably similar. Like many of the settlers of the New World, both Sutpen and José Arcadio are fleeing the exhaustion and corruption of an old world. Each is hoping to forget his past and begin history again, for both are convinced that in a world without a past, the future can be molded to their historical design. As stubborn and strong as they are in holding to their visions of historical renewal, they learn that the moral burdens of the past are not so easily sloughed off. The curse of incest, that classical sin against nature which is laid upon the Buendías in Riohacha, is ultimately realized in the once-arcadian Macondo. (Modern usage has narrowed the application of the word "incest," which derives from the more general Latin word, *incestus,* meaning unclean, tainted.) Incest also follows Sutpen into his new world in the shape of Charles Bon, the mulatto son who will not be repudiated along with the rest of his father's past. In both Macondo and Jefferson, the realities of civil war, economic exploitation of the land by alien usurpers, family tragedy, and crushing personal loneliness eventually overwhelm paradisal visions. Although the generational cycles of the families and the sheer staying power of

Úrsula and Judith would seem to offer the promise of continuity, the promise is false. Sutpen's Hundred is consumed in a holocaust, the fire reeking of "slow protracted violence with a smell of desolation and decay as if the wood of which it were built was flesh" (366). Macondo, overgrown and almost deserted, is blown from the face of the earth, the Buendía predicted from the first swept away with the last. The promised land of America, it would seem, has been irrevocably cursed.

Miss Rosa, Mr. Compson, Quentin, and Shreve in *Absalom, Absalom!*, and Melquíades and Aureliano Babilonia in *One Hundred Years of Solitude*, like the biblical apocalyptists, survey the story of an entire civilization from an atemporal point beyond its end. There is an ironic disjunction between Sutpen's and José Arcadio's initial optimism and the apocalyptic hindsight of those who tell their stories. For the narrators, the worlds which to their founders seemed endless have in fact ended. The uncharted future has become a schematized and unyielding past. Their apocalyptic narrative perspectives telescope time, mocking intentionality by juxtaposing the youthful optimism of beginnings and the harsh reality of cataclysmic ends. Here, then, they depart from apocalyptic convention, for these narrators' accounts of historical endings are not tempered with countervisions of new beginnings, or their cataclysmic visions with millennial ones. There are, at most, vestigial memories of innocence betrayed, of opportunity wasted. Nevertheless, it is the temporal scope of their apocalyptic perspective, their ability to see history whole, which allows them to confer meaning upon both history and biography.

In *Absalom, Absalom!*, Miss Rosa initiates the narration of Sutpen's history, and her cataclysmic vision dominates the novel. It is she who draws Quentin into that history, and she who causes Mr. Compson to expand on her version to his son. Standing beyond the end of her story, she and her auditor are always visible. Just as John in his Revelation frequently begins his sentences with "And behold, I John saw . . .," so Miss Rosa begins hers with the slightly more subdued but equally obtrusive phrase, "I saw," or concludes with, "That's what I found." Medieval apocalypse tapestries and manuscripts often place the figure of John at the side of the scene which he describes, an expression of distress upon his face as he watches the terrors of history (and God's will) unfold. Time is the vehicle of divine purpose, but in Miss Rosa's history, there is no reward – only retribution – at time's end.[23]

Miss Rosa's self-imposed exile in the "dim coffin-smelling gloom" of her "office" is consonant with her apocalyptic narrative stance. The biblical apocalyptist is always an outsider. He deplores the world he describes, and yet also has an urgent moral stake in that world and in its collective end. This ambivalence is reflected in the mediating and distancing devices of the apocalyptic text, devices intensified by the narrator's sense that he is the medium of forces beyond his own ability to understand or control. Messengers speak through other messengers, sealed scrolls must be opened, signs interpreted, phrases revised and reiterated. The apocalyptist's is thus an ambiguous kind of omniscience, for he disavows all personal claims to knowledge, describing only what has been told to him. History is at once an open and a closed book, a tension embodied in the historical narrative which he in turn creates. Miss Rosa and Mr. Compson in *Absalom, Absalom!* are also distanced from and yet desperately involved in the history they tell, and their strategies of indirection may be understood in terms of apocalyptic narrative. Because they seek in the history of Sutpen (and the South) some ultimate moral and ethical significance, the difficulties in historical decoding and recoding are magnified and intensified, as is the importance of their role as narrator, which they sense to be charged with responsibility far beyond that of mere historian.

Like Miss Rosa, Mr. Compson is constantly visible beyond the end of the story he tells, filtering his account of the degeneration and destruction of Sutpen's historical ideal through his own philosophical despair. His apocalyptic perspective is also fundamentally dualistic and deterministic. Human history is impelled by a moral dialectic between opposing forces, both personal and cosmic in character, which vie for control of this world. The progression of events may vary from one apocalypse to another – from Miss Rosa's version to Mr. Compson's – but it is controlled by this moral dialectic. Speaking from a point beyond the end of time, the apocalyptist reveals the predetermined schedule for the rest of time, over which humanity has little or no control. Thus Sutpen's "innocence" of historical necessity – his belief that he could manipulate history by the exercise of his own indomitable will – jars against Mr. Compson's and Miss Rosa's deterministic view of an essentially retributive history. For Mr. Compson, the historical "innocence" upon which Sutpen's Hundred is founded is the very cause of its destruction. Historical necessity – the pressure of time itself – is Sutpen's invincible adversary. Mr. Compson tells Quentin that General Compson hears Wash Jones's granddaughter, in labor with the last possible heir to Sutpen's name, scream "steady as a clock"; shortly afterward, Sutpen is killed with a scythe, his history abruptly truncated with the symbolic tool of Father Time. Mr. Compson's apocalyptic perspective allows him to probe the relation between freedom and historical necessity, to weigh human desire against human limitation and find the scale steeply pitched toward the latter.

Although there are elements of tragedy in Sutpen's history, and Mr. Compson often employs the metaphors of Greek tragedy in his narration, the tale he tells is less tragic than apocalyptic, because tragedy sees a future arising out of the violence of the past, a moral order reasserted and even invigorated after the terrible turbulence of tragic events.[24] Whereas the future envisioned in apocalypse exists by virtue of a radical break with the present, in tragedy, the world is carried on by the exhausted survivors. Such a future as tragedy envisions is nowhere evident in *Absalom, Absalom!*. The howls of Jim Bond, Sutpen's only surviving offspring, heard above the roar of the flames that destroy Sutpen's house, serve to emphasize the irrefutability of the end. And if Quentin's desperate need to understand and communicate Sutpen's history might seem to make *him* a survivor of that history, his survival is only temporary: within six months Quentin will drown himself in the Charles River at Cambridge, Massachusetts. (Only Shreve, the Northerner who bears no relation to Sutpen's world, is granted a future which promises continuance.[25]) Furthermore, apocalypse, unlike tragedy, implies the death not of an individual hero, but of a people, a world. When Mr. Compson, like Miss Rosa, links the destruction of Sutpen's Hundred to the destruction of the South and the New World, we are hardly surprised.[26]

The primary chronicler of Macondo's 100 years of solitude is Melquíades. He too stands beyond the end of the world he describes, surveying its entire history from his apocalyptic perspective. Like Miss Rosa in her "office," Melquíades removes himself from history to his "timeless room," escaping death in order to record the mortal condition of the Buendías and their world. His narrative is an enunciation, at once successive and cumulative, of all that has been and all that will be in Macondo. He both predicts and remembers events, proposing in advance the contents of the future. The novel begins, "Many years later, as he faced the firing squad, Colonel Aureliano Buendía was to remember that distant afternoon when his father took him to discover ice" (11).[27] The presumed present of the firing squad, itself an apocalyptic moment that would seem to obviate Aureliano's future in any case (but does not, for we learn that the Colonel survives that moment and dies of old age), quickly gives way to the narration of events long preceding the presumed present, the founding of Macondo and before. Melquíades's continual shifts through time, like Miss Rosa's and Mr. Compson's, weight the present with wistful anticipation or mournful recall; the remote past and the distant future intrude on the running present; the generations of Buendías reflect one another forward and back until the end of Melquíades's narrative, which is also the end of the world he narrates.

The importance of Melquíades's narrative record of Macondo is suggested early on, in the incident of the insomnia plague. The loss of sleep is not the most serious effect of this plague, but rather the loss of memory that accompanies it. Whoever was afflicted forgot "the identity of people and even the awareness of his own being, until he sank into a kind of idiocy that had no past" (50). In this pristine new world, which would seem to lack a past in any case, such a threat might be inconsequential were it not that Visitación and Cataure, the Indian servants in the Buendía household, identify the illness, even before its effects are evident. They have suffered from this illness already, having forgotten their own cultural past with the pressures of the colonization of Macondo; the Indians' loss presages Macondo's loss of its own Edenic past in the turbulence of civil war and economic colonization by the Yankees. A temporary antidote to the plague is discovered, however. It is the written word. Every object is labeled and its use recorded: "Thus they went on living in a reality that was slipping away, momentarily captured by words, but which would escape irremediably when they forgot the values of the written letters" (53). Obliteration is forestalled. José Arcadio understands that the very existence of Macondo depends upon words, and he decides to build a memory machine which would review the totality of knowledge acquired during one's lifetime, "from beginning to end" (54). It is precisely as José Arcadio struggles with his spinning dictionary that Melquíades returns to Macondo and begins to record 100 years of solitude.

Whereas we are constantly aware of the presence of the narrators who unravel Sutpen's history, we learn only in the final paragraph of *One Hundred Years of Solitude* that it is Melquíades, rather than an omniscient narrator as we have been allowed to believe, who has preserved the history of Macondo beyond its cataclysmic end. Aureliano Babilonia, the last of the Buendías, realizes just before Macondo is swept off the face of the earth that Melquíades's parchments are both history and prediction. The novel ends with this realization: "it was foreseen that the city of mirrors [or mirages] would be wiped out by the wind . . . at the precise moment when Aureliano Babilonia would finish deciphering the parchments . . ." (383). That the narrator is revealed to be a character in the novel, one who is obliterated with the town and the family that his parchments commemorate, suggests an indissoluble mixture of lived and written orders in Macondo, a suggestion which in turn emphasizes the totality of this world of words. Whereas an omniscient narrator is everywhere and nowhere in his narration, his existence presupposing another reality – that of the author – outside of the narration, the fiction that encompasses its own narrator and destroys him with the destruction of the fictional world no longer admits a context that is external to it, or that survives it. That García Márquez withholds the identity of his narrator until the final moments of Macondo's 100-year history serves to heighten our sense of the inevitability of individual and collective ends, and of the necessity of fictions to oppose oblivion.

If the narrators' words describe the annihilation of Macondo and Sutpen's Hundred, their words also defy time's destruction. Language is for the apocalyptist the sole remaining defense against historical chaos. His hermetic symbols and series testify to the conviction that language may yet order and communicate important, even saving truths to those who can

read and interpret them. Melquíades retires to his room in the newly enlarged Buendía house, spending hours on end "scribbling his enigmatic
literature" on the parchment that is brought to him. He tells José Arcadio:
"I have found immortality" (68), by which he means that his verbal embodiment of the Buendías – not the Buendías themselves – will endure *per
omnia saecula saeculorum*.[28] José Arcadio misunderstands him completely; it
is left to the last Buendía to perceive the significance of Melquíades's statement, as it is left to Quentin to perceive significance in the various versions
of Sutpen's history.

Miss Rosa, like Melquíades, is destroyed in the final destruction of the
world she describes. She dies as a result of the holocaust that consumes
Sutpen's decaying house and his barren offspring in December, 1909, her
death nearly simultaneous with that of the last vestige of Sutpen's historical
design. Thus to Quentin, her elected audience, is left the artist's task of
opposing oblivion with words. At night in the "tomblike" air of his "ice-
box" room at Harvard, where time itself seems frozen, as it is in Melquíades's room, Quentin attempts to the fullest extent of his narrative
power to elucidate Sutpen's world from its origin to its end. One thinks of
Roland Barthes's description of myth as "frozen speech," "arrested
speech": "On the surface of [mythic] language something has stopped
moving."[29] Faulkner's evolutionary history is set against his narrator's impulse to arrest time: So Quentin both describes the decay and destruction of
Sutpen's world and preserves it forever. The narration of history in these
novels represents a gesture toward eternity even as apocalypse unfolds.

It is Aureliano Babilonia, the decipherer of Melquíades's parchments,
who, more than Melquíades, shares Quentin's artistic burden. Both Aureliano and Quentin look backward upon worlds that have been created and
then destroyed; from the fragments of those shattered worlds, both narrators strain to construct new orders with their verbal artistry. Both are
obsessed by the histories they survey, at once observers and reluctant participants; both search desperately, as it is said of Aureliano, for "an entrance
that went back to the past" (379). Melquíades chooses Aureliano, as Miss
Rosa has chosen Quentin, to translate the past into art, charging him with
the responsibility of decoding his parchments. Like the biblical apocalyptist,
Quentin and Aureliano must decipher multilayered texts which are mediated by other narrators, distanced by time, and shrouded in seemingly
impenetrable series of events.

Aureliano, the illegitimate child of Meme Buendía and Mauricio Babilonia, has spent his life in captivity, incarcerated by his puritanical grand-
mother in a "decadent paradise." Nevertheless, he has wide knowledge of
the world beyond Macondo, is a medieval scholar like Melquíades, and is,
like Quentin, infinitely dedicated to his task of deciphering the past, of
narrativizing it into coherence. Furthermore he, like Quentin, understands

clearly the economic exploitation and moral abuses that have subverted the original potential of the land, for Aureliano alone believes José Arcadio Segundo's true version of the banana company's massacre of the workers. Thus, Aureliano withdraws to Melquíades's room, much as Quentin encloses himself in his room at Harvard, nailing the doors and windows shut in order to immerse himself in his art. And though their narratives will conserve the communal histories they tell, neither Aureliano nor Quentin deludes himself about his own individual permanence. Aureliano knows that the apocalypse about which he is reading in the past will soon engulf him in the present, and Quentin asks his father why Miss Rosa is so obsessed with Sutpen's destruction, when he knows that they all will be destroyed in any case. Even his Canadian roommate, Shreve, understands that the story Quentin has constructed must somehow lead to holocaust. He says that his account "clears the whole ledger, you can tear all the pages out and burn them . . ." (378). Shreve's conclusion has been foreshadowed by a similar image: Faulkner's omniscient narrator says of the roommates' narrative endeavors, "All that has gone before just so much that had to be overpassed and none else present to overpass it but them, as someone always has to rake the leaves up before you can have the bonfire" (316). The narrators' imposition of an order and an end upon history (their raking of leaves, as Faulkner has it) is the source of the meaning imputed to Sutpen's blazing mansion. Conclusion is first a fact of narration, then, perhaps, of history.

The biblical apocalyptists distinguish very specific patterns in the flow of time and infer meaningful connections among events in their desire to assign significance to history. In Revelation, the Beast reigns for forty-two months, the messianic kingdom lasts exactly 1,000 years, there is silence in heaven after the breaking of the seventh seal, "about the space of half an hour" (Rev. 13:1). Without a pause in the narrative flow, John describes event after event in series of sevens – the seven seals, the seven trumpet woes, the seven vials of wrath: That God should impose such orderly chaos upon the wicked world is cause for reassurance. Apocalyptic narrative achieves its authority by plotting a comprehensive explanation which traces effects to causes and enchains events along the way.

Similarly, in their attempts to create an explanatory narrative structure, Quentin and Aureliano schematize the events and characters of memory, as have Miss Rosa and Melquíades before them. The generational repetition of the Buendías, the alternation of Aurelianos and José Arcadios, the cycles of civil wars, the unrequited loves take their place in a schematized and structured history. Indeed, Aureliano only makes sense of his own relationship to that history when he sees simultaneously the origin and end of Macondo, the completed whole. The italicized epigraph which concludes the apocalypse provides a fullness that is rarely provided by unauthored temporality:

"The first of the line is tied to a tree and the last is being eaten by the ants" (381). Quentin too identifies patterns of repetition and duplication within time's forward movement, which link him to the past: Shreve and Quentin *become* Bon and Henry as they create them with their narration, and Quentin suggests that he and Shreve are in fact *all* of the people to whom they have given substance by their verbal retrospection. More than any of the other narrators, Quentin knows that the self is bound in illusory relations, and that his only hope is to situate himself within the symbolic order of the apocalyptic history he both observes and creates. So the individual allies himself to the grander design he intuits, giving significance to his own history by linking it to a history that is intelligible because it is complete.

If the individual gains support from this alliance, so does the community. The biblical apocalyptist sees himself as providing a communal service in mediating between the source of his text and its audience, between God and his believers: He conveys divine voices, texts, scenes to a select audience so that they may hear or read or see and thereby maintain their communal identity, ensure their communal salvation. Quentin and Aureliano Babilonia are also motivated by their sense of community, not so much wishing to warn the community or save it as to understand it themselves, and pass that understanding on to others. In their secular history of a family and a town, each conveys the accumulated voices and actions of generations. The individuals in their stories are described in relation to the community, and their individual fates are largely determined by that relation. It may be because they tell stories of *failed* communities that Quentin and Aureliano feel so strongly moved to attempt their recapitulation of the collective. Ironically, Quentin's communal history centers on a man unable to join (or create) the community that he desperately desires, and Aureliano describes a community that is ultimately united by nothing but the common solitude of its inhabitants. Indeed, their immediate audiences also exist in ironic relation to their communal ideals: Shreve is not a part of the community that Quentin addresses, and Aureliano speaks only to the absent Melquíades, one of the few outsiders ever to have been allowed entry into the Buendías's world.[30]

This relation between individual vision and communal destiny is also central to the narrative structure of García Márquez's novel, *Chronicle of a Death Foretold*.[31] Although the narrator of this novel tells the fated history not of an entire world but of an individual, Santiago Nasar, like Quentin and Aureliano Babilonia, his perspective and tone are that of the apocalyptist. Twenty-seven years after Santiago's murder, he hopes to make sense of the "senseless" death by means of his narration. Though Santiago's death does not imply the end of a community or a family, it is nonetheless a group drama. The narrator's concern, even beyond questions of the moral responsibility of murderers or victim, is the role of the community in the death, and the nature of their communal guilt. It is precisely *because* Santiago's death is foretold, *because* everyone shares the foreknowledge of his imminent murder, that the narrator is moved to undertake his investigation. Why did no one prevent his death? Could no one intercede in the "announced" scenario of events leading to catastrophe? Does announcement imply irrevocability? And will the narrator's written account (the death "aftertold") modify the future, even if it cannot undo the past? These tensions – between foreknowledge and human volition, between individual responsibility and communal history – are inherent in all apocalyptic narration, and García Márquez's investigative narrator places them in the foreground as Aureliano Babilonia does not.

The biblical apocalyptist assumes that his narration will affect his listeners' beliefs and behavior, even as he shows that it is too late, that individual and communal destinies are foretold and hence presumably final. Yet his emphasis on the reforming power of language (in Revelation, Christ is imaged *as* the Word) implies that his own verbal account may yet modify the history it foretells. This too is the implication of the narrator's account in *Chronicle of a Death Foretold*. If Aureliano Babilonia's and Quentin's narrations survive the end of Macondo and Sutpen's Hundred and mitigate their tragic finality, so the narrator's "chronicle" is the mitigating circumstance of Santiago's murder. His dedicated effort to confer meaning on the events he recounts is in fact rewarded. Through the process of returning, researching, ordering, telling Santiago's history, the narrator understands what he has suspected all along, that the murder was inevitable and that it cannot be justified – only accepted. The meaning of Santiago's death lies in this acceptance – an acceptance reflected in the narrator's final, powerful description of the murder. So he writes the ending that the facts will not concede, and concludes Santiago's history with his own text.

Others of García Márquez's narrators are less fortunate. Despite mythic alliances and communal aspirations, the past eventually weighs too heavily on both García Márquez's and Faulkner's appointed apocalyptists. We are told that Aureliano becomes "unable to bear in his soul the crushing weight of so much past" (381) and Quentin, calling himself a ghost, says, "I am older at twenty than a lot of people who have died" (377), and "I have heard too much" (207). Aureliano is described, and Quentin might well be also, surveying "the last that remained of a past whose annihilation had not taken place because it was still in a process of annihilation consuming itself from within, ending at every moment but never ending its ending" (371). But the end does arrive, despite the seemingly interminable decline and decay which they describe. For both Aureliano and Quentin, there is simultaneously a sense of prescience and déjà vu, the ends of their narrations revealing what was suspected from the beginning. Both are caught in the destruction of the worlds they decipher and describe, worlds that their narrative efforts have in some sense created.

The narrators of these novels understand too well the fragility of the words with which they forestall the inevitable apocalypse. Each is greatly burdened by the pressures and strictures of history, felt the more intensely in their American contexts, where space and time had seemed so endlessly expansive only a few generations before. Their prose reflects this burden. Although in very different styles, their sentences are often constructed with a running inevitability to them, the narrative never pausing but flowing on and on, as if impervious to the events it relates, synthesizing everything as it flows toward its predetermined end. I have already noted the eschatological pressure inherent in Melquíades's narration. His phrase, "many years later," which begins the novel becomes "some years later," "a few years later," then "a few months later"; and Aureliano, approaching the end of Melquíades's parchments, accelerates his reading, even skipping pages in order to keep up with time itself as Macondo hurtles toward its end. The narrative thus reiterates cosmic process. Faulkner's narrators also embody in their narrative styles the implacable fate that they believe to be driving events forward, Miss Rosa using her Puritan vernacular of predestination, guilt, and damnation, Mr. Compson the imagery of Greek tragedy. Quentin's narration is punctuated, but never slowed, by Shreve's constant injunction to wait: "Wait, I tell you!" *"Will you wait?"* Thomas Sutpen himself is moved to finish telling his story to General Compson when he sees that time is about to overtake him. It is as if the stories of the Buendías and the Sutpens were being told in a single breathless sentence, spoken with the knowledge of the annihilating forces at work in history, and thus with the sure knowledge of the need for haste.

The apocalyptic ending of a novel is as fictional as its beginning or any other part of its fictional history. However, the novelist's choice of such an ending is important because the paradigms of apocalypse impose an ending that confers historical significance. Of course all fictional narration imposes some degree of order on the chaos of temporal reality, and the end of all stories implies the cessation, if not the termination, of the fictional world embodied therein. But the apocalyptic perspective that I have attempted to define looks back to record the entire history of a world, not simply to carve out a slice of that history from the flow of time. In *One Hundred Years of Solitude* and *Absalom, Absalom!*, the narrators' apocalyptic stance allows them to integrate memory and anticipation, past and future, into the narrative present. Such temporal integration explains Melquíades's and García Márquez's concentration of "a century of daily episodes . . . in a single instant" and surely reflects as well Faulkner's conviction that "there is no such thing as *was* – only *is*. If *was* existed, there would be no grief or sorrow."[32] This inclusive narrative perspective, its comprehensive finality seeming to suspend time, underlies the transformation of history into myth which one senses with certainty in both novels. Their narrators share in the modernist thirst for myth, for explanatory masterplots which may justify their individual plots. With the loss of belief in the sacred masterplot of apocalypse, in which the secular leads to and is recuperated by the sacred, Quentin, Aureliano, and the rest are left to create their own fictions of apocalypse. There remains, after the end of the worlds they describe, the description itself, and the implicit sense that language is an antidote to past suffering, that a situation may be salvaged by being put into words. The intensity of their apocalyptic narrations underlines their yearning for the restoration of social and psychic order, and they are directed to that end.

I have suggested that the destruction of the fictional world and the narrator along with it seems to obviate a context that is external to that world, or that survives it. Of course this defies common sense, for we readers undeniably *do* survive García Márquez's biblical hurricane and Faulkner's holocaust, the novels still in our hands, ready to read again if we choose. (Surely we are able to suspend our disbelief more completely than the readers of *Moby Dick,* who, when through an error the novel was first published in England without the epilogue, asked with indignation who was left to tell the tale if everyone had gone down with *The Pequod.*[33]) In our role as survivors, we are perhaps akin to Shreve, for whom it is not history's predestined patterns but its fluidity that terrifies. That Shreve grants to Quentin (as do we, to Quentin and to Melquíades) something like total recall, however filtered through personality, represents our own desire for such a comprehensive perspective, for an end which will transform mere duration into a meaningful whole. The myth of apocalypse narrativizes history and provides for Faulkner and García Márquez a means of reclaiming in words their particular part of the American territory.

III.

Apocalypse is inextricably tied to political realities; it both responds to and imaginatively embodies social and political upheaval. The biblical apocalyptic visionary mode developed in response to political and moral crises, as I have said, and its forms have flourished when the established understanding of the history of a community is challenged. Apocalypse proposes radical changes in the organization of future world governance, in reaction to existing inadequacies and abuses. García Márquez is well known for his oppositional political stance, and he has observed (correctly, I think) that Latin American writers are, almost by definition, dissidents. He says that if he were not a Latin American, he might not feel the need to write politically charged fiction and nonfiction. However, he continues, in Latin America "underdevelopment is total, integral, it affects every part of our lives. The problems of our societies are mainly political. And the commitment of a writer is with the reality of all of society, not just with a small part of it. If not, he is as bad as the politicians who disregard a large part of our reality. That is why authors, painters, writers in Latin America get politically involved. I am surprised by the little resonance authors have in the U.S. and in Europe. Politics is made there only by the politicians."[34] If in *One Hundred Years of Solitude* hope resides in the survival of the narration itself, in *The Autumn of the Patriarch* García Márquez uses the myth of apocalypse more explicitly to protest political corruption and propose political reform.

The Autumn of the Patriarch presents the chaotic and violent ambience of a pre-apocalyptic world, a world without moral discrimination that is denied temporal coherence by the tyranny of political force. The nameless Latin American country where the novel is set is suffocating under the domination of an aging dictator, a political Antichrist; the wasteland that he creates with his brutality corresponds to the period just before the end of the world described in biblical Apocalypse. In Revelation, this transitional time does not properly belong to either the old world or the new, but is an interregnum which has its figural embodiment in the three and one-half year reign of the beast.[35] John describes the beast: He is "like unto a leopard, and his feet were as the feet of a bear, and his mouth as the mouth of a lion" (Rev. 13:2). He is specifically a political scourge. Commentators agree that he is meant to represent the state, with its seven heads symbolizing the seven Roman emperors who had been given divine honors and were thus guilty of blasphemy.[36] The mood of the transitional period is that of nightmare. The dislocation of personal and public relationships, the confusion of reality and appearance, fear of the future are its features. The general of García Márquez's novel is at home here.

The chaos of the general's realm is everywhere apparent. Each of the six chapters begins with a description of the "fabulous disarray" of the palace after the general's death, related by the collective narrative voice of the people who have survived the general and have timorously entered the "rubble pits of the vast lair of power." The disorder of the government house is rendered from many points of view. An American ambassador, in his "banned memoirs," describes the "dungheap of paper scraps and animal shit and the remains of the meals of dogs who slept in the halls," and "the reception room where hens were pecking at the illusory wheat fields on the tapestry and a cow was pulling down the canvas with the portrait of an archbishop so she could eat it. . . ."[37] Even the general's own comments are punctuated with the phrase, "What a mess!" In apocalyptic narration, the physical realm figures moral realities. In Revelation, John describes the poisoning of the water, the drying up of the sea during the period of transition. The general here actually sells the sea to the Americans to pay off the national debt. Nautical engineers carry it off to Arizona in numbered pieces, and the country is left a flickering inferno, reminiscent of Satan's realm in *Paradise Lost*. And lest we imagine that the contrary of political disorder is order, or that the moral degeneration of the general's world is reversible, García Márquez introduces José Ignacio Saenz de la Barra. The diabolical political terrorist establishes order in the form of a remarkably efficient organization, the better to torture and murder. He describes his activities as "peace within order" and "progress within order," and justifies his cruelty in terms of that order. So complete is the moral and political corruption of the dictator's world that it subverts and destroys the very conception of order.

The general is in absolute control of the lives of his subjects: he controls the country's resources, its weather, even the time of day. He is often described in terms of divinity (either as God's enemy or his replacement), and his activities are an ironic parody of Christ's. He is "besieged by mobs of lepers, blind people and cripples who begged for the salt of health from his hands, and lettered politicians and dauntless adulators who proclaimed him the corrector of earthquakes, eclipses, leap years and other errors of God . . ." (8). When his boat enters the rural settlements, the people receive him with Easter drums, thinking that the "times of glory" have arrived. The general is the Antichrist who orchestrates the last days, and he is ruthless in exercising his authority. With the slightest hint of insubordination – and often without it – the general wreaks reprisal. He rapes a woman and then has her husband cut into small pieces because he would be an enemy if allowed to live. When a faithful underling is suspected of treason, the general has him roasted, stuffed with pine nuts and aromatic herbs, steeped with spices, garnished with cauliflower and laurel leaves and a sprig of parsley in his mouth, and served to his comrades for dinner.

It is obvious from these examples that *The Autumn of the Patriarch* is a novel of hyperbolic extremes. With its outlandish images and exaggerated horrors, García Márquez's magic realism employs strategies akin to those of biblical apocalyptic symbolism. The naturalistic setting and causal sequences of *One Hundred Years of Solitude* are abandoned in *The Autumn of the Patriarch* for a more expressionist aesthetic. Repeated patterns of poetic association, fantastic imagery and grotesque gesture replace the discursive movement of Melquíades's manuscript. For example, a series of metonyms portrays the general: the gloved hands, the huge "graveyard feet," the buzzing ears, the herniated testicle, the sound of the single gold spur. These partial descriptions suggest the paranoia of the general (he never stands fully in view of the people), his insidious and stealthy exercise of power, and the veiled nature of evil itself. Although the general is more specifically described than the beasts and monsters of Revelation, like them, he becomes a universal symbol of political repression and hence, inversely, of human suffering. García Márquez shares the apocalyptist's intuition that only through grotesquely exaggerated and fantastical imagery can the political evils of his time be fully apprehended and embodied.

As in *One Hundred Years of Solitude,* García Márquez's apocalyptic vision in *The Autumn of the Patriarch* allows him to explore individual and communal ends. The general is terrified by time's passing, and his obsessive concern is how not to die, how to prolong his era. Biblical apocalypse posits time as the medium for the fulfillment of divine purpose, and temporal progression as necessary for the ultimate destruction of evil: García Márquez's general knows that for him, time is not a redemptive force but a destructive one. Time becomes his personal enemy, the only opposition that has ever threatened his absolute power, the only assassin who will inevitably succeed. The general's reign will end, the "last frozen leaves of his autumn" will fall. Nevertheless, for decades and even centuries, the general attempts to deny that fact. When he asks what time it is, he receives the answer, "whatever you command general sir . . ." (88). Indeed, for when the general decides to rearrange time, he does so. In one elaborate temporal maneuver, the insomniac general orders the clocks advanced from three to eight in the morning: "it's eight o'clock, God damn it, eight o'clock, I said, God's order" (68). Night and day are reversed at the general's whim, and cookie-paper stars and silver-plated moons are hung in the windows to attest to his power over time, but they serve rather to reveal the extent of his self-deception.

As the general imagines he can deny the reality of present time, so he attempts to deny both past and future. Like the absolute dictator in Carlos Fuentes's novel, *Terra Nostra,* the general substitutes for facts a grotesque fiction of his own making. He revises history to obscure his illegitimate beginnings and conduct, employing "the artifices of national history" to entangle and destroy "the threads of reality." In order to deny the responsibility for the death of 2,000 children, he simply denies their existence. So inclusive is his self-delusion that he writes his own graffiti on the walls of his bathroom, "long live the general, long live the general, God damn it . . .," and surrounds himself with adulators who proclaim him "undoer of dawn, commander of time, repository of light," "general of the universe," with "a rank higher than that of death." As he grows increasingly terrified, he begins to insist that his sycophants call him "the eternal one," and their shouts of "long live the general" are taken in the most literal sense. When his double dies and everyone thinks that it is the general, he reappears and kills his cabinet members for the crime of imagining that they had survived him. The general attempts to read his future in cards, coffee grounds, his palm, and basins of water, for he is desperate to know his future. He finds a fortune teller who can tell him the circumstances of his death, and then strangles her because he wants no one to know that he is mortal.

The general's attempts to transcend time are cast in ironic light by the structure of the novel. Each chapter opens with an account of the general's death – so, in fact, he seems to die not once but six times. On the first page of the novel, the general's survivors freely enter his palace, stirring up the "stagnant time," the "lethargy of the centuries" created by the general's fear of the future. This structural irony is reinforced by the general's own sense of the futility of his efforts to deny his end. In a final fleeting moment, the general does grudgingly accept his temporal condition, and thus briefly becomes a human being rather than a monster. In this moment, he faces the full extent of his self-deception and understands that he is a victim of his own sect of emperor worship, that he has believed his followers with their placards and slogans. He understands that his desire to reign "until the end of time . . . was an endless vice the satiety of which generated its own appetite until the end of all times general sir . . ." (267). In short, the general understands the temporal reality of his human condition, but it is, of course, too late. He is indeed time's victim.

The people too have been misled by their own placards and slogans. Even when the general's death appears to be irrefutable, they cannot believe that he has in fact died. They are unable to fathom that the general's seemingly infinite autumn has ended. For decades, centuries, they have experienced what Frank Kermode describes as the "intemporal agony" of the period of transition, which becomes an age in itself as crisis succeeds crisis. The people have accepted the notion that their stage of transition is endless, that they live, as Kermode puts it, "in no intelligible relation to the past, and no predictable relation to the future."[38] When they finally realize that the general's oppressive reign is over, they ecstatically celebrate "the good news that the uncountable time of eternity has come to an end" (269).

With these words the novel ends, the emphasis not on the final annihilating cataclysm, as in *One Hundred Years of Solitude,* or on the individual death, as in *Chronicle of a Death Foretold,* but on the better future which will succeed the general's death. As in biblical apocalypse, *The Autumn of the Patriarch* suggests that virtue can outlast persecution, that new worlds can supplant old ones. The people, to their surprise, live to celebrate the demise of their persecutor; end and ending do not coincide, time does not cease but moves forward in the hands of the survivors. And having survived, the people understand their temporal condition. They know that life is "arduous and ephemeral," and that if time's movement from past to present to future is a human contrivance, it is a contrivance that responds to a basic human need and is not to be carelessly abused. García Márquez, leftist journalist and social activist as well as apocalyptic novelist, endows the end of this novel with a future, as he does not with the other novels I have discussed here. In *The Autumn of the Patriarch,* the survivors know who they are (unlike the general, "who is left never knowing forever"), and we are given to understand that they will use that knowledge to the good. On the contrary, in *One Hundred Years of Solitude* and *Chronicle of a Death Foretold,* the fated ends and emphatically final endings seem to obviate such historical potential. Though we may rejoice that the *records* of those ends remain, we must also lament Santiago's murder, and the obliteration of Macondo in a hurricane of years, days, hours, minutes. In these two novels, García Márquez explicitly poses the permanence of narration against the terrible transience of human life. Words, he suggests, may almost overcome the temporal loss that they so poignantly describe.

It is the "almost" in the preceding sentence which García Márquez's 1982 Nobel Prize acceptance speech seems to cancel. The Nobel speech is often the occasion of a strange mix of genres, as García Márquez recognized when he said of his speech before it was written that he wanted it to be "a political speech presented as literature."[39] As if to dispel the idea that his most famous novel reflects a view of a doomed future, García Márquez used the forum provided by the Nobel speech to address the issue of his own literary apocalypticism and the apocalyptic nature of our time. He begins his speech by invoking the utopian visions and fantastic images inspired by the discovery of the New World: El Dorado, the fountain of eternal youth, a giant in Patagonia described by a sailor on Magellan's voyage. With familiar temporal sweep, the author moves immediately from such beginnings to a consideration of ends, quoting a statement made by William Faulkner when he received the 1949 Nobel Prize for Literature:

> On a day like today, my master William Faulkner said, "I decline to accept the end of man." I would feel unworthy of standing in this place that was his if I were not fully aware that the colossal tragedy he refused to recognize thirty-two years ago is now, for the first time since the beginning of humanity, nothing more than a simple scientific possibility.[40]

But even as he contemplates the end of humanity by nuclear holocaust, García Márquez oscillates back to envision its opposite, asserting that it is not too late to undertake the creation of "a new and leveling utopia of life where no one can decide the form of another person's death." Here we witness a marked shift in emphasis from the negative to the positive side of the apocalyptic myth, and a shift as well in García Márquez's relation to the Latin American literary tradition of historical idealism.

García Márquez's Nobel statement is decidedly more optimistic than anything that has yet been embodied in his fiction (as was that delivered by Faulkner, when he accepted the prize in 1949). In *One Hundred Years of Solitude* and *Chronicle of a Death Foretold,* it is the survival of the narration, not of Macondo or Santiago, that suggests temporal continuance and serves as saving counterbalance to communal and individual annihilation; and in *The Autumn of the Patriarch,* the future hardly holds out the extravagant promise of "a new and leveling utopia." The Nobel speech, however, offers a resounding affirmation of historical and human potentiality: "Neither floods nor plagues nor famine nor cataclysm nor even the eternal wars throughout centuries and centuries have managed to reduce the tenacious advantage of life over death." The emphasis has shifted, but García Márquez's speech, with its dialectic of cataclysm and millennium, remains a part of the apocalyptic tradition as I have described it. It is precisely his expressed hope that historical renewal – even utopia – may yet be possible, despite enumerated past disruptions and present dangers, that is most characteristic of apocalyptic dicta.

García Márquez ends his speech with a playful yet profound revision of the concluding sentence of *One Hundred Years of Solitude,* invoking not the historical cataclysm of his novel's ending, but historical renewal instead. In his speech, he describes a utopia where "races condemned to one hundred years of solitude will have at last and forever a second opportunity on earth." Here García Márquez dismisses the very idea of irrevocability, in history and in fiction. Nothing need be irremediable, to use a word that often appears in his novels. By proposing in his Nobel speech this new version of the apocalyptic conclusion of his masterpiece, García Márquez enacts the renovating activity he describes, calling into question the nature of finality itself, be it the finality of biblical hurricane, nuclear holocaust, or novelistic structure.

3

APOCALYPSE AND ENTROPY:
PHYSICS AND THE FICTION OF
THOMAS PYNCHON

Thermodynamics has won at a crawl.

Naked Lunch, William Burroughs

THOMAS PYNCHON ELABORATES an avowedly modern revision of apocalyptic narrative. Trained in electrical engineering, Pynchon finds in his technical and scientific background the methods and metaphors with which to explore contemporary mass society. Unlike García Márquez's primal world of myth and magic, where apocalyptic imagery serves to describe ultimate hopes and fears, Pynchon's urban settings evoke the technological realities of a world where scientific laws provide the only operative mythology. It is the law of entropy rather than the patterns of apocalypse that structures Pynchon's fiction and describes his vision of the end of the world. The eschatology based on the law of entropy is far more pessimistic than conventional apocalyptic eschatology, for the anthropomorphism of traditional apocalypse, with its implicit sense of a purposeful history responding to human as well as to divine actions, yields to the bleak mechanism of a purely physical world that is irreversibly running out of energy. Yet having made this distinction, one also immediately senses the kindred compulsions (both global and ultimate) of entropic and apocalyptic visions, with their shared oppositions of order and chaos, of present and future. Octavio Paz's synthesizing perspective is useful here. He comments in *The Labyrinth of Solitude:* "Contemporary man has rationalized the myths, but he has not been able to destroy them. Many of our scientific truths . . . are only new ways of expressing tendencies that were embodied earlier in mythical forms. The rational language of our day can barely hide the ancient myths behind it."[1] Conditioning Pynchon's entropic vision are the mythic forms of apocalypse, and his departure from or concealment of those forms will prove to be significant.

Paz's observation is applicable not only to Pynchon's fiction but also to the work of a number of U.S. writers, among them Nathanael West, Joan Didion, William Burroughs, James Purdy, Susan Sontag. In fact, writers have explicitly invoked the law of entropy as a metaphor for the end of time to a far greater extent in the United States than in Latin America. This may be due to the more thoroughly urbanized and mechanized nature of U.S. society, with its different attitudes toward technological progress, as well as to the fact that the intellectual progenitors of the social application of the concept, Bertrand Russell and Henry Adams, were particularly English or Anglo-American in their orientation and influence.[2] Pynchon's world of steel and concrete is far from García Márquez's overripe tropics and, for that matter, from Faulkner's decaying South, where human nature, not the laws of physics or technology, is causal. For contemporary U.S. novelists of entropy, the real doomsayers of our time are the physicists and mathematicians – Clausius, Kelvin, Bolzmann, Gibbs, Planck, Einstein, Heisenberg – whose work has led to the ultimate cosmic *memento mori,* the second law of thermodynamics.

Irving Howe, in his well-known essay "Mass Society and Post Modern Fiction," discusses the difficulties of portraying contemporary U.S. reality. He describes mass society's "amorphous symptoms," the dissolution of social relationships, the disintegration of individual belief and taste in the face of mass-produced, homogenized culture.[3] Hannah Arendt also refers to contemporary mass society, principally as a consumer society that, with its gargantuan appetites, is in danger of consuming its own cultural bases of existence. For Arendt, the difference between "society" and "mass society" is that society wanted culture, whereas mass society wants entertainment. Although she uses a metaphor from biology rather than physics to make her point, her sense of mass society is clearly cognate to Pynchon's.[4] It is precisely such a society that Pynchon is able to describe in terms of the law of entropy. At his best, he uses the metaphor of entropy to embody the situation Arendt describes and to overcome the problem Howe posits. He captures, in Howe's phrase, "the hovering sickness of soul, the despairing contentment, the prosperous malaise" of the contemporary culture he has chosen to depict.

Although Pynchon almost never comments on his work, he departs from custom in the introduction to his collected short fiction, saying that, "When we speak of 'seriousness' in fiction ultimately we are talking about an attitude toward death. . . ."[5] The law of entropy describes the gradual death of the universe, and is indeed the metaphoric source of "seriousness" in Pynchon's fiction.[6] Entropy refers to the statistical probabilities of various molecular distributions in a thermodynamic system. It also refers to the irreversible tendency of a thermodynamic system to move from the least probable to the most probable molecular distribution, that is, from a state of molecular organization capable of producing work to a state of random, disorganized, uniform molecular movement. Entropy reaches its maximum when the position and velocities of molecules are distributed uniformly and completely at random. Any spontaneous changes in the system will be in the direction of increasing entropy, of increasing randomness and disorganization: The law of entropy requires that the total amount of entropy in the system increase. At the end of the entropic process, heat energy will be nontransferable because everything will contain an equal quantity of energy. This equilibrium, which represents the maximum molecular disorder, the greatest molecular homogeneity, is called heat death. To paraphrase T. S. Eliot, the world will end not with the bang of apocalyptic cataclysm but with the whimper of entropic chaos. Pynchon describes a world drifting "into the graceful decadence of an enervated fatalism."[7]

The concept of entropy has a highly specific application. It refers to a long-range microcosmic process which is theoretical rather than observable and which occurs only in a closed thermodynamic system with no sources of energy external to itself. To translate this idea from the molecular realm which it properly describes to society and human relationships is a dangerous jump for any novelist to make. And even given the jump, individual human beings and cultures are not necessarily closed systems and are therefore not inevitably subject to entropy. Furthermore, certain biological functions provide an enormous local *decrease* in entropy: The process of photosynthesis or the growth of an animal represent complicated forms of physical organization with very moderate energy transfer. Indeed, the process of biological evolution itself seems to contradict the law of entropy, for organisms have not obeyed the entropic movement from organization to disorganization but rather have progressed from simple organisms to complex ones, from undifferentiated unicellular creatures to highly differentiated species. Yet another difficulty in using the concept of entropy outside its specific microcosmic context arises from the occurrence of homeostasis. Animals and vegetables possess information systems that sustain an orderly state within the organism through the balancing of opposing forces, thus maintaining temperature, oxygen, water, sugar, salt, fat, calcium at suitable levels in the body. The autonomic nervous system of animals, and the tropism and taxis of lower forms of life, control the apparatus by which the organism differentiates itself from its surroundings and carries out its entropy-reducing processes. Such mechanisms allow both the individual and the species to resist entropy and adapt to short- and long-term environmental changes, and represent the antithesis of the unopposed tendency toward tension reduction implied by entropy. Although these facts would seem to limit the applicability of entropy as a metaphor for anything beyond the realm of physics per se, Pynchon nonetheless uses the concept very effectively in his early short stories, in *V.* (1963), and in *The Crying of Lot 49* (1966) to describe what he sees as the progressive disintegration of contemporary U.S. culture, its lack of individuality, its tendency toward conformity and passivity. In *Gravity's Rainbow* (1973), the metaphor is considerably less successful.

I.

As I have already said, the entropic vision is far more extreme in its hostility toward human value and potential than is the apocalyptic vision. In the physics of entropy, as in the myth of apocalypse, temporal movement is unidirectional and irreversible, envisaging a future that is qualitatively different from the past or present. But, unlike apocalyptic temporality, the entropic vision admits no possibility that time may prove redemptive or regenerative. Nor is there any logical causal relationship between past, present, and future. As history moves irrevocably toward heat death, it admits no human influence. Absent are the anthropomorphic embodiments of moral values, the Christ and Antichrist, the Whore of Babylon and the Bride, symbols of the ethical dialectic that is understood as the motivating force of time. Humans can only wait passively, like the characters in Pynchon's short story "Entropy," for "the moment of equilibrium . . . when the hovering, curious dominant of their separate lives should resolve into a tonic of darkness and the final absence of all motion" (292).

In Pynchon's stories, an apocalyptic vision of history *is* initially invoked, only to be explicitly supplanted by the wholly pessimistic eschatology inherent in the law of entropy. "Under the Rose" introduces Pynchon's readers to Porpentine, a British agent in Cairo on an intelligence mission during the final years of the nineteenth century. Pynchon has recently commented in the introduction to his collected stories that he was influenced by writers who "allowed World War I in my imagination to assume the shape of that attractive nuisance so dear to adolescent minds, the apocalyptic showdown" (18). Porpentine belongs to the past era of British supremacy, where good meant the pursuit of the interests of empire, and evil meant their opposition. From that era of confident colonialism to the "dogdays of '98," Porpentine has watched the disintegration of an order which for him and many like him was a kind of universal principle. In his bewilderment, the middle-aged gentleman clings to his understanding of history as a dialectic between opposing forces the course of which he may possibly influence. He still considers himself a "veteran spy" and remembers back to times when he and other "veteran spies" dealt with political crises which "could be given the name of sure apocalypse."[8] But no longer is the simple dualism of an "apocalyptic showdown" an adequate response to the moral chaos of history, as "the century rushes headlong to its end" (224).

Porpentine is a pathetic figure in a world where "The Rules" have changed from a comprehensible dualism (where a man knew who he was because he knew who he wasn't) to an ambiguous multiplicity. He belongs to the past, as the character in *V.,* Stencil, Sr., recognizes that he also does: "to a time where which side a man was on didn't matter: only the state of opposition itself, the tests of virtue, the cricket game."[9] Porpentine senses the accession of an unnameable power which now operates in the world, a ubiquitous but unspecific force which obviates action and ensures destruction and death. He recognizes that it is "no longer single combat" (248), and curses himself for wanting to believe in a fight according to the duello. "But they, – no, it – had not been playing those rules. Only statistical odds. When had he stopped facing an adversary and taken on a Force, a Quantity?" (249). It is the force of entropy that has replaced the clearly defined oppositions of apocalypse, a fact which becomes explicit as Porpentine sees a bell-shaped curve against Cairo's night sky. "The bell curve is the curve for a normal or Gaussian distribution. An invisible clapper hangs beneath it. Porpentine (though only half-suspecting) was being tolled down" (249). The Gaussian curve measures probability, that central reality of entropy which dictates the increase of randomness and the decrease of order. The curve forms a bending invariant, a geodesic, a suffocating lid from which there is no escape. William Burroughs, whose characters, like Pynchon's, are subject to decay and disintegration in an entropic world, uses the same image in *Naked Lunch:* "The black wind sock of death undulates over the land, feeling, smelling, for the crime of separate life, movers of the fear-frozen flesh shivering under a vast probability curve. . . ."[10] At the end of Pynchon's story, Porpentine surrenders passively to the younger agents, who understand the new rules of the game. As he shrugs and grins and tosses his pistol on the ground, he pays them a compliment that reflects the old order: "You have been good enemies" (250).

A greatly changed "Under the Rose" becomes Chapter 3 of Pynchon's first novel, *V.,* subtitled, "In which Stencil, a quick-change artist, does eight impersonations." The narrative material has been diffused by being rendered through eight points of view, those of the native serving class, rather than through the omniscient narrator of the earlier story. Events are unexplained, seemingly unrelated, certainly not made clear in terms of cause and effect. Our sense of the characters is also diffused, for we see them not directly but tangentially, from peripheral perspectives. The gradual loss of differentiation of increasing entropy implies the loss of individuality. And significantly, the word "apocalypse," which appears numerous times in the short story, has been eliminated from the chapter. It is as if Porpentine's realization in "Under the Rose" – that apocalyptic certainties have been replaced by a complex field of probabilities – has been incorporated into the style and structure of *V.* . The character of Porpentine in the story becomes in *V.* no more than a veiled reference in Stencil's journals. The rest is, as Stencil says of twentieth-century history in general, "impersonation and dream."

Because entropy posits the encroachment of chaos and sameness on all systems of organization and differentiation, paranoia is an inevitable response. Pynchon's characters attempt almost pathologically to distinguish JUpatterns of meaning, significant relationships, relevant connections beneath the increasingly homogeneous surface of mass culture. In *V.*, young Stencil accumulates "history's rags and straws" in the hope of creating a viable version of his own history, but succeeds only in gathering random, disconnected facts. In *The Crying of Lot 49*, the underground organization which Oedipa Maas seeks is called W.A.S.T.E.; a used-car lot described in the opening paragraph of the novel echoes F. Scott Fitzgerald and becomes emblematic of Oedipa's world – "a salad of despair, in a gray dressing of ash, condensed exhaust, dust, body wastes. . . ."[11] Detritus proliferates in the war-torn world of *Gravity's Rainbow* as characters attempt to map strategies and decode rocket patterns. All of Pynchon's characters are to some extent victims of encroaching objects and information – undifferentiated masses of things and words which are inert and unresponsive. Indeed, so insidious is the operation of entropy in the physical sphere that the boundaries between inanimate objects and human beings are often disturbingly unclear. Whereas the objects of material reality have traditionally been the building materials out of which the novel is constructed, the entropic vision sees in them rather a dumb and lifeless fatality, relics of a past more real than the present because less abandoned to entropy. Preceding Pynchon in this view are Henry Adams, who writes of a world in which the "ash heap is constantly increasing in size,"[12] and Nathanael West, who in *Miss Lonelyhearts* (1933) places his character in a pawnshop, where he futilely attempts to reanimate his world by imagining implicit patterns in the piles of junk.

Octavio Paz contrasts Mexico and the United States in terms of the unresponsive world which Pynchon portrays. For Paz, the reality of the United States is perceived by its inhabitants as having been invented by them. The resident of the United States "has built his own world and it is built in his own image: it is his mirror. But now he cannot recognize himself in his inhuman objects. . . . His creations, like those of an inept sorcerer, no longer obey him. He is alone among his works . . ." (20–1). According to Paz, the contemporary Mexican does not feel that he has created his own world, but he too is isolated in a labyrinth of solitude, for a different reason. The source of his world is perceived as a divine center in which he once dwelled but no longer does. His search for his mythic origin is foreign to Pynchon's technological eschatology, but his sense of displacement is not. This Mexican search for a mythic center will occupy our attention more fully in my final chapter on the fiction of Carlos Fuentes.

In "Mortality and Mercy in Vienna" (1959), Pynchon locates his labyrinth of solitude not in a dark corner of the entropic world but in the mind of his characters. The detached narrator of this story finds himself the de facto host at a party of people whom he does not know. As he enters the room, a character called David Lupescu leaves, with the comment, "Mistah Kurtz – he dead."[13] Joseph Conrad's short story, "The Heart of Darkness," from which the phrase is taken, and T. S. Eliot's poem, "The Hollow Men," which uses the phrase as an epigraph, echo through Pynchon's story, as they have more recently in Francis Ford Coppola's film, *Apocalypse Now*. Indeed, despite its title, Coppola's film is motivated less by an apocalyptic vision than by an entropic one, chronicling as it does the paranoid tendency to build mental structures with which to surround and isolate the terrified self. In *Apocalypse Now*, this tendency is evidenced by just about everyone, from the generals in Washington who, Coppola suggests, created the Viet Nam war, to the character played by Marlon Brando in his hostile Cambodian forest. The movie proposes no apocalyptic renewal or self-conscious narrative ordering, though the story is told retrospectively by one of the participants. Rather, there is a relentless descent into a world without moral or ethical distinctions, where everything is equally suspicious, everyone equally terrifying. Coppola finds his perfect visual correlative for paranoia in the silent horde of Montagnards who surround Brando in his enclave, their masks of paint identical, and their postures of hostility indistinguishable one from the other.

The paranoia generated by an entropic vision of history, whether in Coppola's film or Pynchon's fiction, differs in essential ways from the assumptions underlying apocalyptic visions. Although we see Pynchon's characters responding to the same impulse that moves the apocalyptist – to decipher historical reality and endow it with significant form – their attempts do not lead to any comforting dualities (Porpentine's "state of opposition itself") or resolutions, but rather to an ultimately unsearchable subterranean world. Their increasingly random and disorderly world engenders fantasies and hallucinations of malign conspiracies. (One avoids the terms "fiction" and "imagination," for Pynchon rarely suggests that his characters' mental constructs might be positive.) Whereas the locus of evil is well known and quite transparent to the apocalyptist and to his audience, its locus in an entropic world is everywhere and nowhere. The paranoid fear of Pynchon's characters is, one senses, a kind of inversion of the spiritual longings of the biblical apocalyptist, for whom it is the power of good that is unfathomable, not the power of evil.

In Pynchon's story, "Entropy," the shift from apocalypse to entropy is complete. That the world is in the final throes of heat death is recognized by the character Callisto,[14] a student of thermodynamic theory who attempts, despite his knowledge of its impossibility, to oppose entropy, to create for himself and his mistress, Aubade, an enclave of order in the midst of increasing chaos. Callisto understands the imminence of entropic equilibrium because the temperature outside has remained unchanged for three days. Despite the fact that he is "leery at omens of apocalypse," he possesses what for him represents at once the omen and proof of the imminent end. He holds a small, sick bird in his hand, attempting to warm him. Callisto understands that as long as a transfer of energy is possible, thermal equilibrium has not yet set in and heat death has not yet occurred. But the bird dies, indicating that the world has indeed degenerated to a state of inert equilibrium, ticking, like the heart of the bird, "a graceful diminuendo down at last into stillness" (292). End and ending coincide, as they do in García Márquez's *One Hundred Years of Solitude* and *Chronicle of a Death Foretold,* but there is no manuscript to survive the end, no friend to outlive his fated companion, to look back and infer meaning. Whereas the apocalyptic perspectives of Melquíades and the narrator of *Chronicle of a Death Foretold* suggest that narration may yet renovate history, Pynchon's entropic perspective proposes no such extenuating narrative circumstance.

So we see that entropic time, like apocalyptic, invests history with direction, but not with purpose. It is linear and unrepeatable, the future qualitatively different from the past or present, but change is inevitably for the worse. Time increases entropy, destroying order and structure until a point is reached when time is conceived of as standing still. Until the second law of thermodynamics was postulated in 1852 by William Thompson, time was not considered by physicists to have a direction. In Newtonian physics, the past and the future were identical in essence, for there were continuing laws of cause and effect, continuing laws of energy which operated in the universe. With the transition from Newtonian reversible time to the irreversible time implied by the law of entropy, the end of the world becomes as inevitable from the scientist's point of view as it is from the biblical apocalyptist's. It is ironic that the entropic end should resemble the apocalyptic end in the eternal, changeless equilibrium it foresees. This end, which represents for the biblical apocalyptists the final reign of God, represents for Pynchon's characters the final horror. That entropic equilibrium should be presented as so disturbing is perhaps the result of the positivist faith in progress that is engrained in the thinking of the industrialized nations of the West. It is difficult for residents of the twentieth-century United States to dismiss the notion, widely held but also widely distrusted, that "progress" and "development," responding to individual and communal volition, is the only desirable temporal construct. This circumstance explains in part the continuing attraction of the apocalyptic vision and the implicit undertow of apocalyptic eschatology in Pynchon's fiction, despite his explicit metaphoric use of the second law of thermodynamics.

II.

In his first novel, *V.* (1963), Pynchon presents a novelistic history calculated to reflect the realities of our century. It is by now a cliché that the horrors of recent history have far outstripped the imagination of the novelist. Earl Rovit, in an essay entitled, "On the Contemporary Apocalyptic Imagination," puts the point succinctly: "The overwhelming course of the Enlightenment and the empirical tradition have tended to enclose our world into comprehensible capsules of why-and-because. And the shock of the twentieth century on our tender rational sensibilities is caused – as much as by anything else – by the increasing irrelevance and unreliability of the answers we are able to produce. Why the death camps? Why the dread of nuclear annihilation? Why our loss of rational control over our private and public lives? Why the quality of dissociated terror and loneliness that seem pervasive beneath the mannered surfaces of our behavior?"[15] Pynchon acknowledges fully the irrelevance of traditional explanations for the events of our time, capturing in *V.* the irrationality and self-destructiveness of the events the novel describes. Pynchon often blurs and limits the outlines of history in his novels, but if the author chooses to portray the twentieth century in the last throes of entropic death, then "impersonation and dream" are perhaps the only means left with which to express historical reality. Such is the possibility we are continually asked to consider as we read *V.* .

The character most concerned with the "impersonation of lost times" is Herbert Stencil, "born in 1901 . . . the century's child," son of Sidney Stencil, British foreign service functionary who dies in unknown circumstances in 1919. The elder Stencil leaves to his son his journals, the events of which fill the younger Stencil's life as he attempts to make sense of "a past he didn't remember and had no right in" (51). He can find no historical continuities, no links between past and present which might reveal the nature of his future, but it is nonetheless the journals that provide him with whatever sense of direction and identity he possesses. But identity in any traditional novelistic sense is irrelevant. Stencil, like Callisto and their literary precursor, Henry Adams, refers to himself in the third person, aiming at a kind of self-dissociation: "Herbert Stencil, like small children at a certain stage and Henry Adams in the *Education* . . . always referred to himself in the third person. This helped 'Stencil' appear as only one among a repertoire of identities. 'Forcible dislocation of personality' was what he called the general technique . . ." (51). Stencil's "technique" is consonant with the gradual loss of differentiation that increasing entropy implies. In a world moving toward equilibrium, personality is subject to the same process of homogenization that affects all matter. As his name suggests, Stencil has no specific individuality but rather multiple disguises which are but reactions to and reflections of a given situation.

It is one particular reference in the journals which determines Stencil's activities in the novel. Stencil searches for the mysterious V., realizing that his obsession is more than simply the challenge of discovering the identity of his father's reference. V., or rather, the search for V., allows him the hope that there is discoverable significance beneath the surface of the past, a meaningful progression of events which, whatever they might reveal, would at least reveal something. Thus Stencil's chase of the Lady V., in all her various apparitions, provides him with an "acquired sense of ani-mateness" which he can maintain, it seems, only by continuing to search. Even after Stencil has followed V.'s career to its end, he continues to search for the inert material which comprised her robot body and which was dismantled and scattered. The irony of Stencil's chase is that in pursuing V. he pursues what he most fears. His attempt to counter entropy by imposing the patterns of significance upon V.'s activities leads him instead into its very realm.

Stencil discovers quickly – one suspects he knew from the beginning – that V. is allied with the chaos, wars, hatred, and perversion that charac-terize twentieth-century history, with "those grand conspiracies or fore-tastes of Armageddon" (141). V. manifests her presence in Cairo, during the Fashoda crisis in 1898; in the Venezuelan uprising of 1899, as Victoria Wren; in racial violence and brutality in South West Africa in 1904; in Paris as the Lady V. in 1913, with intimations of the Russian Revolution and World War I; in 1918 and 1919, as Veronica Manganese in Malta and Italy; in 1922, again in South West Africa as Vera Meroving and Hedwig Vogelsang; in 1934, in the sewers of New York, with intimations of World War II; in 1943, in the bombing of Malta, with the death and dismantling of the "Bad Priest," who is the Lady V. in her final inert state. In 1956, Stencil continues to "approach and avoid" as he leaves Malta in pursuit of a Madame Viola. V.'s constantly changing roles and shifting identities, like Stencils's, are at the heart of the historical nightmare that Pynchon depicts.

Pynchon uses the phrase "Jacobean etiology" to describe the sea of ran-dom events in which his characters drift, the unmotivated cruelties they perpetrate and suffer. One character ponders the impossibility of gaining a historical perspective: "Perhaps history this century . . . is rippled with gathers in its fabric such that if we are situated, as Stencil seemed to be, at the bottom of a fold, it's impossible to determine warp, woof or pattern anywhere else. By virtue, however, of existing in one gather it is assumed there are others, compartmented off into sinuous cycles each of which come to assume greater importance than the weave itself and destroy any con-tinuity. . . . We are accordingly lost to any sense of a continuous tradition"

(141). Fictions of historical coherence have been replaced by an entropic vision which rejects historical explanation: Stencil is unable, despite his search for causal connections, to give destruction "a name or a face." The utter ambiguity of V. is thus essential to Pynchon's portrayal of our times.

V. is presented as a graphic example of entropic decline into inert matter. She begins as a girl, Victoria Wren, and ends as a machine, flesh and blood replaced by plastic and vinyl circuitry. Her final apparition is on the island of Malta during World War II, where she is dismantled by curious children. She has a wig which covers a bare scalp tattooed with a crucifixion scene, artificial feet with slippers attached to her legs, "the two sliding out as a unit, lug-and-slot . . .," false teeth, a glass eye with the iris in the shape of a clock, and a star sapphire in her navel. But even this is not the end of V., for she lives on in Stencil's distorted fantasies. In 1956, he envisions the product of continued entropic decline, complete with nylon limbs, butyrate veins, and photoelectric eyes. Here, the author's literal objectification of the female body would be more repulsive if it were not part of a world which is in its entirety moving toward inanimateness. Stencil focuses his own progressive objectification and that of his culture in his image of V. His fantasy is yet another manifestation of "the politics of slow dying," the entropic movement toward annihilation.

The violence which surrounds V., and which exudes a kind of sick fascination for Stencil, unfailingly results from the surrender of human value and moral distinctions, and is another effect of entropic leveling. One could list example after example where perversion and brutality reign. Perhaps one, the atrocities visited upon the native population of South West Africa by the German colonial administrators during the first years of this century, will do. General Lothar von Trotha, after demonstrating "a certain expertise at suppressing pigmented populations," murders 60,000 Herero men, women, and children. Foppl, the political and moral successor of von Trotha, describes the grisly means by which the annihilation edict was effected. The relish with which he tells of the slow strangulation of the Hereros suggests that such inhumanity may provide a kind of perverted catharsis for the murderers. Foppl speaks of his love for his mentor, von Trotha: "He taught us not to fear. It's impossible to describe the sudden release; the comfort, the luxury; when you know you could safely forget all the rote-lessons you'd had to learn about the value and dignity of human life. I had the same feeling once in the Realgymnasium when they told us we wouldn't be responsible in the examination for all the historical dates we'd spent weeks memorizing . . ." (234). Foppl's analogy is instructive. To be released from historical dates and the continuities that they imply is to be released from moral responsibility. If the past can be dismissed, so can the present and the future: Every act becomes an isolated event without consequence and without moral content. The undoing of historical distinctions is complete when Foppl tells a servant whom he is brutally beating that the second coming is at hand. In a grotesque parody of apocalyptic imagery, Foppl describes the second coming – of General Lothar von Trotha. Speaking to the suffering man, he says: "Your people have defied the Government . . . they've rebelled, they have sinned. General von Trotha will have to come back to punish you all. He'll have to bring his soldiers with the beards and the bright eyes, and his artillery that speaks with a loud voice. How you will enjoy it, Andreas. Like Jesus returning to earth, von Trotha is coming to deliver you. Be joyful; sing hymns of thanks. And until then love me as your parent, because I am von Trotha's arm, and the agent of his will" (222). Moral equilibrium, the concomitant of physical heat death, has set in.

Despite the "impersonation and dream" which shrouds history for Stencil, there is nothing subjective about the passage of time, nor would we expect there to be in a novel that repeatedly posits the thermodynamics of entropy as its operative metaphor. In a setting that might lend itself to naturalistic description, Pynchon insists instead on the mechanical. A character comments on the futile attempts of the inhabitants of the Egyptian desert to keep back the sand: "The desert moves in. It happens, nothing else. . . . And now the house begins to fill with desert, like the lower half of an hourglass which will never be inverted again" (70–1). Another character thinks of human beings as "the weights of a fantastic clock" (216), necessary only to keep time in motion. Yet another character expresses a twentieth-century view of temporal mechanics: "The party, as if it were inanimate after all, unwound like a clock's mainspring toward the edges of the chocolate room, seeking some easing of its own tension, some equilibrium" (41).

Stencil is only one among several characters in this novel who are obsessed with the problem of interpreting history. Fausto Maijstral is more trustworthy than Stencil in his reading of history for, unlike Stencil, Fausto's experience is not merely vicarious. He has lived through World War II on the island of Malta and looks back, not so much to make sense of his own past – he knows that he cannot – as to communicate to his daughter the importance of that past as well as of the future. From the outset, Fausto advises her to accept the past as she finds it, a St. Giles fair, a balloon floating upward on the gusts, "illustrating the colorful whimsy of history." Unlike the journals bequeathed to Stencil, which seem to suggest a conspiracy of evil centered around V., Fausto's journal insists upon "life's single lesson: that there is more accident to it than a man can ever admit to in a lifetime and stay sane" (300). Whereas Stencil vainly attempts to decode the underground messages he vaguely perceives, and fit them into patterns he himself creates, Fausto accepts the world that is. Instead of paranoia, Fausto recommends perseverance as the appropriate stance vis-à-vis historical indeterminacy. Fausto understands the kind of retreat into passive paranoia which attracts Stencil, the entropic drift toward the inanimate which Stencil can't avoid, because as a young man Fausto was caught in that same current of "slow apocalypse." The "slow apocalypse" to which he refers is in fact entropy, a movement toward the time "when like any dead leaf or fragment of metal they'd be finally subject to the laws of physics" (301). The mature Fausto knows that entropy is inadequate and misleading as a metaphor for human activity. He also rejects the metaphor of apocalypse, finding its humanized history fallacious, its fiction of a great struggle unacceptable. For Fausto, both metaphors – entropy and apocalypse – confuse the human with the nonhuman. Apocalypse invests the physical universe with human significance; entropy dehumanizes humanity. Rather, one must separate the animate from the inanimate, recognize the difference, and live in "a universe of things which simply are."

Although Fausto rejects the metaphors of apocalypse and entropy, he does not reject metaphor altogether. For his own operative metaphor, he chooses the immovable rock which is the island of Malta, and the invincibility which that image implies. To assert one's rockhood is, paradoxically, to assert one's humanity, and deny entropy as a force in human affairs. To refrain from investing history with mysterious powers, and acknowledge that life is an accumulation of small accidents, is the only viable approach to contemporary history. One must live despite the lack of guarantees. Fausto is unique among Pynchon's characters in his growth toward self-awareness and in his sensitivity: Chapter 11, "The Confessions of Fausto Maijstral," stands in distinct contrast to the "impersonation and dream" of the other chapters, in which the characters and their world move "from the quick to the inanimate."

Counterpointing Stencil's search for V. in the past and Fausto's use of the past to understand the present is the activity of Benny Profane and his friends. The Whole Sick Crew, as they refer to themselves, epitomizes Pynchon's criticism of mass culture.[16] They are part of a "technologically splintered humanity," not individualized but homogenized, not directed in their movement but peripatetic, frenetic. Each is related, socially, psychologically, often spiritually and sexually, to some machine or other as he or she becomes increasingly dehumanized. And, conversely, machines become more and more human. The interchangeable, even indistinguishable, nature of the mechanical and the human becomes horrifyingly explicit when SHOCK and SHROUD, computers that provide alter egos for Benny Profane, remind him of the Jewish corpses at Auschwitz, stacked up like car bodies in a junkyard. If Stencil's chase of V. is an attempt to postpone inanimateness even as he pursues just that, so Benny's "yo-yoing" keeps him moving despite his lack of direction or destination. His attempt, like

Stencil's, is futile: In a world of increasing entropy, random motion is the harbinger of heat death. Benny's movement becomes more and more mindless, until at the end of the novel he succumbs totally to entropy and is carried into the sea by "momentum alone."

The members of the Crew belong to one of two categories, the "hothouse" or the "street," and each is removed in its own way from the realities of the present. On the one hand, the hothouse group lives in a hermetically sealed world of the past, and, on the other, the radically activist street group exists in the "dreamscape of the future." In these chapters dealing with Benny and the Crew, experience is presented as either a retreat into the past or an escape into the future. Despite Pynchon's keen sense of modern history, and his ability to describe in blackly comic terms just about anything U.S. culture has produced in this century, this oversimplification limits the success of these chapters. It is possible that much contemporary chaos is the result of one skewed temporal perspective or the other, but the very cultural multiplicity which Pynchon evokes so effectively in the novel as a whole obviates the easy categories the Crew represents.

The language of the Whole Sick Crew, filled with clichés and with the formulae of contemporary mass media, foreshadows the subject of Pynchon's subsequent novel, *The Crying of Lot 49*. If in *V*. entropy has most obviously invaded history and personality, its invasion of language is the focus of Pynchon's second novel.[17] Just as molecular organizations are prey to increasing disorganization, so is the information carried in any given message. Entropy is a measure of disorganization, and the information contained in a message is a measure of organization. Messages, like other forms of organization, may be conceived of as tending toward disorder in a world where there is a low probability of thermodynamic order. Whereas Faulkner's and García Márquez's apocalyptic narrators have little left *except* their faith in the capacity of language to order the historical chaos they confront, Pynchon's narrators and characters no longer count even upon that. The search of Oedipa Maas, the main character of *The Crying of Lot 49*, for a "revelation" amidst the roar of electronic popular culture is a central irony of the novel – the analogue of Stencil's search for historical form in the polymorphous V. Like Stencil, Oedipa attempts to oppose the entropic drift of her world, but she is no more successful than Stencil. The novel ends with Oedipa awaiting the crying of Lot 49, the auctioning of a group of forged stamps which she hopes (vainly, we suspect), will yield some revelation of historical meaning.[18]

As in *The Crying of Lot 49*, the issues raised by the use of entropy as a metaphor for social phenomena are left unresolved in *V.* . The characters' attempts to reconstruct the historical material of the novel end inconclusively, subverted by the novel's theme-and-variation effect and by the novelist's insight into the obsessiveness he depicts. Fact and fiction blend in endlessly self-perpetuating paranoid fantasies. Of course apocalyptic narratives may also be read on some basic level as paranoid fantasy but, unlike Pynchon's entropic vision, they are not endless or unresolved. On the contrary, they propose an emphatic end to persecution, whether real or imagined, and temporal rescue and/or recuperation provides their primary motivation. Nevertheless, *V.* and *The Crying of Lot 49* do succeed in conveying political and cultural and technological abuses. If the "slow apocalypse" of *V.* contrasts with the headlong pace of time sensed by Faulkner's and García Márquez's narrators, and if both *V.* and *The Crying of Lot 49* are inconclusive in ways that the apocalyptic fictions of Faulkner and García Márquez are not, it is because Pynchon's novels accurately reflect an unresolved tension at the heart of contemporary U.S. culture. In their dramatized ambivalence toward (and ultimate rejection of) technology as an unalloyed agency of progress, Pynchon calls into question the very definition of the future in the United States. He portrays a consumer culture whose appetite for novelty is insatiable, and which is devoid of a genuine historical sense for this reason. Although his characters move incessantly from place to place, and his descriptions of popular culture literally sizzle with electric voltage, Pynchon's images of entropic decline and stasis are well suited to his intuition of the bankruptcy of the U.S. positivist project.

III.

With *Gravity's Rainbow* (1973), Pynchon's use of entropy as a social metaphor, and his own entropic vision of human reality, fail him. The application of the metaphor in *V.* and *The Crying of Lot 49* is successful because Fausto and Oedipa provide the structural means by which to measure entropic disintegration; the reader has the perspective necessary to follow the entropic process operating in the context of the novels. In *Gravity's Rainbow* the reader senses the entropic disintegration of the novel itself.

I have already suggested that the use of entropy as a metaphor for human affairs is limited in its application. As a metaphor upon which to base novelistic interactions, it can suggest the chaos of contemporary society, but it can also lead to narrative and thematic confusion, as it does in *Gravity's Rainbow*. Entropy is a quantitative determination of the natural tendency of molecules, the *statistical* measure of microscopic behavior when all constraints are absent and when all elements in the system assume an equal position in the whole. Entropy may be used to suggest order and disorder, as Pynchon uses it, but it is *not* in fact a measure of spatial disorder as such, and certainly not its cause. Rudolph Arnheim, in his study entitled *Entropy and Art: An Essay on Disorder and Order,* states that it is easy to mistake entropy for a natural force, when in fact it does not describe a natural process; rather, it measures the *effects* of a natural process. "It is a standard measurement like the gram or the meter. . . . The physics of entropy tends to consider only the initial and final state of a process, not the dynamic events leading from one to the other."[19] The quantitative rather than qualitative nature of entropic law is obvious as we realize that it encompasses no means by which to differentiate among the various elements in a system, no means to account for causal factors. Thermodynamics exhibits no curiosity; certain statistical characteristics obtain at the outset and others emerge according to the laws of statistical probability, without regard to either the mechanisms of the process or the nature and character of the various molecular species concerned. The inability to assign relative importance to relative phenomena is also the chief characteristic – and the source of the failure – of *Gravity's Rainbow*. Whereas in his earlier work Pynchon does impute value to characters, behavior, and relationships, in *Gravity's Rainbow,* characters, events, relationships, and a great weight of erudition are poured into the novel, to emerge like the identical atomic particles measured by the law of entropy.

The equating of events which are not at all equal is, I think, the most serious confusion into which the metaphor of entropy leads Pynchon. Because the relation of cause and effect is not by definition integral to the law of entropy, there is a tendency, when using entropy as a metaphor, toward the leveling of all elements to the same moral plane (if the novelist does not specifically create exceptions to the general compliance with the law of entropy, as he does in Fausto and Oedipa). *Gravity's Rainbow* is set in the last few months of World War II in Europe and in the subsequent period of occupation. All of the participants in the war, according to Pynchon, are equally guilty (or is it innocent?), for all of them supposedly respond to exactly the same economic motivation. The death and destruction of war is simply a secondary effect:

> Don't forget the real business of the War is buying and selling. The murdering and the violence are self-policing, and can be entrusted to non-professionals. The mass nature of wartime death is useful in many ways. It serves as spectacle, as diversion from the real movements of the War. It provides raw material to be recorded into History, so that children may be taught History as sequences of violence, battle after battle, and be more prepared for the adult world. Best of all, mass death's a stimulus to just ordinary folks, little fellows, to try 'n' grab a piece of the Pie while they're still here to gobble it up. The true war is a celebration of markets.[20]

Thus, the killing of Jews in concentration camps is no different from killing on the front; the German aggression in Europe and the American retaliation in Germany are all the same thing. Though the reader imagines at the outset that such a statement is meant to be ironic, it becomes more and more evident that broad statements of quantitative, rather than qualitative, behavior are all that Pynchon is willing to construct. The leveling is complete with a statement that follows the one quoted above: "So, Jews are negotiable. Every bit as negotiable as cigarettes, cunt, or Hershey bars" (105). A war which was radically ideological becomes, under the influence of what we might call the entropic fallacy, a kind of physical process in which all acts and events are simply statistical phenomena in a field where there is no moral differentiation or value.

Characters, like events, are treated without moral distinction. Just as the war is propelled by economic interests, so all of the characters are propelled by sex, or more accurately, by Freudian clichés about sex. Pynchon has commented in the introduction to his collected short stories that in his early fiction, sex and death are linked; this is characteristic of *Gravity's Rainbow* as well. The ubiquitous V-2 rocket is of course a towering phallic symbol, and every character has his or her particular sexual relationship to the rocket. Messenger of death and destruction, it is a symbol of sex not as procreative but as destructive, as a kind of death wish, a total loss of self. A character comments casually about Slothrup, whose particular reaction to the V-2 has provided the major plot device of the novel. Referring to Slothrup and a supposed German psychiatrist–scientist, the voice says, "There never was a Dr. Jamf . . . Jamf was only a fiction, to help him explain what he felt so terribly, so immediately in his genitals for those rockets each time exploding in the sky . . . to help him deny what he could not possibly admit: that he might be in love, in sexual love, with his, and his race's death" (738). Blicero, a German commander and the most perverted character of the novel, also has his sexual relationship to the rocket, sending his young lover, Gottfried, up in one of the V-2s, one of those "bright angels of death," in order to possess him more completely. It is typical of this novel that there is no assignment of relative significance to the juxtaposed accounts of Blicero and Slothrup. Each is merely and simply "in love with death." No matter that one has imposed death on countless victims and that the other is a kind of blundering innocent.

Freud, whose concepts, when they are reduced to a set of monologic symbols as they are in this novel, is a particularly amenable source of support for the entropic vision of human beings. In defining what he called the Nirvana principle, Freud expresses his belief that the psyche strives to keep tension at a minimum or to eliminate it entirely, that the instincts are all directed toward a return to the inorganic state. An oversimplification of this concept leads to the conclusion that the inherent goal of life is death, that life-sustaining instincts are mere detours, hesitations, imposed reactions to disturbances. David Riesman, for example, has asserted in an essay on Freud: "It seems clear that Freud, when he looked at love or work, understood man's physical and psychic behavior in the light of the physics of entropy and the economics of scarcity."[21] Though I do not subscribe to this statement, I cite it because it seems to describe the understanding operating in *Gravity's Rainbow*. The combination of simplified Freudianism and thermodynamic theory can be used, or rather abused, to justify a vision of individuals as endless waves of humanity created for death rather than life. Blicero is an example of such reasoning.

With Germany obviously only days from losing the war, death is more than ever the principal force operating in this character's history. It is not, however, Blicero's own death or those which he has caused, but the death of the world which occupies his attention. He says:

> And sometimes I dream of discovering the edge of the World. Finding that there is an end. . . . But it has cost me so much.
>
> America was the edge of the World. A message for Europe, continent-sized, inescapable. . . . America was a gift from the invisible powers, a way of returning. But Europe refused it. . . .
>
> In Africa, Asia, Amerindia, Oceania, Europe came and established its order of Analysis and Death. What it could not use, it killed or altered. In time the death-colonies grew strong enough to break away. But the impulse to empire, the mission to propagate death, the structure of it kept on. Now we are in the last phase. American Death has come to occupy Europe. . . . Will our new Edge, our new Death kingdom, be the Moon? (722–3)

To Blicero, with this planet in a shambles, only another world altogether removed from this one seems likely to offer a future. This thinking is an ironic inversion of the apocalyptic optimism originally associated with America by Europeans as a place for a new beginning: the future that Blicero projects will be nothing more than an extension of the present, "our new Death kingdom." So Blicero withdraws from the dying world into his jealously guarded alienation.

Earl Rovit, in his essay on modern apocalyptic messianism from which I quoted earlier, suggests that to see the world as a wasteland responsible only to death is to move from the historical to the hysterical, "from history to mystery . . . from history to the sacred mysteries of crematorium smoke, of broken bodies as discarded phrases of a romantic poem that failed, of an abortive drama of destiny. . . ."[22] To consign the world to death as Blicero does is to dismiss the reality of the present and arrogate to oneself powers that will expedite the cosmic consummation. Blicero's devaluation of historical reality leads him to create his own, a reality in which he controls both life and death, a game in which he decides the fate of the players:

> he has chosen the game for nothing if not the kind of end it will bring him, nicht wahr? . . . He only wants now to be out of the winter, inside the Oven's warmth, darkness, steel shelter, the door behind him in a narrowing rectangle of kitchen-light gonging shut, forever. The rest is foreplay.
>
> Yet he cares, more than he should and puzzled that he does, about the children – about their motives. He gathers it is their freedom they look for, yearningly as he for the Oven, and such perversity haunts and depresses him. . . . (99)

The confusion of history with private mysteries is the fascist's justification. Death is the awaited reality; life is only "foreplay." Pynchon's entropic novel is filled with such death dreams, and there is no life-confirming vision, whether historical or narrational, to counterbalance them.

Gravity's Rainbow succumbs to entropy in its style as well as in its content. Whereas Oedipa, in *The Crying of Lot 49,* is aware of the possibility of words as vehicles of meaning – even of revelation – despite the noise that surrounds her, for the characters in *Gravity's Rainbow* there is only noise. I have described messages as patterns of organization, subject to entropy like other forms of organization. Since, in the realm of thermodynamics, entropy increases with the probability of a molecular state, it would seem that information, if it is to resist entropy, must be improbable. The more probable the message, the less information it supposedly carries. Poems mean more than clichés. Herein lies another entropic fallacy to which Pynchon accedes. Not only great poems but also totally disordered sequences of words are improbable. Certainly the great variety and frequent shifts of tone and style in *Gravity's Rainbow* are improbable, but improbability does not in this case imply heightened meaning. The plethora of styles, the technical and mathematical talk, the redundancy, the songs, and verbal pyrotechnics are offered as if to affirm that language has reached the late stages of entropy. What at the outset of the novel seems to be a certain stylistic vivacity exhausts its energy in frenetic attempts at novelty.[23]

Despite the variety of perspectives, tones, styles in *Gravity's Rainbow,* its prose remains strangely distant and unmoving. There is a detachment on the part of the narrative voice which does in fact achieve the "forcible dislocation of personality" to which Stencil aspires in *V.* . The author has been praised for his sense of theater in this novel. Again and again segments occur where the speaker seems to watch him- or herself acting, playing a part in which he or she has no vested interest other than implicit narcissism.

Such a scene is this one, in the car of a theater manager on the Santa Monica Freeway:

> Laughter surrounds you. Full, faithful-audience laughter, coming from the four points of the padded interior. You realize, with a vague sense of dismay, that this is some kind of stereo rig here, and a glance inside the glove compartment reveals an entire library of similar tapes: CHEERING (AFFECTIONATE), CHEERING (AROUSED), HOSTILE MOB in an assortment of 22 languages, YESES, NOES, NEGRO SUPPORTERS, WOMEN SUPPORTERS, ATHLETIC – oh come now – FIRE-FIGHT (CONVENTIONAL), FIRE-FIGHT (URBAN), CATHEDRAL ACOUSTICS. . . .
>
> "We have to talk in some kind of code, naturally," continues the Manager. "We always have. But none of the codes is hard to break. Opponents have accused us, for just that reason, of contempt for the people. But really we do it all in the spirit of fair play. We're not monsters. We know we have to give them some chance. We can't take hope away from them, can we?" (756)

Funny as this scene is in parts – indeed, as funny as the novel is in parts – the detached attitude toward language as canned response or incomprehensible code, both serving the purpose of manipulating a mass audience, is not at all funny. Again, we might wish to find some structural or narrative device that would cast ironic light on such passages as the one above, but again, there is none. This lack of any moral or historical or narrative order against which to measure the disorder deprives the novel of much of its intellectual and emotional impact. Whereas Pynchon uses the physics of entropy in his early works to mold the amorphousness of mass society and the atrocities of modern history into novelistic form, the same physics becomes a mode of retreat in *Gravity's Rainbow*. Perhaps the sense of increasing entropy leads away from serious treatment of the world to private fantasies of the self. Indeed, it is for this reason that the metaphor of entropy is explicitly rejected by both Ernesto Sábato,[24] and by Walker Percy, as we will see in Chapter 6.

IV.

I began my discussion of Pynchon's fiction by asserting that entropy is not a metaphor of common currency in contemporary Latin American fiction. There are Latin American metaphoric analogues to this thermodynamic *mundus senescit,* of course, but they are naturalistic rather than mechanistic or technological. The jungle signals in several novels the steady loss of organization in the civilizations upon which it relentlessly encroaches. One thinks of Mario Vargas Llosa's *The Green House* (1965), Alejo Carpentier's *The Lost Steps* (1953), García Márquez's *Leaf Storm* (1955) and *One Hundred Years of Solitude,* in which Macondo's apocalypse is preceded by its inhabitants's prolonged and futile battle against the aggressive fecundity of the usurper tropics. In contrast, Pynchon's description of the encroachment of the Egyptian desert on a settlement of houses, in the passage from *V.* which I cited earlier, does not demonstrate the futility of human effort, but rather the purely physical laws to which the world and its human occupants are subject: Human energy, like every other kind, must dissipate and, once dissipated, is quite simply gone. As I have said, thermodynamic law is not weighted by moral or ethical distinctions: Energy is by definition merely spent, never misspent. Human effort to oppose oblivion can have no tragic consequences for Pynchon's characters, as it does for the Buendías or Quentin Compson.

If the jungle eats at the city from the outside in Latin American fiction, the cities themselves are often portrayed as natural wastelands of desolate and powerful grandeur. In several works, urban decline is concentrated symbolically in a dilapidated house. The insubstantial structure stands at the center of the city in question, suggesting past eras of familial and national pride and wealth, but now possessed only by a palpable nostalgia for those irretrievable times. In the previous chapter, I mentioned the Buendía house; other examples are Consuelo's house on Donceles Street in the oldest part of Mexico City in Carlos Fuentes's *Aura* (1962), and the mansions-become-tenements in his story, "These Were Palaces" (1981); the grandparents' house in Santiago in José Donoso's brilliant novel of autobiographical reminiscence, *This Sunday* (1965), as well as the house in his *The Obscene Bird of Night* (1970); and the Olmos Acevedo house in Buenos Aires in Ernesto Sábato's *On Heroes and Tombs* (1962).

These Latin American metaphors depart from the metaphor of entropy not only in their naturalism but also in the synecdochal relation to the novelistic world in which they are located. Whereas entropy is used to suggest the generalized tendency of the whole, from which the tendency of the parts may be inferred, the Latin American metaphors suggest the tendency of the parts, from which we may infer the direction of the whole. The totalizing impulse characteristic of Latin American fiction is served by this metaphorical strategy. The end of the Buendía house or the Olmos Acevedo house *is* the end of the world. The microcosm has been carefully designed to stand for, and then supplant, the macrocosm.

Cuban novelist José Lezama Lima epitomizes these Latin American visions of progressive decay with another metaphor taken from nature. He speaks of a crepuscular or twilight vision ("lo crepuscular"), as opposed to an apocalyptic vision ("lo apocalíptico o catastrófico"), and suggests that in the evolution of culture, the crepuscular sensibility follows upon and replaces the apocalyptic.[25] According to Lezama, after the collapse of apocalyptic oppositions and expectations, there is a sense of resignation, almost of relief, at the certainty of the approaching night. Like the entropic vision, this twilight vision described by Lezama contains no dazzling,. potential New Jerusalem, no sense that the world may yet begin again. Nevertheless, his naturalistic metaphor, like those in the Latin American novels I have just named, endows the end with an acceptability, almost a benediction, that is not present when entropic chaos engulfs a fictional world.

The contrast I am proposing here between Latin American naturalistic metaphors and U.S. postmodernist, mechanistic metaphors is offered as a generalization. As such, it has its exceptions and is therefore not to be insisted upon. Nevertheless, it allows me to return for a moment to the question of William Faulkner's influence on contemporary Latin American writers. It is easy to accept Faulkner's influence – remarkably strong fifty years and more after the publication of *Absalom, Absalom!* – on the grounds of the shared historical and cultural experiences of the U.S. Southerner and the Latin American which I have already mentioned. What is surprising is that more recent, highly original, postmodernist U.S. writers such as Pynchon are so rarely cited as influences, or even mentioned as significant, by Latin American writers. Clearly Faulkner's philosophical naturalism is consonant with a Latin American sense of time and history, as the mechanistic understanding inherent in much postmodern U.S. fiction is not. These differences may be traced back to two divergent twentieth-century philosophical strains.

If the essential influence on Pynchon's thinking about time, and an important one for U.S. postmodernism generally, is Henry Adams, for Faulkner it is, as he himself said in an interview, "Bergson, naturally."[26] Henri Bergson's organic view of time is based on biology, as Henry Adams's mechanical view is based on physics; Bergson's definitional term for the propelling force of time is vitalism, Adams's is dynamic mechanism. The title of Bergson's *Creative Evolution* suggests his preference for the dominant scientific vision of the nineteenth century, whereas Adams explicitly dismisses Darwinism in favor of the essential twentieth-century sciences, physics and mechanics. The affinity of Faulkner for Bergson's organic conception of time is certainly part of what Hugh Kenner means when he writes that Faulkner is the last American "mutation" of the novelistic procedures that stem from the nineteenth century.[27]

I have already noted that Darwinism projects a model of temporal progression which contradicts the entropic model: Evolution moves from the simple structure to the more complex. For Bergson, too, time is directional ("We perceive duration as a stream against which we cannot go"), and effectual ("if [time] *does* nothing, it *is* nothing").[28] But his primary interest is in time as it is filtered by the experiencing consciousness, a process that is historical but not logically (or mechanically) so. Following his metaphor of organic evolution, Bergson argues that *la durée* is not rationally predictable but rather accretive and intuitional: "Duration is the continuous progress of the past which gnaws into the future and which swells as it advances. And as the past grows without ceasing, so also there is no limit to its preservation" (45). He dismisses mere rational understanding of time under the term *radical mechanism:* "As soon as we go out of the encasings in which radical mechanism . . . confines our thought, reality appears as a ceaseless up-springing of something new, which has no sooner arisen to make the present than it has already fallen back into the past; at this exact moment it falls under the glance of the intellect whose eyes are ever turned toward the rear" (53). Radical mechanism is rational, and therefore an external, retrospective view of time; whereas, Bergson argues, our mental experience of time is a far more complex and elusive thing.

Faulkner, like Bergson, explicitly rejects a mechanistic understanding of time. In *The Sound and the Fury,* Quentin Compson removes the hands from his watch in an attempt to escape "the mechanical progression" of time, remembering his father's comment that "time is dead as long as it is being clicked off by little wheels; only when the clock stops does time come to life."[29] The organic conception of time which compels Faulknerian narration is epitomized in *Absalom, Absalom!* by Quentin's well-known comparison of the process of narration to a pebble tossed into a pool, with its resulting ripples moving and spreading through the water from pool to pool, one attached to the next by "a narrow umbilical water-cord" (261). And yet, despite Quentin's Bergsonian accretive narration in *Absalom, Absalom!,* he fails to escape mechanical time. Though Faulkner's characters refuse to yield to mechanical temporal progression, their refusal is no less fatal than the passive acceptance of entropic inevitability by most of Pynchon's characters.

To relate Bergson's organicism to Faulkner's apocalypticism and to my own discussion, we must consider the philosopher's rejection of what he calls *radical finalism,* a concept that he associates with radical mechanism. According to Bergson, radical finalism and radical mechanism both presuppose a historical plan that has been previously arranged. Their basic presumption is that the future and the past are calculable functions of the present . . . that all is given. This is of course precisely the presumption of both the apocalyptic and the entropic visions of universal history, though the biblical apocalyptist bases his "calculation" not on physical principles but on what he believes to be divine revelation, and modern apocalyptists, on their own narrative projections of historical pattern. Bergson rejects such overarching temporal patterns and projections on the basis that they sacrifice experience to a system and thus obviate humanity's participation in duration.

Bergson's rejection of such teleological time schemes as apocalypse would seem to call for the revision of my argument in the preceding chapter that Faulkner's character Quentin is an apocalyptist. But just as Bergson seems most emphatic in his rejection, he concedes an essential point. The absence of an end does not obviate our wanting one. Or creating one. Here Bergson anticipates by more than half a century the current literary critical distinction between the lack of historical ends and the necessity of fictional endings. He recognizes that in order to act we must invent ends: "the human intellect, inasmuch as it is fashioned for the needs of human action, is an intellect which proceeds at the same time by intention and by calculation, by adapting means to ends and by thinking out mechanisms of more and more geometrical form. . . . In so far as we are geometricians, then, we reject the unforeseeable" (50, 52). So the vitalist Bergson uses the image of geometry to argue for the necessity of artifice, an argument that brings us back to Quentin. In *Absalom, Absalom!*, Faulkner portrays Quentin as creating a fiction of radical finality precisely because he realizes that history is never conclusive. Bergson concludes his own discussion with the observation that we are *all* born artisans, born geometricians.

If one of our last modernists, William Faulkner, is the most appreciated of U.S. writers by contemporary Latin Americans, it is Jorge Luis Borges, arguably the first Latin American postmodernist, who has been most influential on contemporary U.S. writers. If Faulkner's naturalism explains in part his appeal to Latin American writers, Borges's mechanistic vision may in turn explain his position of importance for U.S. postmodernists writers. In Borges's contemplation of the mechanical operations of the cosmos, in his understated despair about the potential for anything other than chaos in a post-Newtonian world, and in his wistful backward glances at the vestiges of past worlds, the Argentine writer is akin not to Bergson and the modernism of which Faulkner's fiction is the culmination, but to the postmodernist temporal attitudes of which Henry Adams is harbinger. This is a proposition I will entertain more fully in my next chapter on the postmodernist fiction of John Barth.

4

ART AND REVOLUTION IN THE FICTION OF JULIO CORTÁZAR

Art is the community's medicine for the worst disease of mind, the corruption of consciousness.

R. G. Collingwood

THE USE OF THE MYTH of apocalypse by writers as different as García Márquez and Pynchon reaffirms its wide artistic appeal. In considering its appeal to the Argentine writer Julio Cortázar, we will not look at the fictional potential inherent in the historiographic patterns of the myth, as we have in the preceding chapters, but rather at its esthetic and political implications. Cortázar is attracted to the visionary energy of the myth of apocalypse, to its revitalizing power: Its transformative vision becomes for Cortázar the central metaphor for the artistic imagination operating under extreme conditions of personal and/or political crisis.[1] The apocalyptic imagination is subversive in its recognition that present forms of thought and action are inadequate, and revolutionary in its impulse to create a new synthesis out of psychic or social dislocation. The apocalyptic artist seeks to relocate his or her creative synthesis within a revitalized community, to connect an individual vision to a shared future. Literature is for Cortázar a revolutionary act, an instrument of esthetic and political renewal.

There is no shortage of critical commentary on the nature and processes of the apocalyptic imagination. Austin Farrer, in his seminal study of poesis in the Book of Revelation, discusses apocalyptic images and "the process of inspiration by which they are born in the mind";[2] Kenneth Burke, in his introduction to the reprinted edition of Farrer's study, also emphasizes the insights provided by Revelation into the psychology of creativity. D. H. Lawrence anticipates Farrer's study in his own extended commentary on the Book of Revelation, published in 1931. In this very personal exegesis, Lawrence dismisses the temporal projections and historical explanations of apocalypse in favor of the imaginative activity that it both describes and inspires.[3] He recognized his own affinity (and that of the modern artist

76

generally) to the biblical apocalyptist, struggling against repression and fragmentation to achieve spiritual and symbolic wholeness. Lawrence is particularly attracted to the expansive spatial form and content of the apocalyptic vision. Addressing the open form which the apocalyptic artist is likely to create in his rejection of the constraints of social and literary convention, he argues that the apocalyptic work of art resists completion, that it is constantly struggling to say something that it does not know how to say, something that cannot be said.[4] In Julio Cortázar's fiction, a creative impulse operates that is apocalyptic in these Lawrencian terms. His visions of apocalypse inspire spatial symbols and open narrative structures which challenge the accepted conventions of both artistic and political forms.[5]

In an homage to Julio Cortázar at the time of his death in 1984, Carlos Fuentes praised the Argentine writer's dedication to a dual revolution, internal and external. Fuentes develops this characteristic of Cortázar's by referring not only to the Argentine writer, but also to Octavio Paz. He writes that Cortázar and Paz were both born in 1914 and, for the next generation of writers, they "gave a sense to our modernity and allowed us to believe a bit longer in the adventure of the new. . . . Both Cortázar and Paz spoke of something more than novelty or progress – they spoke of the radically new and joyful nature of every instant, of the body, the memory and the imagination of men and women."[6] Though Cortázar's political commitment differed greatly from that of Paz, their esthetics are, as Fuentes suggests, closely linked. In the following discussion, I will refer to essays by Paz to illuminate the creative process which Cortázar dramatizes in his early fiction on art and artists. Furthermore, we will find that Paz's essays on the nature of revolution are very applicable to Cortázar's later political fiction, the ideological differences of these writers notwithstanding.

Until the mid-1960s, Cortázar was primarily concerned with the portrayal of characters, often artists, who are struggling to bring about revolutionary change in their art and their lives. However, reflecting his growing commitment to liberal political reform in Latin America, Cortázar began to create characters who were not confronting psychic or esthetic limitations, but rather political repression. Cortázar has commented on this transition, saying that at this time, "I realized that as an author, though maintaining my interest in literature, in aesthetics, I could not skirt a very elementary, simple, and important thing: I am Latin American."[7] Cortázar had lived in France since the mid-1950s, so this realization was more than a manner of speaking. It represented his increasing support of Latin American political solutions to what he insisted were pecularily Latin American political situations, namely Castro's Cuba and, more recently, the Sandinista regime in Nicaragua. During the 1970s, the worsening political repression in Argentina made Cortázar aware that his exile in France could no longer be considered voluntary. Much of his late fiction deals with political violence such as that documented in Argentina, and with exile, a condition he portrays as existing under a repressive regime, even when his characters do not leave their country. Thus, the emphasis of Cortázar's revolutionary concerns shifts from art to politics, though never are the two completely separated. Because the apocalyptic imagination addresses both individual and communal ends, we may trace its workings throughout his fiction, underlying and integrating his esthetic and political idealism.

I.

Cortázar's most explicit early portrayal of the artist as apocalyptist is in his story, "The Pursuer" (1964). Johnny Carter is a jazz saxophonist, and it is with his music that he attempts the apocalyptic "explosion" which Cortázar believes to be the artist's function.[8] Jazz provides for Johnny a means of transcending the limitations of time and space, the means of freeing himself from the rational, analytical tendency of Western thought. He seeks to synthesize rather than analyze, to use the chaos of human experience as the substance of his vision, for he conceives of art as created from, not in spite of, chaos. He is aware of the creative work that he must perform, internally, in order to find the holes, as he puts it, through which to project his expansive art.

The apocalyptic movement of Johnny's art is described in spatial terms. It is centrifugal, spinning upward and outward, sending flying fragments into space. His best music is produced in a dreamlike state which is referred to as a spin. His style is "like an explosion in music . . . the crust of habit splintered into a million pieces."[9] This spatial expansion seems limitless: "Incapable of satisfying itself, useful as a continual spur, an infinite construction, the pleasure of which is not in its highest pinnacle but in the exploratory repetitions, in the use of faculties which leave the suddenly human behind without losing humanity" (208). Here, Cortázar describes the open form to which his artist/characters aspire, as he does in his own fiction. This form is never final or definitive because it is neither linear nor stable. The narrator describes Johnny's art as a structure of desire, always searching for "ultimate possibilities" in its continuous creation. And it is both highly individualized and at the same time a source of universal symbols.

The epigraphs of "The Pursuer" address the apocalyptic impulse underlying Johnny's art. The first is from Rev. 2:10: "Be thou faithful unto death."[10] Johnny lives in the presence of death, dreaming of walking the cemeteries of the earth and finding burial urns in the fields. He renounces the limitation of death as he does the limitations of time and space, considering death not an end but a metamorphosis, a means of regeneration. Johnny rejects the notion of life as moving progressively toward a given end, and embraces instead the intimations of eternity, the moments of mystic communion with the universe, that his art provides. Through his music, Johnny attempts to encompass all things in their totality, to reveal a world beyond the reach of rational analysis, a world gained only through the intuitive powers of the mind.

The epigraph is not the only reference in this story to Revelation: Johnny refers to himself in terms of John's imagery, quoting Rev. 8:10, which describes one of the seven trumpet woes: "The name of the star is called wormwood" (234). Wormwood, or absinthe, is associated with bitterness and drunkenness. The star, "burning as it were a lamp," falls into the rivers and fountains, and "Many men died of the water" (Rev. 8:10–11). In apocalyptic writings, angels and stars are often linked. In this case, the star – an angelic being – unlocks the fearful judgment but remains under the control of God. Johnny identifies both with the victims of the star and with the star itself: "they see that you belong a little to the star called wormwood" (235). In this passage, Johnny mixes his verb tenses. Like the biblical apocalyptist, who alternately speaks in the prophetic future, the accomplished past, and the timeless present, Johnny also attempts to overcome the incongruity between the temporal limitations of language and his own encompassing vision. The character's choice of astrological images from Revelation is instructive. The author of Revelation, a political prisoner when he wrote his visionary text, describes expansive celestial vistas which are in inverse proportion to his actual situation and testify metaphorically to his desire to break the bonds that hold him captive. Cortázar's character adds esthetic and psychological levels to the original content of these images. Johnny reminds us that human existence always involves bondage, and that artistic assaults upon that bondage, even if they are short lived, are necessary to sustain our fictions of freedom and our belief in worlds beyond the mind's enclosure. So Cortázar uses the myth of apocalypse to create his own myth of the artist.

It is appropriate that jazz should be Johnny's artistic medium, for jazz is based not only on melodic sequence and synchronized rhythmic patterns, as is most classical and popular music, but also on syncopation and the superimposition of conflicting rhythms. Its structure depends on the apprehension of many unstable elements simultaneously. The connection made between Johnny's art and the myth of apocalypse confirms my assertion that Cortázar, in his early fiction, is interested not in the historical implications of the myth but in its spatial imagery as a metaphor for the imaginative activity of the artist. The affinity of Cortázar's musician for myth is perhaps more completely understood in the general terms suggested by Claude Lévi-Strauss in his "Overture" to *The Raw and the Cooked*. Here Lévi-Strauss compares the temporal structures of myth and music, asserting that both transcend articulate expression and yet require, like speech, a temporal dimension in which to unfold. Myth, like music, exists in tension between experienced time and a "permanent constant" realm, between external, serial time and internal, psychophysiological time.[11] Cortázar emphasizes this paradoxical temporality by having his musician refer to apocalypse, a myth which describes time's movement toward a timeless end.

The second epigraph of this story is Dylan Thomas's phrase: "O make me a mask."[12] Johnny refers several times to Dylan Thomas in the story, and to his own search for a mask which will allow him to transcend his limited point of view, extend his consciousness into space, and surrender himself to cosmic process. His identification with universal truths explains Johnny's vatic intensity, and it also approaches an explanation of his alternation between abjection and euphoria. The authority of the individual vision is often problematic in expression that is presented as inspired. Susan M. Bachmann, in her study of the narrative strategies of Revelation, points to John's vacillation between self-emergence and self-deprecation, and to his shifting narrative motivations, from individual expression to communal imperative, and ultimately, of course, to divine revelation.[13] John speaks of the "annihilating wonder" of his vision (Rev. 1:17), repeatedly asserting that he is merely a vehicle of cosmic truth, a revealer of God's plot rather than a creator of his own. Yet, at the same time, he frequently asserts his own authority as seer and hearer of the text which he himself has written. This narrative ambivalence reflects the ambivalent origin of his revelation – divine and therefore universal, yet also poetic and therefore personal. For Cortázar's artist/characters too, the problem is how to approach the unfathomable source of their vision, and how to find the medium by which to express it.

I do not mean to imply that Johnny Carter's artistic inspiration is in any way ascribed to God, or that his purpose is the same as the biblical apocalyptist's. Nevertheless, the search of Cortázar's visionary artists for an expressive medium is related to the narrative ambivalence of Revelation. Octavio Paz explores the relation between religious utterance and artistic expression in *The Bow and the Lyre,* and his understanding of the psychology of creativity coincides in a number of ways with Cortázar's. Though Paz's primary interest is in poetry, his comments on poetic inspiration are, as he insists at the outset, generally applicable to the many languages of art, including music. In chapters titled "The Poetic Revelation," "Inspiration," and "The Other Shore" (a phrase also used by Cortázar to suggest the movement of the artistic consciousness, both in "The Pursuer" and in his 1963 novel, *Hopscotch*), Paz develops his argument for the congruence of poetic inspiration and religious revelation: "Poetry is knowledge, salvation, power, abandonment. An operation capable of changing the world, poetic activity is revolutionary by nature; a spiritual exercise, it is a means of interior liberation. Poetry reveals this world; it creates another."[14] Paz follows this assertion with an almost breathless incantation of words suggesting the special nature of the new world created by the artist: prayer, litany, epiphany, presence, madness, ecstasy, logos, nostalgia for paradise. Similarly, Johnny Carter, referring to his music, says that he makes his own God, and the narrator of the story confirms the analogy, avowing that when he listens to Johnny's music, he understands why prayer demands that one fall instinctively to one's knees.

Like Cortázar, Paz emphasizes not the temporal progression which a poetic or religious vision may describe, but the timelessness of the visionary experience itself. Though Paz acknowledges that without history and community, poetry would have no meaning, he nonetheless insists that the poem "consecrates" the timeless instant of the poet's revelation: "chronological time – the common word, the social or individual circumstance – suffers a decisive transformation: it ceases to flow, it stops being succession . . ." (169). Paz recognizes what Cortázar dramatizes in his fiction, that this transformation is more problematic for the modern artist than for the religious visionary, because the possibility of inspired revelation contradicts our current conception of the world. Like Cortázar, Paz wishes to counterbalance the emphasis of Western culture on scientific rationalism, and he finds in religious revelation the analogy which he needs to do so. As García Márquez finds in the myth of apocalypse the means to structure his magical histories, Paz and Cortázar find in it the means to usher the idea of inspiration back into the world.

Paz again describes what Cortázar dramatizes in his assertion that artistic revelation is never final or circumscribed. Both authors locate the basis of "the open work" in the universalizing function of poetic inspiration. The artist's search for adequate expression of his or her vision transcends the self and opens up the work of art – both structurally and substantively – to a multitude of meanings. Paz writes: "[Poetry] re-creates man and makes him assume his true condition, which is not the dilemma: life or death, but a totality: life and death in a single instant of incandescence" (139). In Paz's statement, the significance of the two epigraphs of "The Pursuer" may be integrated. Johnny Carter is faithful unto death in this apocalyptic sense of the simultaneous death and rebirth inherent in the moment of vision; his artist's mask, the self-transcendence represented in the universality of his art, is the product of that faith. Here, the "annihilating wonder" of religious vision and artistic inspiration coincide.

Cortázar's artists share the apocalyptist's search for the medium to express his vision, and they share as well an acute sense of the dangers of their undertaking. In Revelation, the power of language is constantly symbolized, but so is its potential perversion. God's word is figured as a double-edged sword, both redemptive and destructive, and also double-edged in the sense that God's enemies may use it to subvert his text. The narrator of

Revelation is obsessed by the possibility that he himself may bear false witness, and he repeatedly symbolizes evil as monsters who speak blasphemous words and dragons who devour truth and spew lies. Language also proves to be double edged in "The Pursuer." The story is narrated by Bruno, a jazz critic whose reputation rests on his definitive verbal analysis of Johnny's jazz style. Bruno wants to make controllable, closed structures of both Johnny's life and art, the same impulse that motivates García Márquez's first-person narrator to recount Santiago's murder in *Chronicle of a Death Foretold*. But unlike that narrator or Johnny Carter, Bruno is not interested in death because it will open up possibilities for rebirth and renewal, but because it will close them off. He hopes Johnny will die so that his analysis will not be undermined by new directions in Johnny's art. So the apocalyptic esthetic Johnny represents in "The Pursuer" is not embodied in the structure of the story itself, for multiplicity and fluidity are threats to the narrator's analytic control. Rather, it is thematized in the description of Johnny's esthetic medium and aspirations, and dramatized ironically in the simultaneous development of the narrator's opposing attitude toward the language of art.

The irony implicit in this story conveys the fact that Johnny's vision is not tenable for long in a culture where reason, rather than passionate transcendence, is the rule. The art critic, the voyeur, easily outlasts Johnny, the voyant. Johnny dies, the book on Johnny's art is published to popular acclaim. That Johnny fails to sustain his unbounded vision does not invalidate it, however, for continual aspiration rather than the finality of achievement is what characterizes Cortázar's apocalyptic esthetic. Although the critic tells us he is sure that Johnny will continue searching after death, he admits that he is delighted not to have to try to understand that search. The story ends with a play on the ambivalence between sealing and unsealing which we have observed in apocalyptic texts. The critic boasts about his "ultimate analysis" of an artist whose art is characterized by its resistance to closure and, hence, to final definition.

There are in Cortázar's fiction a number of artist/characters who confront their limited points of view; like Johnny, each manages momentarily, in a conscious apocalyptic act, to deny the limits of his individual perspective and project himself into an expanded spatial dimension.[15] In "Blow-up" (1964), the photographer Robert Michel finds that his unbounded vision is not accompanied with unbounded powers of expression. The visual language of his blow-up, like the verbal language with which he struggles to write his story, is ultimately inadequate. For Horacio Oliveira, the Argentine intellectual and novelist manqué in *Hopscotch* (1963), apocalyptic visions again serve to focus artistic desire rather than fulfillment. The novel is a graphic spatial projection of a spiritual process. The geometrical pattern of the game of hopscotch – a chalk grid, a small stone, the words "heaven" and "earth" in the boxes at the ends of the grid in the Argentine version of the game – becomes a figure for the elusive transcendental reality that Horacio pursues. It symbolizes his intermittent moments of esthetic transcendence, and his ultimate esthetic failure. It is, furthermore, a figure for the structure of the novel itself, and reflects Cortázar's own apocalyptic impulse to abolish the boundaries of narrative genres and conventions. In place of linear narrative progression, spatial relativity becomes the novel's basic structural principle. Cortázar offers a quantity of temporally disconnected narrative fragments which depend for their significance and their synthesis upon the reader's perception of their relationships. If his characters, Johnny Carter, Roberto Michel, and Horacio Oliveira, manage momentarily to create an expanded spatial dimension in their art, Cortázar's multitiered text, *Hopscotch,* offers itself as a lasting example of such art.

Cortázar refers generally to spatial patterns like his hopscotch grid as *figuras*. Whereas John Barth uses geometrical figures, as we will see, to create closed narrative structures, Cortázar's *figuras* are, on the contrary, central to his conception of the open narrative structure. *Figuras* represent systems of relations, intuitive constellations of meaning in which people, events, places relate to each other across time and space in patterns that transcend discursive, diachronic reason. In these patterns of relation, the artist may transcend at least momentarily the limitations of the self to discover an integrated vision – a "crystallization," as Cortázar calls it – such as is symbolized for Johnny Carter by the astrological skies of Revelation. Morelli, the mature novelist in *Hopscotch,* explains that by means of a crystallization, the artist attempts to create "a work which may seem alien or antagonistic to the time and history surrounding them, and which nonetheless includes it, explains it, and in the last analysis orients it towards a transcendence within whose limits man is waiting."[16] This is also the paradox that exists at the heart of apocalyptic narration. The apocalyptic order opposes the historical moment and yet encompasses it, is limited by it yet transcends it. Though Horacio Oliveira does not achieve his artistic crystallization, his failure is presented in a novel which is itself an example of such a creation. The open structure of Cortázar's novel itself remains dynamic, never reaching a point of temporal or spatial stasis, never making a definitive whole out of the fragments. In this novel, and again in *A Manual for Manuel* (1974), Cortázar masters the paradox with which his characters struggle, creating verbal structures that challenge the linear enclosures of diachronic discourse.

I have said that Johnny Carter's situation is analogous to the imprisoned apocalyptist's, and I would extend my assertion to include Roberto Michel and Horacio Oliveira. Cortázar's artist/protagonists occupy an analogous epistemological stance. Each feels imprisoned within a hostile environment which he seeks to transcend by imaginative flight. His transcendence depends upon the mind's mediation, which promises to transform time and place into a timeless, limitless realm. The artist's vision, however, requires language, whether words or another artistic vocabulary, and language, when required to express the inexpressible, inevitably falls short, for it can evoke such a realm only in images which are temporal and in forms which are of necessity limited and specific. Thus, Roberto's animated blow-up becomes a self-reflexive window, Johnny's music is reduced to his critic's verbal summary, and the "heaven" of Horacio's hopscotch pattern is necessarily drawn on the ground. By means of these characters and their experiences, Cortázar integrates into his fiction a rhetoric of self-criticism, a commentary on the problematic endeavor of creating expansive apocalyptic structures in a time-bound world. In his characters' failures, Cortázar demonstrates his awareness of the limitations as well as the possibilities of the artist's shaping mind. These works remind us that transcendent artistic structures lead back to a world of language where bondage is the rule, but they are nonetheless apocalyptic in their assault on the limitations of consciousness and artistic form. Their visionary and narrative energy is directed to overcoming those limitations, to creating new realms of consciousness and new forms in which to express them.

II.

In his essay of eulogy in 1984, Carlos Fuentes wrote of Cortázar that he had more than one dream, that he believed in more than one paradise.[17] Coming from Fuentes, praise for utopian visions is rare, because he knows that such visions may be exclusive, hierarchical, and veer easily toward totalitarianism. However, Fuentes recognizes that Cortázar's idealism is plural and relative. It is not the potential perfection (hence singularity) of utopia his characters seek, but its multiple freedoms – artistic, political, social. The freedom to discover new forms of expression and action is what motivates Cortázar's characters. In fact, Cortázar insists upon the connection between artistic invention and political change: "by revolutionary we must understand not only those who fight for revolution but also those who have inaugurated it in themselves and transmit it through words or sounds or pigment, not to mention those who combine those activities, those assassinated in the Bolivian jungle with a copy of Pablo Neruda's *Canto general* in their pocket till the end."[18] In Cortázar's implicit reference to his countryman Che Guevara, and in his explicit reference to Latin America's great poetic epic of cultural self-definition, he joins the goals of revolution and literature. As in the fiction of García Márquez and Fuentes, visions of apocalypse in Latin American are likely, sooner or later, to be construed as communal mandates.

In the last fifteen years of his life, Cortázar came to insist upon the interconnectedness of artistic and political renewal in ways that he had not before. Specific political aims and activities are not an issue in his early work. Indeed, his character Horacio Oliveira explicitly rejects political engagement. Recall his soliloquy in Chapter 2 of *Hopscotch* on his unwillingness to participate in communal activity, and his quotable commitment to noncommitment: "I'm not renouncing anything, I simply do what I can so that things renounce me" (193). Cortázar, in an interview the year before his death, commented upon his own apolitical stance during the 1950s and early 1960s in Paris, the time of *Hopscotch,* and the change that occurred when he began to sense the significance of the Cuban revolution.[19] Not surprisingly, one of his first stories to embody this change is about the Cuban revolution. In "Reunion" and the other short fiction I will discuss in this section of my chapter, Cortázar's apocalyptic vision acquires a new sense of revolutionary purpose.

As its title suggests, "Reunion" is about a community – in this case, a community that is alienated from the existing social and political system, and that shares a vision of a better future. The narrator of the story is a member of a guerrilla group fighting to enact the ideals of the revolution; though the characters are never explicitly identified, we are given the evidence to deduce that among them is Che Guevara himself. These characters are concerned primarily with survival and strategy, not with artistic expression, as we have seen Cortázar's earlier characters to be. Octavio Paz's distinction between the rebel and the revolutionary is useful in tracing this shift in Cortázar's characters, and in defining their different though related desires. Paz defines the rebel as "the accursed hero, the solitary poet, lovers who trample social conventions underfoot," a definition that easily applies to Johnny Carter or Horacio Oliveira.[20] It is, however, Paz's definition of the revolutionary that applies to Cortázar's characters in "Reunion." Revolutionaries object to the existing social order and believe in the possibility of changing it by means of communal action. The revolutionary, not the rebel, attacks tyranny and envisions sudden leaps forward for society as a whole. Paz concludes: "Art and love are rebels; politics and philosophy revolutionaries" (142).

The narrator of "Reunion" is clearly a revolutionary in Paz's terms, and yet he often reverts to the metaphor of art to describe the collective consciousness and historical aims of the revolution. It is music to which he refers – not jazz this time, but the structural order of the classical sonata. He says, "We have wanted to transform a torpid war into an order which makes sense, justifies it, and ultimately carries it to a victory which will be like the reinstatement of a melody after so many years of hoarse hunting horns, will be a final allegro which follows the adagio like an encounter with light."[21] The order, progression, and resolution of the classical sonata form, rather than the open and improvised structure of jazz, better evokes the revolutionaries' more defined social and political future. The final paragraph of the story reiterates the image of the culminating allegro of history, to which the narrator adds the description of "a star in the middle of the design" (86). This luminous point, "small and very blue," seems calculated to reinforce the vision of the ideal end toward which Marxist history moves.[22]

Like Cortázar's earlier artist/characters, his revolutionaries are aware of historical potential, but much more than the artist, it is the revolutionary's particular compulsion to choose a future and then play out the consequences of this choice. So we detect a changing conception of the goals of both history and narration as Cortázar begins to focus on actual social and political ends. It is Marxist ideology which provides the author with the philosophical means to transpose his early interest in the alienated visionary artist to his subsequent revolutionary political concerns.

As Cortázar knew well, Marxism explicitly connects alienation and revolution. Georg Lukács was the first to call attention to the importance of the Hegelian conception of alienation in Marxist philosophy. In his preface to the reprinted edition of *History and Class Consciousness,* Lukács quoted Hegel to show that the philosopher regarded alienation not as a mental construct or a "reprehensible reality" but "as the immediately given form in which the present exists on the way to overcoming itself in the historical process."[23] Marx follows the thread of this Hegelian argument, Lukács tells us, basing his theory of class-struggle on the tenet that those alienated from existing society – the proletariat – could call into question old forms, create new ones. In humanity's alienation lay the potential to transform the whole of society.

For Cortázar, this is not a utopian ideology in the sense of proposing an unrealizable ideal. Marx understood the human mind as a reflection of the material world, and human history as a dialectical process based on the exigencies of economic and social relations – a model that Cortázar believed to be essential in approaching the political and social realities of contemporary Latin America. But of course Cortázar is also attracted to the utopian idealism inherent in Marxism. He recognized that Marxism *is* idealist in its understanding of history as progressing toward world revolution and world renovation: The goal of history is an egalitarian society which will be instituted by revolution. Marxist historiography is thus allied to apocalyptic eschatology in its emphasis on the teleological nature of temporal movement: Despite Marx's criticism of religion, his vision of the eventual reconstitution of society by the disenfranchised carries the clear traces of biblical apocalypticism.[24] Cortázar makes use of this complementarity of apocalypticism and Marxist idealism in his story "Apocalypse at Solentiname."

The narrator of "Apocalypse at Solentiname" is meant to conjure up

Cortázar himself; among the autobiographical details provided to establish the narrator's identity are a reference to his story "Blow-up," his friendship with the Nicaraguan poet Ernesto Cardenal, his permanent residence in France. He tells of his visit to Solentiname, Ernesto Cardenal's commune on an island in Lake Nicaragua. While there, the narrator sees some paintings by the peasants who form part of the community, and is so impressed that he takes slides of a number of them. They are naive representations of the activities and natural surroundings of the community: The childlike innocence of their Edenic vision is made explicit by the narrator's observation that the paintings are "once more the first vision of the world."[25]

When the narrator returns to his apartment in Paris, he projects the slides he has taken of the paintings, only to have them change before his eyes into scenes of torture and murder. The sudden, irrational explosion of horrifying images from behind the pastoral surface of the paintings seem to burst forth from the narrator's unconscious; they represent the fears, and perhaps the realities, that the narrator has entertained during his visit to Nicaragua. The intensity of the collision between the images of the ideal community of Solentiname and their opposite, the hellish landscape of political repression, reiterates the structures of the opposing images of heaven and hell in traditional apocalyptic narration. The moral tension inherent in the photographs has the effect of suggesting the inevitability of violence in Central America, just as the moral opposites in Revelation – Christ and Antichrist, Whore and Bride, Babylon and New Jerusalem – point to Armageddon.

This story provides a useful pivot for tracing Cortázar's shifting fictional concerns, because its plot is parallel to that of "Blow-up," but the narrators' concerns in the two stories are markedly different.[26] Both narrators are artists, but the essential problem of the narrator in "Blow-up" is how to *tell* his story, whereas how to *tolerate* his story is what torments the narrator of "Apocalypse at Solentiname." The earlier story describes a single potential crime which is averted by the narrator's action, the later story describes accomplished acts of political terrorism. The narrator's action in "Blow-up" results in the rescue of the intended victim, whereas the narrator of "Apocalypse at Solentiname" can only watch passively as the paradise of his photographs assumes the shape of totalitarian hell.

Yet there is nonetheless a hopeful element in the apocalyptic vision of the later story, and that is in its homage to the political and artistic activity of the Nicaraguan poet Ernesto Cardenal. Cardenal has inherited Neruda's place as the foremost Latin American poet speaking for the ideological left; his poetry is known for its social criticism and its advocacy of radical political change. If Cortázar's use of apocalyptic elements in his story is secular, Cardenal's apocalyptic poetry is deeply rooted in the Catholic tradition. Cardenal studied under Thomas Merton at the Trappist novitiate at Gethsemani Abbey in Kentucky during the late 1950s, and eventually completed his studies for the priesthood in Mexico and Colombia. His community of Solentiname was founded on his revolutionary interpretation of Pauline Christianity and on contemporary "theologies of liberation"; before it was destroyed by Samoza, it was a part of the movement of *concienciación* which promotes social and religious awareness on the lowest economic levels of Latin American society.[27] Cardenal's poetic versions of biblical material convey his political and social vision of renewal: His Psalm 21 ends, "A banquet will be set before the poor / Our people will celebrate a great feast / A new people will be born."[28] His poem, "Apocalypse," to which Cortázar specifically alludes in his story, describes the end of the world through political unreason. The poem's narrator uses the images and cadences of Revelation to describe a technological Armageddon but, true to the biblical genre, he concludes by envisioning the regeneration that apocalyptic cataclysm implies.[29] Cardenal insists that in Latin America, spiritual attitudes toward time (hence, salvation) cannot be dissociated from political and social realities; his poetry embodies his desire to overcome the separation between individual hope and collective fulfillment. That the autobiographical narrator of "Apocalypse at Solentiname" sees the realities of violence and death behind the Edenic paintings from Solentiname suggests the extent to which Cortázar has come to conceive of art as serving a political function in Latin America.

"Apocalypse at Solentiname" was published in Spain in 1977; the political content of this story and others in the same collection explains its publications outside of Argentina. The two volumes of short stories which follow it (the author's last) – *We Love Glenda So Much* (1980) and the as-yet untranslated collection, *Deshoras* (1983) – were published in Mexico, and they also contain examples of what one critic has labeled Cortázar's "literatura de denuncia."[30] Though many of the stories in these collections can be fruitfully read on a psychological or esthetic level, they also yield political insights; private relations unmask the realities of politics, and vice versa. Cortázar's stated aim, to demonstrate the common ground of literature and politics, impels the fiction in each of these volumes.

The torture and public violence which irrupt into the Solentiname paintings are the subject of a number of Cortázar's recent stories. "Second Time Around" suggests the politics of torture but never calls it by its name. The author presents a scenario in which a young man simply disappears, thus evoking the horrible reality of thousands of "desaparecidos," people who were arrested in the late 1970s by the military regime in Argentina and were not heard from again.[31] The story is presented from the viewpoints of both victimizers and victims. The victimizers sanitize their language into vague euphemisms in order to deny the moral responsibility – indeed, the reality – of what they are doing, and the language of the victims is equally vague through ignorance and/or fear. Arrest and torture become "procedures," the sites of such activities "offices," and the people summoned to those offices likened to patients sitting in doctors' waiting rooms. Abuses are sanctioned by yet other deformations of language, like "governmental efficiency" and "the good of the country." But if language is the mechanism behind which evil hides, it is also a means of uncovering evil. These stories communicate the unspeakable with dreadful clarity. As I have said, narration, to be properly considered apocalyptic, must entertain the notion of amelioration as well as damnation; it must denounce injustice as it describes it. Like the Solentiname paintings, Cortázar's late stories present images of paradise irretrievably lost and utopias yet to be established. Beneath the descriptions of wrong, the right is always implicit, always potential.

Such is also the case in "We Love Glenda So Much," which addresses totalitarianism in the realms of both art and politics. I have cited Carlos Fuentes's statement that Cortázar believed in more than one paradise. "We Love Glenda So Much" presents characters who believe in only one, and would impose it upon the world. It is as if Cortázar wished to examine the dangers inherent in his own idealism and in the utopian ideology to which he committed his hopes for renewal in Latin America. The first-person narrator of this story describes a group of admirers of the movie actress Glenda Garson. So devoted are they to her work that when she retires they go quietly about the business of collecting all the copies of all of her films and editing them to conform to their conception of her art. They cut scenes that they consider to be inferior, substitute sequences, change their order. Through these activities, which the narrator refers to as their "mission," the fans seek the illusory promise of static perfection: "Glenda's last image in the last scene of the last movie."[32] Their goal is a changeless and hence totally controllable ideal.

The finality of their image of Glenda is threatened, however, when the actress announces that she will come out of retirement to make more films. The narrator, one of her most devout fans, sighs, "a poet had said under Glenda's same skies that eternity is in love with the works of time" (15). Although murder is not mentioned, the reader is given to understand that her disciples will not tolerate any disruption of the static image they have created. Their only means of assuring perfection is to stop time, or at least the life-time of Glenda: "We loved Glenda so much that we would offer her one last inviolable perfection" (16). So they tell themselves that they have no choice. The narrator's insinuation is insidiously indirect, but clear enough. The distinction between "fan" and "fanatic" begins to blur. The implications of their blind devotion and uncritical commitment are social and political as well as esthetic.

Because of their desire to suppress divergences from their own unanimously held ideal, Glenda's fans and their spokesperson (who narrates in the first-person plural) inevitably assume an ideological stance. The achievement of their single, unchanging ideal depends upon absolute obedience to that ideal, and upon the suppression of any possible alternative. The ideological unison of the group's activities is stylistically embodied in their rhythmic repetition of the phrase "we love Glenda so much." The narrator speaks derisively of differences of opinion or moral objections within the group itself ("analytical voices contaminated by political philosophies"), but he assures the reader that such "heresy" has been eradicated. And when certain moviegoers protest that they remember Glenda's films differently, the narrator dismisses public memory as fickle and transitory: "people are fickle and forget or accept or are in search of what's new, the movie world is ephemeral, like the historical present, except for those of us who love Glenda so much" (13).

A seemingly casual narrative juxtaposition – the movie world and historical reality – is significant, for the group's cinematic revisionism and the historical revisionism practiced by repressive political regimes is closely related. As the fans modify cinematic images and hence the public memory of Glenda's art to conform to their requirements, so dictatorship attempts to revise reality by depriving people of their relationship to the remembered past and to the "ephemeral" temporal continuum of human history. The group's editing seems calculated to suggest governmental censorship, and their vision of esthetic totality to suggest political totalitarianism.

It is interesting that another exiled artist, the Czech writer Milan Kundera, indicts political censorship with an image similar to Cortázar's. Kundera begins *The Book of Laughter and Forgetting* with the description of a photograph from which the figure of a discredited Czech leader has been airbrushed into oblivion by the revisionist historians of the Communist Party. Of the agents of this revisionism, Kundera's narrator says, "They are fighting for access to the laboratories where photographs are retouched and biographies and histories are re-written."[33] For Kundera, the images of memory are the essence of individual and communal identity, reference points in the flow of time which differentiate among human beings and cultures. The self is constituted by what we remember, so when the past is intentionally distorted or destroyed, when its names and faces are changed to suit the present, then distinctions among people and nations are lost. Not only would Cortázar's characters in "We Love Glenda So Much" change the face of the past: They are themselves nameless and faceless. Their lack of individualized features and names suggests both the unanimity and the anonymity required by their repressive methods. Of course one might argue that the characters in Cortázar's stories are often nameless, so cerebral and psychological is the fictive interaction among many of them that the sociological identification, the name, is irrelevant. Here, however, the characters seem willfully to have assumed faces without features in order to dissemble their defacing of the past. Their facelessness is a principal source of the malignity that pervades the story.

The retouched image of reality which Glenda's fans create is called by quite another name in the story. The narrator refers repeatedly to the "perfection" that the group seeks. Revision, falsification, intolerance, even murder, are justified in the present for the sake of future "perfection." The narrator explains that "we loved Glenda so much that above and beyond ethical or historical disagreements the feeling that would always unite us remained, the certainty that perfecting Glenda was perfecting us and perfecting the world" (14). What event or idea or person cannot be dismissed as an "ethical or historical discrepancy" if it should happen to conflict with the group's definition of perfection, jostle their static ideal?

Again, Milan Kundera's literary vision resembles Cortázar's, for Kundera describes in similar terms the abuses spawned by an idealized conception of the future which overrides the reality of the present. In an interview with Philip Roth published at the end of *The Book of Laughter and Forgetting,* Kundera says, "Totalitarianism is not only hell, but also the dream of paradise – the age-old dream of a world where everybody would live in harmony, united by a single common will and faith, without secrets from one another. . . . If totalitarianism did not exploit these archetypes [of paradise], which are deep inside us all and rooted deep in all religions, it could never attract so many people, especially during the early phases of its existence. Once the dream of paradise starts to turn into reality, however, here and there people begin to crop up who stand in its way, and so the rulers of paradise must build a little gulag on the side of Eden" (233). Whether it is the "rulers of paradise," as Kundera calls the contemporary Czech leaders about whom he writes, or Glenda's fans who attempt to impose their own absolute definition of the perfection onto the past and the future, they do violence to the multiplicity and variability – the "discrepancies" – of present experience. Cortázar, whose celebration of artistic revelation and political idealism has been a constant theme, dramatizes here the tragic countertruth that visionaries are often blind to all but their own version of the end.

The word "perfection" by definition contains the notion of unanimity and temporal stasis. Words that suggest change over a period of time – progress, growth, development, decay – are in some sense its opposite. Such definition is implicit in Judeo-Christian myth, which proposes that perfect worlds are necessarily outside of time altogether. On either side of history lie the eternal realms of Eden and Israel, or the New Jerusalem. ("Eternal" in this context does not mean "endless" or "forever," but rather "atemporal," "timeless.") Nevertheless, I have said that the biblical apocalyptist, for all his concern with the next world, is passionately engaged in this world – describing its injustices and interpreting God's activity to end injustice. But when the apocalyptic vision shifts from an engagement with the present to focus on a future realm of absolute and unchanging unanimity, there are likely to be abuses such as those perpetrated by Kundera's dictators and Glenda's fans, and, as we will see, by Walker Percy's character, Lancelot. The abuses of dogmatic utopianism are also a central concern in the fiction of Carlos Fuentes.

Those who would impose their vision of perfection on the political or esthetic realm are particularly interested in the consummation of their ideal, in the terminal point of time or form. Throughout "We Love Glenda So Much," the narrator emphasizes "the completed work," "the last, inviolable perfection." In his last sentence, ending and end, form and content seem to coincide, for the finality of his image, placed in the final structural position of the narration, reinforces the group's search for timeless ultimacy: "On the untouchable heights to which we had raised her in exaltation, we would save her from the fall, her faithful could go on adoring her without any decrease; one does not come down from a cross alive" (16). The image justifies the mythic interpretive context in which I have placed the group's fanatic idealism. That the crucifixion image is applied to a contemporary movie star emphasizes the inversions and perversions of such fanaticism; that it is used to conclude the story serves as ironic commentary on the group's intentions to put a stop to time, for the crucifixion is, in its usual Christian context, a symbol not of death but of rebirth. If the cross traditionally represents the subversion of finality, here Cortázar manipulates the meaning of the symbol to imply its opposite. The forceful closure of his account is calculated by the narrator to deny any illusion of temporal continuance or development beyond the ideal which the group has imposed.

It is for this reason that the epilogue to the story, published three years after the story itself, comes as an interesting surprise. "Epilogue to a Story" takes the form of a letter to Glenda Jackson, the model, Cortázar tells us, for his character Glenda Garson, and is labeled with place and date, Berkeley, California, September 29, 1980, where in fact Cortázar was teaching at the time. The author, in an ironic return to his own story, considers the problematic enterprise of detaining a moving medium, whether film, narration, or human history.

In his letter, Cortázar retells the plot of "We Love Glenda So Much" to Glenda Jackson, emphasizing the dialectic in the story between temporal movement and stasis. He reiterates his character's retirement in terms of the group's ideal of arrested movement, her retirement "bringing to a close and perfecting without knowing it a labor which repetition and time would have finally sullied."[34] He describes the group's opposition to Glenda's return in similar terms, explaining that the group is determined to maintain the image they have created, "closed, definitive." But, writes Cortázar to

Glenda Jackson, the continuity of life undermines the finality of fiction. A film called *Hopscotch,* in which she stars, has appeared just after the publication of "We Love Glenda So Much," as if to defy the absolute end which the story proposes. That the new film should have the same title as his best-known novel seems to Cortázar to add force to the defiance. As Glenda Jackson's film undoes the fictional seal on Glenda Garson's art, so Cortázar's epilogue reverses the finality of his story and challenges the very possibility of complete closure in any esthetic structure. The epilogue ends with a reference to Glenda Jackson's next movie.

III.

The ending of Cortázar's novel about revolution, *A Manual for Manuel,* (1974) contains elements comparable to the ending of "We Love Glenda So Much," and it is with a brief discussion of those elements that I will conclude this chapter. The novel describes a revolutionary group, several of whom are Argentines, in Paris. We read of their political and their personal relations, in particular those of a character named Andrés, who begins as an observer but during the course of the novel makes a commitment to the activities and goals of the revolution. Andrés keeps a record of the group and of contemporary events to give someday to the baby son of one of the members of the group. The record is in the form of a scrapbook, with short entries comprising an open narrative structure like that which Morelli describes in *Hopscotch.* Interspersed among the short narrative sections that describe the characters' revolutionary activities are actual, dated newspaper clippings, reproduced government records and diagrams, interviews of cases of torture as reported in the Forum for Human Rights. This factual material locates the novel at the intersection of history and fiction, a self-conscious narrative positioning, as Cortázar's introduction to the novel makes clear.

I have cited Octavio Paz's statement that art and love are "rebels," politics and philosophy "revolutionaries"; in this novel, however, Paz's distinction does not apply. The roles of rebel and revolutionary in fact converge, for erotic liberation and political liberation are closely identified by Cortázar and his character Andrés; furthermore, in this novel, Cortázar's esthetic concerns consciously reflect his political philosophy. The atmosphere that Cortázar creates here is related to the theory of revolution proposed by Norman O. Brown.[35] Brown's use of apocalypse as a metaphor for political and sexual liberation is well known, and his insistence on the interdependence of repression in these areas coincides with Cortázar's understanding of the nature and necessity of revolution. If Brown's writing now seems hyperbolic and somewhat dated, too much a product of the prevailing romanticism of his time, Cortázar's novel escapes that fate by virtue of its inventive narrative techniques, its particular brand of Cortázarian humor, and its dramatization of the complexity of human relations, whether political or sexual or both.

The novel ends after the revolutionaries' violent confrontation with government forces. The scene shifts to the silent stillness of a morgue, where a corpse, presumably one of the revolutionaries, is lying. The description of the scene recalls the famous photograph of Che Guevara lying dead in a stark room in the Bolivian jungle. If the indirect reference to a corpse at the end of "We Love Glenda So Much" is meant to figure the fanatic narrator's desire to negate potentiality, here the corpse, alluding as it does to revolutionary involvement, suggests a far more complex relation to the historical future. Of course a dead body is an obvious and irrevocable terminal point. We are told that in the morgue "all marks of history" will be washed away. However, the novel is not the closed temporal structure that the concluding scene in the morgue would seem to imply. The member of the revolutionary group who attends the body says: "Rest easy, there's time,"[36] as if to assure his companion (and himself) that he hasn't died for nothing, that the revolutionary struggle will continue. This final scene of individual death implies collective continuance, collective betterment.

The reader has known all along that the novel he or she is reading implies another: *A Manual for Manuel* is a book about the preparation for a book which will be undertaken after this one ends, and which will to a large degree reiterate its contents. Thus the temporal context of the novel explicitly extends beyond its own ending, not only into a political future but also into a literary one. At the beginning of the novel, the narrator addresses this process, commenting on Andrés's accumulation of narrative fragments: "he had gathered together a considerable amount of notes and clippings, waiting, it would seem, for them to end up all falling into place without too much loss. He waited longer than was prudent, evidently . . . that neutrality had led him from the beginning to hold himself as if in profile, an operation that is always risky in narrative matters – and let us not call it historical which is the same thing. . . . All this, of course, so that all those notes and scraps of paper would end up falling into an intelligible order . . ." (6). Andrés has not, at the beginning of the novel, committed himself to the revolution, and therefore he can only wait: The "neutrality" of his stance, it is implied, initially prevents him from creating the literary order which his subsequent involvement in revolutionary activity will allow. Cortázar's novel describes the political engagement that permits artistic engagement. The existence of Manuel's book depends upon Andrés's commitment to history, as the existence of *A Manual for Manuel* depends upon Cortázar's.

The book that Andrés will begin after the end of Cortázar's novel will preserve a record of the past for the baby Manuel in the future, and is thus a gesture of historical affirmation. Much as a family photo album or scrapbook is assembled to preserve a record of the past for the future, fixing on its pages the visual and verbal images of moments of familiar history, so Andrés wishes to fix in Manuel's book a historical record of a more public sort. The fact that Andrés will include *verbatim* documentary evidence of the past suggests his wish to impede the kind of revisionism, the retouching of history, practiced by Glenda's fans and Kundera's rulers of paradise. The newspaper clippings and government reports that will be integrated into his book are meant to be authoritative, objective. Political and social abuses must be remembered and recorded precisely. Regard for the past and visions of a better future fuse in the revolutionary order, an order symbolized for Andrés by the book he will yet create.

Andrés's literary intention conveys his understanding of revolution as far more than a total break with the past or the initiation of a unanimous future. Here again, I return to Octavio Paz's observations on revolution. Paz has commented on the concept of time contained in the word as it was originally conceived, as opposed to its modern usage. "Revolution is a word that implies the notion of cyclical time and therefore that of regular and recurrent change. But the modern meaning of the word does not refer to an eternal return, the circular movement of worlds and stars, but rather to a sudden and *definitive* change in direction of public affairs."[37] Whereas the original etymology of the word implies the primacy of the past, its modern usage postulates the primacy of the future; the known past has been replaced by the unknown future as the object of modern revolutionary desire. It is clear, however, that Cortázar, in his description of Andrés's literary project, wishes to combine the two meanings of the word, and thus to undermine the contemporary conception of revolution as instituting a singular future. So we understand that Andrés is both a relativist and a revolutionary. Like Cortázar, he knows that there is more than one paradise, more than one means of working toward the fulfillment of historical desire.

In order that the fragments of Manuel's book may "end up falling into an intelligible order," as Andrés intends them to, Cortázar's narrator tells us that Andrés must find a narrative stance outside of time, "an hour outside the clock so that all of a sudden fate and will can immobilize the crystals in the kaleidoscope. Etc." (7). Like the apocalyptist, the novelist Andrés is aware that he must place himself beyond the end of the history he recounts and impose his narrative vision upon it (as have the characters Quentin and Aureliano and Stencil). If Cortázar's characters in his early fiction reflect their author's esthetic concerns, here Andrés reflects Cortázar's concern with revolutionary process and how to narrate it. The image of the kaleidoscope, and the "Etc." which ends the phrase quoted above, suggest that Andrés will create an open structure like the one in which he has himself been placed. We are given to believe that his manual will, like the fiction of Cortázar, self-consciously embody the truth of Henry James's assertion in his preface to *Roderick Hudson:* "relations stop nowhere and the exquisite problem of the artist is eternally but to draw, by a geometry of his own, the circle within which they shall happily appear to do so."[38] I have already cited Henri Bergson's analogous insistence that, in the absence of historical ends, our need to create fictional endings makes us all geometricians. It is narrative geometry of another kind, the configurations of the closed narrative structures of John Barth, that will concern me in my next chapter.

5

THE APOCALYPSE OF STYLE:
JOHN BARTH'S SELF-CONSUMING
FICTION

It is one of the peculiarities of the imagination that it is always at the end of an era.

The Necessary Angel, Wallace Stevens

JOHN BARTH'S FICTION is permeated with considerations of beginnings and ends. His characters move from innocence to experience, from Eden to the end of the road. Yet meaningful endings are often subverted and denied. Barth's discussion of fiction focuses upon the "apocalyptic ambience" of contemporary literature. In a much noticed essay, Barth suggests that "the novel, if not literature generally, if not the printed word altogether, has by this hour of the world just about shot its bolt. . . ."[1] He implies that the very enterprise of storytelling is apocalyptic in nature, and at the same time may be a means of forestalling the apocalypse. In his essay, "Muse, Spare Me," several examples of "narrative ultimacy" serve to illustrate Barth's point. He cites Canto 19 of Dante's *Inferno,* where the Florentine assassins are described: "Head–downwards in a hole and sentenced to be buried alive, the murderer postpones his fate by drawing out his confession to the attendant priest."[2] In the *Decameron,* the storytellers escape their own society, which is literally dying in the plague of 1348, by creating their own enclave of fiction. And in *The Thousand and One Nights,* Scheherazade's survival depends absolutely upon her storytelling ability; it is only the Sultan's fascination with her stories that keeps him from killing her as he has the maidens before her. Barth writes: "her talent is always on the line: not enough to have satisfied the old cynic once, or twice; she's only as good as her next piece, Scheherezade; night by night, it's publish or perish." Comparing himself and modern writers in general to Scheherazade, he characterizes himself as spinning, "like the vizier's excellent daughter, through what nights remain to him, tales within tales within tales . . . until he and his scribblings are fetched low by the Destroyer of Delights" (444). If we have agreed with Bergson and Kermode that endings are among the imagination's consolations, we may also agree with Barth that Scheherazade represents another of its consolations. The postponement of endings which are associated metaphorically with death.[3] Like Scheherazade, Barth suggests, the modern writer must be aware of the approaching end and use narrative ingenuity to put it off. Postponement, however, is not always possible or even desirable, as we will see in several instances in Barth's fiction.

Barth's essay, "The Literature of Exhaustion," contains perhaps the first important acknowledgment of the influence of contemporary Latin American fiction on U.S. fiction (the influence in the other direction having long been assumed).[4] Barth asserts that the subjects, themes, and narrative techniques of the novel have been used up, that original work is, for the most part, no longer possible. Barth cites Jorge Luis Borges as a prime example of an author who has recognized this apocalyptic situation, confronted it, and turned it to narrative advantage. Vladimir Nabokov and Samuel Beckett are also invoked to illustrate the point. Beckett moves toward silence, Nabokov's *Pale Fire* and Borges's *ficciones* are "not only footnotes to imaginary texts, but postscripts to the real corpus of literature" (277). The modern writer is left little alternative other than allusion or ironic imitation; he or she must represent "not life directly but a representation of life." Adopting a phrase from Borges, Barth prescribes for this late moment in literary history a style that "deliberately exhausts (or tries to exhaust) its possibilities and borders upon its own caricature" (277). Confronted with the baroque reality of the present moment, it is the "virtuoso," the master of technique who will be "the chosen remnant" of the literary apocalypse.

Barth's essay suggests implicitly another Hispanic literary precursor, José Ortega y Gasset, and his essays on literary modernism. Ortega was an early observer of the modernist tendency toward self-reflexiveness, noting in various contexts the shift in emphasis away from representational structures based on human and social relationships toward abstract structures expressly removed from such relationships. Of specific interest here is the echo in Barth's essay of Ortega's well-known early formulation of the death of the novel. In "Notes on the Novel" (1925), Ortega asserts that "the genre of the novel, if not irrevocably exhausted, has certainly entered its last phase, the scarcity of possible subjects being such that the writers must make up for it by the exquisite quality of the other elements that compose the body of a novel."[5] Though I am not proposing that Barth was necessarily familiar with Ortega's essays, Borges surely was, as he was with Ortega's German philosophic bases. Borges was critical of Ortega, but it is nonetheless interesting to entertain the possibility that Barth's early appreciation for Borges is due in part to Borges's participation in the modernist tradition about which Ortega wrote and, in so doing, focused and encouraged.[6]

Since, according to Barth, the "felt ultimacies" of our time are esthetic, narrative endings are bound to supersede historical ends as matters of consequence. Nevertheless, Barth's early fiction does deal with the individual's experience of temporal ends, and the narration of that experience: *The Floating Opera* (1956) and *The End of the Road* (1958) present complex treatments of human temporality and its various artistic embodiments. Both novels are stories about stories, representations of representations of life which parody traditional novelistic conventions. Both narrators have the a priori certitude that the basis of reality is linguistic, that language can control and indeed create reality. But this does not obviate their interest in historical phenomena. Each is involved in a literary attempt to explain his past – to explain, more precisely, the irruption of death into that past. Each narrator senses that he must keep writing fictions in order to survive; each refers to the death grip that reality has upon him. The narrative process thus becomes in Barth's first two novels the means by which the narrators attempt to understand their situations and the fact of human mortality. For Todd and Jake, verbal artifice holds out the hope of continuance, despite the finality of the deaths that both of them describe.

Todd Andrews provides at once a paradigm of the apocalyptic situation of the storyteller and a parody of it. He is born in 1900 and given a name heavy with apocalyptic overtones. *Tod* means "death" in German; Andrew derives from "man." Todd says, "Todd is almost *Tod* – that is, almost death – and this book, if it gets written, has very much to do with almost-death."[7] Todd has a heart condition which he takes to be the central fact of his life: He may at any moment expire. Todd's sense of personal apocalypse is exaggerated to the point of the ridiculous, but he nonetheless conveys Barth's sense of the contemporary condition. In "Muse, Spare Me," Barth relates just such an individual apocalyptic situation to that of society in general: "For though the death of one person is not the death of a people, even mankind's demise will have to consist of each of our dyings; in this respect all apocalypses are ultimately personal – an important fact, since it validates apocalyptic visions age after age despite the otherwise awkward circumstance that the world has, so far, persisted" (443). Todd's sudden death, like that of the world, has been long awaited. The permanent suspicion of an imminent end – his own – is the fact with which he lives.

The irony of Todd's apocalyptic preoccupation is that his bad heart is quite likely a fiction which he has fostered and expanded, rather than a medical fact (and his reappearance in Barth's later novel, *LETTERS* [1979], at the ripe old age of sixty-nine supports this hypothesis). He was told of his condition by an army doctor thirty-five years earlier and has never been to another doctor to have the diagnosis confirmed or refuted. He obviously enjoys his bad heart, for it justifies his good-humored solipsism and allows him his detached perspective. Todd pays for his lodging not by the week or the month, but by the day, a ritual gesture which symbolizes his awareness of his precarious position on the edge of the end. In this, Barth suggests, Todd is essentially and crucially contemporary.

Despite this awareness and because of it, Todd writes inquiries into his past. Against the temporary quality of his own existence, he counterposes his literary constructs. (Todd's Latin American analogue is Artemio Cruz, Carlos Fuentes's narrator in *The Death of Artemio Cruz* [1962], who is in fact on his deathbed, narrating his life not in the hope of prolonging it – his physical state, unlike Todd's, permits no such illusions – but in the hope of revising it.) Todd is involved in investigations of his father's suicide and his own suicide attempt. He undertakes these projects because he knows that they are impossible, that he will never complete them. Indeed, it is that fact which most attracts him:

> One needs, even in my position, something to counterbalance the immediacy of a one-day-at-a-time existence, a life on the installment plan. Hence my *Inquiry,* properly to prepare even for the beginning of which, as I see it, would require more lifetimes than it takes a lazy Buddhist to attain Nirvana. My *Inquiry* is timeless, in effect; that is, I proceed at it as though I had eternity to inquire in. And, because processes persisted in long enough tend to become ends in themselves, it is enough for me to do an hour's work, or two hours' work, on my *Inquiry* every night after supper, to make me feel just a little bit outside of time and heartbeats. (50–1)

In creating his fictions, Todd imaginatively forestalls death even as he explains it. Referring to his symbolic gesture of paying for his room every morning, he contrasts his life to his literary projects: "I begin each morning with a gesture of cynicism, and close it with a gesture of faith; or, if you prefer, begin it by reminding myself that, for me at least, goals and objectives are without value, and close it by demonstrating that the fact is irrelevant. A gesture of temporality, a gesture of eternity" (51).

The novel we are reading is one of Todd's "gestures of eternity," his narrative of death *manquée,* his own attempt to kill himself on the twentieth or twenty-first of June, 1937. In a digressive and mannered fashion, he reveals the events that lead to his decision to end his life, and to his subsequent realization that such a self-imposed end is no more tenable, philosophically speaking, than continuance. This account is *not,* however, the one that Todd intends to give to his dead father (granting, as we must, the theoretical nature of such communication in any case). Todd tells the reader: "I would take a good long careful time, then, to tell Dad the story of *The Floating Opera.* Perhaps I would expire before ending it; perhaps the task was endless, like its fellows. No matter. Even if I died before ending my cigar, I had all the time there was" (252). Todd will continue to create version after version of his nonsuicide; the end of one floating opera is the beginning of another; there are no real conclusions, only continuations. Todd's avoidance of endings is a protest against individual ends, and this would seem to be a tactic of Barth's as well. In the closing paragraph of the novel, another inquiry is proposed which, Todd tells us, is beyond the scope of his floating opera. That inquiry is contained in *The End of the Road,* Barth's subsequent novel. Another narrator takes up where Todd leaves off, or rather, follows a narrative path that forks in another direction, to use Borges's metaphor for endless narration.

Jake, the narrator of *The End of the Road,* is undergoing "scriptotherapy"; he is writing and rewriting the story of the events of the summer of 1953, especially the death of Rennie Morgan, much as Todd is writing various versions of his father's death and his own almost-death. Jake is, however, psychopathic, and depends on his literary attempts to order the experiences that have rendered him incapable of living in the world where time and death exist. He is emotionally paralyzed, capable only of producing one literary account after another of the fatal events he cannot assimilate, replacing (not just describing) reality with language. The version we happen to read, entitled *The End of the Road,* is no real end for Jake but merely one more verbal construct: Jake's last word (and the last word of the novel) is "Terminal," and it is uttered to direct the cab driver to the train station, and on to the retreat where he will write endless versions of the events that led him to the end of the road. His flight to the asylum of timeless fiction represents an attempt to find the order that an ending implies, a point that is confirmed by Jake when the character is resuscitated in *LETTERS.* In this later novel, Jake laments, "if only roads did *end.* But the end of one is the commencement of another, or its mere continuation. . . . I Am Back at the Beginning of mine, where I Was in 1951 . . . only Older; not so much Paralyzed as Spent."[8] Jake's scriptotherapy is doomed to failure, for meaningful conclusions must be based upon temporal realities, realities that Jake simply cannot face. Unlike Todd in *The Floating Opera,* Jake seeks with his narration to seal off the past from the present, to put an end to it rather than to put off its end.

Jake is very explicit about the time at which he is writing: He tells us that it is 7:55 P.M., Tuesday, October 5, 1955. This is important because we learn that all he has to orient himself is the present moment. In his "arrested history," as he calls his narration and implicitly his life, he denies the past as having consequences in the present. He has told his friends the Morgans that he does not believe in choice or in the assumption of responsibility for the events that succeed choice. When he tries – or pretends to try – to take the responsibility for Rennie Morgan's senseless death on the abortion table (which *is* in fact largely his fault), he is unable to accept the tragic consequence of the events he has set in motion. He begins several letters of explanation, hoping to devise written conclusions that will somehow cancel the single fatal conclusion he has just witnessed. But he is not yet practiced enough at self-delusion, and cannot yet make words substitute for reality. He says: "The terrific incompleteness made me volatile; my muscles screamed; but my limbs were bound like Laöcoon's – by the serpents Knowledge and Imagination, which grown great in the fullness of time, no longer tempt but annihilate."[9] It is the "terrific incompleteness" of reality which he hopes to escape with words.

In the Laöcoon, Barth finds the perfect symbol for Jake's immobility. The Greek Laöcoon, brother of Anchises, was bound at Apollo's behest for his impiety, and probably for his attempt to warn the Trojans about the Trojan horse as well. Jake often sees himself as Laöcoon, immobile and agonized, or as a statue in a generalized sense: "My eyes, as Winckelmann said inaccurately of the eyes of the Greek statues, were sightless, gazing on eternity, fixed on ultimacy, and when that is the case there is no reason to do anything – even to change the focus of one's eyes. Which is perhaps why the statues stand still" (74). Jake's understanding of his paralysis is thrice removed from reality, an elaborate artifice to separate himself from the reality he cannot bear. He sees himself in terms of the art historian's "inaccurate" description of Greek statues, that is, in terms of words rather than statues – which are still once removed from their human models. G. E. Lessing, in his famous essay on the Laöcoon published in 1766, points to the half-open mouth of the statue, and wonders why it is not wide open. Perhaps, he suggests, it is because the statue captures a "significant and fruitful" moment just short of the climax of death, a timeless moment implying an end which is always imminent, but which never comes.[10] Jake replaces the Laöcoon with himself, eschewing temporal reality for a static world where one imagines him, his mouth eternally half-open, endlessly refuting the disastrous end to which his actions led. Words, not the twin serpents, are the agents of his bondage.

Jake is an English professor as well as a self-conscious storyteller. He ostensibly recognizes the equivocations inherent in language, but he tells himself that by teaching the fixed conventions of prescriptive grammar, he is confronting reality rather than fleeing from it. He enthuses:

> Articulation! There, by Joe, was my absolute, if I could be said to have one. . . . To turn experience into speech – that is, to classify, to categorize, to conceptualize, to grammarize, to syntactify it – is always a betrayal of experience, a falsification of it; but only so betrayed can it be dealt with at all, and only in so dealing with it did I ever feel a man, alive and kicking. . . . I responded to this precise falsification, this adroit, careful myth-making, with all the upsetting exhilaration of any artist at his work. When my mythoplastic razors were sharply

honed, it was unparalleled sport to lay about with them, to have at reality. (119)

Jake is indeed a virtuoso at manipulating words, and his virtuosity fosters his misconception that he can also manipulate the reality for which the words stand. Of course, words are always to some extent a falsification of reality, and the narration of past events – especially cataclysmic events – is at least partially an imaginative construct. Apocalyptic narration is certainly "adroit myth-making," to use Jake's formulation. But in imaginative recuperations of history, intention matters. Whereas the apocalyptist intends to reveal past and present abuses (and forestall further abuses, in the case of Barth's favorite model of apocalyptic narration, Scheherazade), Jake intends to obscure and ultimately to conceal them. He fails "to do a Marcel Proust on the thing" because his premise, that enough words can efface history altogether, is fallacious.

Unlike Jake, Todd in *The Floating Opera* realizes the problem inherent in relating words to experience and the danger of belying the complexity of reality with verbal constructs. Todd continually stresses the problem of doing justice to contingent reality; his voluminous notes in circular peach baskets provide a wonderful metaphor for the difficulties of imposing fictional endings on human experience, especially his own. He begins his opera with the exclamation, "Good heavens! How does one write a novel! I mean how can anyone stick to the story if he's at all sensitive to the significance of things" (2). Jake, in *The End of the Road*, with his scriptotherapeutic faith in the game of articulation, provides the answer to Todd's question. One must generalize if one is ever to tell a story, suppress one's sensitivity, hone one's "mythoplastic razors," and go to it. He glibly minimizes the distinction between fiction and reality which Todd sees so clearly; his constant use of phrases such as "as a rule," "normally," and "generally" indicates his obedience to his doctor's injunction to ignore particulars and generalize. His doctor encourages Jake's sense of the rupture between things and words, telling him: "fiction isn't a lie at all, but a true representation of the distortion that everyone makes of life" (88–9). Perhaps. But Jake fails to understand that there are degrees and kinds of distortion; and worse, he fails to understand the complexity of the temporal world he is distorting. The world collapses into words. Language becomes for Jake an end in itself, an abstract, ahistorical system.

For Jake in his scriptotherapy, the difference between words and reality has disappeared. There is, however, one point in the novel where Jake cannot delude himself that his verbal constructs are the same thing as his experience. This is in his description of Rennie's death. Jake gives an extremely precise and concrete description of Rennie's body on the abortion table, introducing the description by saying, "And so this is the picture I have to carry with me" (191). There is nothing "incomplete" about his image, and even the equivocations of language cannot deny its reality. Jake inadvertently suggests the nature of his attempt to evade the finality of Rennie's death: "At the moment when Rennie was lowered into the earth, I believe I was explaining semicolons to my students" (195). The semicolon, punctuation of suspended closure, suggests metaphorically the refuge from reality that Jake will seek in language. If in the Marxist context of Cortázar's *A Manual for Manuel,* alienation inspires action and produces a revolutionary writer, here alienation ends in paralysis and the writer's withdrawal from the social and psychological situation the novel presents.

It should be clear by now that Barth's novel, unlike Jake's narrative account, does *not* evade the temporal reality of actions and their consequences. In Jake's flight from historical and literary responsibility, Barth displays the exigencies of the temporal realm in which we exist and of which we must make sense. In *The Sense of an Ending,* Frank Kermode suggests the terms to contrast Barth's verbal enterprise with his character's: "As soon as the serious novel speaks, it imposes causality and concordance, development and character, a past which matters and a future within certain broad limits determined by the project of the author rather than of its characters."[11] Whereas Jake writes in a suspended present, without past or future, denying time's progression toward anything conclusive, Barth's novel presents events that the reader follows to their fatal conclusion. While Jake disavows causality, he admits that certain explanations are evident in his story, and that the reader may draw conclusions, impose endings, even if he himself is unable to do so. He says of his situation, "I presume that anyone interested in causes will have found plenty to pick from by now in this account" (86–7). For Jake, the word "terminal" means train station and the escape to a timeless world without meaningful ends. For Barth and Barth's readers, the word is the suggestive conclusion of a novel about our temporal condition and about the difficulties of translating experience into words.

After completing *The Floating Opera* and *The End of the Road,* Barth has indicated in an interview that he intended to write a third short novel which would, like the first two, deal with the theme of nihilism. That did not happen, however, because of a change in his own attitudes. He explains: "The difference is simply that I didn't think after *The End of the Road* that I was interested in writing any more realistic fiction – fiction that deals with Characters from Our Time, who speak real dialogue. . . . One ought to know a lot about reality before one writes realistic novels. Since I don't know much about Reality, it will have to be abolished. What the hell, reality is a nice place to visit but you wouldn't want to live there. . . . Reality is a drag."[12] Barth's rejection of realism leads him to a narrative mode in which the preconceived rules of a closed verbal field supplant temporal development. In *The End of the Road,* Barth's character Jake tries to free himself from the realities of time and mortality by playing with words which he has detached from the objects of experience they represent. In the novels that follow *The End of the Road,* Barth himself creates abstract verbal patterns, controlling and manipulating them within a closed field. The concern for the "terminal" nature of human experience which grounds the first two novels has been replaced by what I will call Barth's apocalyptic style and narrative structures.

II.

Barth's reassessment of the relation between art and experience after his first two novels results in self-enclosed fictions which point to their own literary forms. The process of writing becomes a primary subject and, more particularly, the idea that the narrative impulse is exhausted and must get along with what little energy remains in demonstrating that fact. Barth's stories in *Lost in the Funhouse* (1968) and *Chimera* (1972) stress pattern, as does apocalyptic literature generally, but in these stories it is not the patterns of history which matter but rather those of the fictional structure. Whereas Pynchon's fiction concerns itself with the futile search for rational patterns which might oppose entropic chaos, and Cortázar's fiction devises narrative strategies aimed precisely at transcending such rational enclosures, Barth's fiction after his first two novels proposes patterns, not for the purpose of engaging the phenomenal world (which is the aim of both Pynchon and Cortázar in their different ways), but rather to reveal the conceptions underlying the artistic structure. Cortázar's fiction focuses upon the tension between the world and language, the inevitable gap between the perception of experience and its description. In Barth's fiction, on the other hand, meaning is no longer generated from the individual's subjective encounter with history but from a pre-existent linguistic or narrative structure. The phenomenological stance of Pynchon and Cortázar is supplanted with what we might call a conceptual stance, where the artist wishes only to make statements about the esthetic structure per se. This emphasis on the arbitrariness of the linguistic model serves to separate the artwork from the individual's experience of temporal phenomena, and particularly, it would seem, from the finality of temporal ends. The self-enclosed novel is not concerned with teleology or eschatology in any external sense. Apocalypse becomes a question of literary style and structure rather than of history.

Again, the ideas of José Ortega y Gasset shed light on Barth's fiction; decades ago, Ortega noticed the predominance of ironic detachment in modern art, and its repudiation of social and political subject matter in favor of the esthetic order as subject.[13] In a progression that reverses the one I have traced in Cortázar's work, Barth reflects Ortega's insight in his shift from historical to esthetic subjects. He begins to create circumscribed fictions which no longer seriously entertain the notion of forestalling death with words, because the fictions have been removed from historical concerns altogether. In *The Floating Opera* and *The End of the Road,* Barth's treatment of literary exhaustion takes the form of narrators who attempt to confront the finality of historical ends with their narration (as have Quentin and Aureliano Babilonia and Stencil and Andrés); in his subsequent fiction, the idea of literary exhaustion manifests itself in the avoidance or subversion of narrative endings. The problematic relationship between verbal endings and historical ends, the subject of his first two novels, is no longer problematic. Except for occasional cracks in the wall, the funhouse of words is the only reality.

Barth's fiction in a closed field sets forth the rules that will operate within a given work. Subjects are affirmed and then closed off; the order and workings of the material within the field are prescribed and limited. Because such fiction has as its primary aim and subject matter the execution of its own internal patterns, the contingency of temporal reality and the finality of temporal ends must be excluded. All prose fiction is to some extent enclosed within the field of its setting and subject matter and narrative strategies, but not all fiction is enclosed as explicitly and emphatically as Barth's. Ironically, it is historical material which isolates *The Sot-Weed Factor* (1960) from historical concerns; its field is delimited by eighteenth-century literary and linguistic and social material. In "Muse, Spare Me," Barth writes that "the use of historical or legendary material, especially in a farcical spirit, has a number of technical virtues among which are aesthetic distance and the opportunity for counter-realism" (440). Indeed, the elaborate imitation of eighteenth-century diction and the weight of historical detail in *The Sot-Weed Factor does* call attention to the patterns of the artifice, increasing its separation from the world outside its esthetic patterns and detracting from the temporal issues which such deliberate use of historical material would ordinarily be expected to engage. I have said that apocalyptic literature is always an imposition of pattern onto history, and contemporary apocalyptic narration often self-consciously redraws the lines of history and fiction, but not for the purpose of dismissing the claims of historical experience, as Barth does explicitly in the last section of this novel. *Giles Goat-Boy* (1966) is also tightly enclosed – by its allegorical plot, its technological jargon, its framed structure. Like *The Sot-Weed Factor,* it ends with an epilogue, or rather a number of epilogues, that undermine and expose all proposed resolution of both structure and substance. Though I do not mean to suggest that the experience of fictional characters and events must perforce be "resolved," the actual experience of the reader must be. These novels resist such resolution by providing the material for the subversion of all that has gone before; their final sections expose the fraudulence of the narrative and undermine any assertions of value that might have been offered. So the artifact contains the means for its own self-destruction. This is apocalyptic fiction in a recognizably postmodern stylistic and structural sense.[14]

Barth's "esthetic ultimacy" is most obvious in *Lost in the Funhouse* and *Chimera,* and it is these works to which I want to refer in some detail. They are not novels but collections of short fictions, without conventional plot structure, loosely allied to the other fictions in the collection yet detached and discrete artifices, apparently approaching Borges's *ficciones.* They often deny their endings and turn back upon themselves in circular fashion while at the same time insisting on the narrative urge/desire/need for conclusion. But the satisfactions of temporal development and conclusion, sequence and consequence, are withheld. Indeed, Barth draws a sharp distinction in "The Literature of Exhaustion" between "the *fact* of aesthetic ultimacies and their artistic *use*" (271, Barth's italics).

In *Lost in the Funhouse,* the funhouse itself, with its labyrinths and mirrors, tumbling barrels and circular passageways, provides the metaphoric enclosure for these stories. They explicitly aim for the coincidence of medium and message, form and content. They are about their own fictional processes, often circular and endless like the structures of the funhouse, beginning in medias res and "leaving off" rather than ending. They conclude only in the sense that they suspend their "strings of letters and empty spaces," and Barth's constant use of "etc." reinforces the reader's sense of suspension rather than conclusion. The "Frame Tale" of the collection is a Moëbius strip which the reader is instructed to cut out, twist once, and fasten end to end. A two-dimensional rectangular piece of paper until it is put together, it becomes a continuous single-sided track. The words on the strip are "Once upon a time there was a story that began" which one may read ad infinitum. Because there is no beginning or end, one may start reading at any point. Narrative progression and narrative conclusion are subverted as the "frame," a twisted circle, encloses and excludes as it turns upon itself. Whereas Cortázar uses the image of the Moëbius strip in a story of that title in *We Love Glenda So Much* to project his narrative beyond death's end and beyond conventional literary endings, Barth uses it to emphasize the enclosure of his artifice.[15]

"Title" is the fiction in *Lost in the Funhouse* which is most preoccupied with ends and which most thoroughly subverts the notion of both temporal and spatial succession. The narrative voice, which converses with another disembodied voice, constantly describes its apocalyptic situation:

Can't we keep on to the end? I think not. Even another sentence is too many. Only if one believes the end to be a long way off; actually it might come at any moment; I'm surprised it hasn't before now.[16]

I can't finish anything, that is my final word. (104)

The voice burlesques doomsday rhetoric while employing it constantly.

> In this dehuman, exhausted, ultimate adjective hour, when every hu-
> mane value has become untenable, and not only love, but decency,
> and beauty but even compassion and intelligibility are no more than
> one or two subjective complements to complete the sentence. . . .
> (103–4)

Rather than selecting specific adjectives, the phrase "ultimate adjective
hour" is used and the sentence is left unfinished. The fiction is, as the
narrative voice says of modern literature in general, "an exhausted parody
of itself" (105); the voice cancels itself and its concern for the impending
apocalypse with ironic self-parody. The end of the story, in both form and
content, subverts finality:

> Let the *dénouement* be soon and unexpected, painless if possible, quick
> at least, above all soon. Now now! How in the world will it ever (110)

The final word is omitted as is the punctuation. The funhouse of fiction is,
as one story says of itself, more climacteric than climactic.
  Examples of such subverted endings multiply. The final period is omitted
from "Autobiography"; the "Anonymiad" returns us to the beginning of
the story when we reach the end; "Petition" ends with a comma; the
fictional author and his character don't end "Life-Story" but are interrupted: "he did at last as did his fictional character end his ending story
endless by interruption, cap his pen" (126). "Autobiography: A Self-Re-
corded Fiction" is narrated by the story itself (engendered by the author and
a tape-recorder, we are told in the author's note), which repeatedly attempts
to stop the narration by turning itself off, and eventually suspends its narration in this way:

> Shark up some memorable last words at least. There seems to be
> time.
>
> Nonsense, I'll mutter to the end, one word after another, string the
> rascals out, made or not, heard or not, my last words will be my last
> words. (37)

Narration is endlessly terminal, permanently liminal, and language itself
always on the brink of extinction.
  The narrative debate about the possibility of endings which I have just

quoted echoes the debate that runs throughout Samuel Beckett's *The Un-namable* (1959). Beckett's novel concludes: "where am I, I don't know, I'll never know, in the silence you don't know, you must go on, I can't go on, I'll go on." Though Barth departs from the affirmation of Beckett's conclusion, he clearly shares with Beckett the conception of language as something arbitrary and external – as a medium which need no longer be representational. Hugh Kenner describes U.S. modernist poetics in just these terms: "[Language's] norms are not imposed by history, they are elected, and if they turn out to be misleading, we can elect new ones . . . a language may be less a heritage than a code, and a code moreover that we are free to change. . . ."[17] Kenner quotes William Carlos Williams's phrase that words need to be "separated out by science, treated with acid to remove the smudges, washed, dried, and placed right side up on a clean surface" – precisely the impression conveyed in Barth's description of his stories as "strings of letters and empty spaces." Barth's fiction accepts the arbitrariness of language, but it is ironic that what for the modernists provided poetic and narrative opportunity is used by Barth to signal his own sense of literary exhaustion. This is perhaps the result of the attempt to extend or refine an esthetic that is already essentially complete. Barth recognizes this as the situation of postmodernism when he says of Beckett and Borges that "The irony (and the problem for their successors) is that each in his way brings narrative literature to a kind of ultimacy, or finishing point. . . ."[18] Or as Beckett has said, "Little is left to tell."

The stories in *Lost in the Funhouse* are the product of a writer who has insisted on the apocalyptic situation of literature and thus seems left with little else to write about. They raise the question of whether fiction can any longer make statements about historical experience, and the answer they propose is almost wholly negative. Again and again, a statement about temporal conclusion is accompanied with a technical or stylistic comment which suggests that the end is made of words:

This last-resort idea, it's dead in the womb, excuse the figure. A false pregnancy, excuse the figure. (107)

We grow old and tired, we think of how things used to be or might have been and how they are now, and in fact, and in fact we get exasperated and desperate and out of expedients and out of words. (109)

Words are the substance of the apocalypse, for the world is limited to language. These fictions illustrate the apocalyptic style described by Barth in his essay. It is a style that "deliberately exhausts (or tries to exhaust) its possibilities and borders upon its own caricature."

The mirrors in the funhouse have changed radically from those in *The Floating Opera* and *The End of the Road,* and the change may serve to epitomize the shift in Barth's attitude toward ends and endings. The mirrors in the earlier fiction do indeed reflect something about the world to their beholders. Todd learns about the comedy of human nature in his bedroom mirror; Jake and Rennie about the hypocrisy of human nature as they watch Joe cavort in front of a mirror in a scene that becomes a turning point in the novel. The distorting mirrors in the funhouse, on the other hand, reflect only Barth's pessimism about the possibility of valid perception in any form; and the facing mirrors, endless reflections of their own reflections, suggest not infinity but rather the extreme limitation of the funhouse, sealed off from all but its own forms. The avoidance of endings in these stories is not at all the same thing as Todd's open-ended narration in *The Floating Opera.* Whereas Todd imagines closure as a kind of death which he, in Scheherazadian fashion, may oppose with more and more precise versions of his story (his "gestures of eternity"), the lack of conclusion in *Lost in the Funhouse* becomes for its characters a source of frustration and despair. The narrator of the "Anonymiad" says in a hopeless tone: "I begin in the middle – where too I'll end, there being alas to my arrested history as yet no dénouement" (164). Barth has commented on his own symbolic identification with the stranded minstrel who narrates this story, confirming the esthetic self-consciousness of this attitude toward endings.[19]

III.

Like the stories in *Lost in the Funhouse,* the three-part fictional *Chimera* is a narration about a narration, a story about itself. The central image, a chimera, is a neat emblem for the coincidence of the form of the artifact and the material it treats; the three-part mythical monster in the fiction, like the three-part fiction itself, is an invention of language (Polyeidus, in attempting to make himself into the word "kamara" mistakenly makes himself into the word "chimera"), and is circular in structure. As Barth's chimera is created by Polyeidus's error (Polyeidus in turn blames Hermes, "famous trickster and inventor of the alphabet . . . lover of puns and practical jokes,"[20] whose sport it is to play with the proximity of the words kamara and chimera), so he is killed with a pencil. As in *Lost in the Funhouse,* words and letters, "strings of letters and empty spaces," are the primary subject of these fictions.

Each of the stories in *Chimera* is structured according to numerical and geometrical patterns which are defined by the narrative voice, and then used to enclose the abstract artifice. Barth's geometrical figures, primarily circles and spirals, allow for the separation of the narration into enclosed units that can be manipulated and rearranged with relation to the other units; the parts remain distinct within the whole, resisting permanent integration. Whereas this geometrical aspect of Barth's literary games might seem to resemble Cortázar's use of *figuras,* it is a resemblance which leads once again to the differences in the authors' esthetics. I have described Cortázar's "figures" as intuitive constellations of meaning where characters, events, locations relate across time and space, which his artist/characters hope to capture in moments of esthetic transcendence, and which he himself embodies in his novelistic structures. Although Cortázar uses spatial metaphors which have geometrical dispositions to describe his concept, one senses that Horacio in *Hopscotch* speaks for the author when he rejects fixed structural models, "this whole A.B.C. of my life . . . the trap of geometry, that method we Occidentals use to try to regulate our lives" (24). Carlos Fuentes also uses the geometrical figure of the spiral, not for the purpose of structuring his fiction but to describe what he considers to be the movement of history. Barth's narrative geometry, however, serves primarily to figure the predicament of literature in an age of exhaustion.

The first of the three stories, the "Dunyazadiad," is Barth's fictional invocation of Scheherazade and *The Thousand and One Nights.*[21] As I have suggested, Scheherazade symbolizes for Barth the apocalyptic situation of the modern storyteller, using her narrative ingenuity to forestall her own death, postponing with words the end of her story and her life. The number 1,001 itself oscillates between closure and continuance: Visually, it constitutes a reflexive pattern, the first two digits mirroring the last two in perpetual self-repetition. Conceptually, on the contrary, it may suggest indefinite continuation. One thousand in Arabic means "innumerable," so 1,001 signifies an infinite number;[22] the number may imply more generally the idea that there is always another story, even after an obvious endpoint has been reached. The "Dunyazadiad" is the story the genie (who looks and sounds like John Barth) tells Scheherazade he hopes to write: "series of, say, *seven* concentric stories-within-stories, so arranged that the climax of the innermost would precipitate that of the next tale out, and that of the next, et cetera. . . ."[23] Added to the series of seven is the numerical structure of *The Thousand and One Nights,* a figure which Barth doubles, making the story of Dunyazade endure for two thousand and two nights. The concentric structure of the stories-within-stories is reinforced by the genie, and then the narrator of the story. The genie compares his narrative processes and his plight in midcareer to a snail that "carries his history on his back, living in it, adding new and larger spirals to it from the present as he grows. That snail's pace has become my pace – but I'm going in circles, following my own trail" (18). The story itself is circular, turning back on itself. The narrative voice which comments on the story says, "Dunyazade's story begins in the middle; in the middle of my own, I can't conclude it . . ." (64). Unlike Scheherazade, the narrator's tone is despairing. Endless narration frustrates rather than consoles.

The "Perseid" is also based on the number seven and on the figure of the spiral. The story is told on a gigantic spiralling mural with seven panels of increasing dimensions, a "heptamerous whorl" with the sixth panel itself containing seven panels of proportions similar to the larger whorl. A second series of murals spirals around the first, doubling the story in a manner similar to the doubling in the "Dunyazadiad." These spirals suggest the endlessness of the artifice, as do the circles in the "Dunyazadiad." Perseus comments on the repetition of his story, which has become a constellation, "silent, visible signs" which "circulate" every night. The stars representing Perseus say to those representing Medusa, "My love, it's an epilogue, always ending, never ended . . . which winds through universal space and time . . . ; to raise you up forever and know that our story will never be cut off, but nightly rehearsed as long as men and women read the stars . . ." (142). Like words, the stars deny conclusion: Perseus and Medusa remain suspended, "always ending, never ended."

The "Bellerophoniad" is based on the previous stories in the collection, particularly the "Perseid," which it imitates. Barth's self-parody is at its height as he distorts even his own critical statements and interviews, adding one fragment to another, one phrase to another, arranging and rearranging the literary puzzle made up of his own previous work. The narrator of the story sets out his geometrical and numerical patterns clearly, again doubling the initial pattern of the story, making "the second half of my life recapitulate ironically the first, after the manner of the *Perseid,* but with the number five (*i.e.,* threes and twos) rather than seven as the numerical basis of the structure, and a circle rather than a logarithmic spiral as its geometric motif" (150). Bellerophon is obsessed with patterns of all kinds, for it is according to the pre-existing patterns of heroic behavior – the "heroical curriculum" – that he hopes to become a hero himself. Like the postmodern writer in an age of literary exhaustion, the postheroic hero can only allude to previous heroes, because all original grounds for heroism have already been occupied. But it is just as well. The pre-existing pattern protects Bellerophon from contingency and the necessity of choice.

The idea of narrative ending is again entertained and undercut in the "Bellerophoniad." Added to all of the story's lists, series, groups of alternatives, diagrams of probability, and schemata is a pattern which is to be produced by a computer and titled the "Final, Revolutionary Fiction." Its creation is described: "the machine was to analyze the corpus of existing fiction as might an Aristotelian lepidopterist the existing varieties of butterfly, induce the perfect form from its 'natural' approximations, and reduce that ideal to a mathematical model, preliminary to composing its verbal embodiment" (260). The "Final, Revolutionary Fiction" is entitled NOTES: "it will represent nothing beyond itself, have no content except its own form, no subject but its own processes. On the other hand, at its Phi-point (point six one eight et cetera of the total length . . .) there is to occur a single anecdote, a perfect model of a text-within-the text, a microcosm or paradigm of the work as a whole . . ." (266). It cannot be coincidental that the description of this proposed "Final, Revolutionary Fiction" falls almost exactly at the "*Phi*-point" of the "Bellerophoniad" text. This is a "revolutionary" text not in the political sense or in the sense of a radically innovative text, but in the original etymological sense of the word. It is circular. Unlike Paz's discussion of the historicity implied by this etymology, to which I referred in the previous chapter, Barth's "revolutionary" text reflects only its own content, turning back upon itself, excluding all that is external to its announced narrative parameters.

Bellerophon, who "rode the heroic cycle and is recycled," is given only a few more words at the end of the story as he plunges through space toward the ground. He says of his story, "It's no *Bellerophoniad*. It's a   " (320). The word he is unable to utter is "chimera." The tail of the story, like that of the beast, points toward its head. The hero, like the story, turns upon itself. The narrative voice complains, "my plot doesn't rise and fall in meaningful stages but winds upon itself like a whelk-shell or the snakes on Hermes's caduceus: digresses, retreats, groans from its utter et cetera, collapses, dies" (205). Bellerophon, his story, and the collection as a whole remain, like Perseus and Medusa, forever suspended in mid-air, forever on the verge of total repetition or total dissolution. The absence of closure suggests not endless individual readings of the text, as Borges's stories often do, but endless repetition of the same reading.

There is obviously a vast difference in spirit between the efforts of Barth's narrators in *Chimera* and the narrative efforts of the original Scheherazade. The difference may lie in the fact that Scheherazade's stories *do* cease, Barth's assertion of her ceaseless narration notwithstanding. 1,001 may symbolize infinity, but the frame story which encloses Scheherazade's stories clearly describes their conclusion. Although Scheherazade wishes to postpone her own end as well as the ends of countless other maidens who will be sacrificed if her stories do not beguile the sultan, she nonetheless understands the necessity of narrative endings. On the thousand and first night of narration, after completing her tale, Scheherazade requests the sultan's permission to stop. She senses that the continuance of her life resides not in perpetual narration but in the three sons whom she has borne to the king during the course of the 1,001 nights. Before terminating her stories, she has them brought before the sultan, asking that she be delivered from death not by more stories but by her children's need for her. They are not a substitute for her literary creativity but concomitant to it, confirming the life-sustaining powers of her narrative artistry. Whereas sexual impotence and literary exhaustion are repeatedly associated in Barth's Perseus and Bellerophon, Scheherazade's confrontation of individual and communal annihilation produces her stories and her children. The sultan grants Scheherazade's request, but not for the reason she proposes. He tells her that it is neither the stories nor the children which have assured her a long life, but her own virtue: "I pardoned thee before the coming of these children, because I saw thee to be chaste, pure, ingenuous, pious."[24]

The frame story of *The Thousand and One Nights* emphasizes Scheherazade's narrative ingenuity less than Barth would have it in his essay "Muse, Spare Me." Scheherazade's story does *not* conclude, as Barth proposes, by saying that she continues to *tell stories* until she is "visited by the terminator of delights and the separator of companions"; it concludes in fact with the assurance that she and the sultan and the people of his empire continue to *live* "in prosperity and joy and delight and happiness" until they are so visited. (Barth's emphasis in the same essay on the "narrative ultimacy" of the Florentine assassins in Dante's *Inferno* is similarly misplaced: Dante's apocalypticism, and that of his characters, was above all political and theological, a narrative "technique" only to the extent that the narrative itself embodied Dante's vision of historical renewal.) Scheherazade's stories, her children, her virtue have served to postpone her end — but not to cancel it: She has escaped murder, not death. Her story concludes upon this point: The narrator, addressing Him who alone "the vicissitudes of time do not destroy, and to whom no change happeneth," prays for "a happy end!" So, it is implied, Scheherazade exits from her framed fiction into temporal flux, delighted with the freedom that such an exit provides. In her acceptance of her own mortal status, she does not resemble Barth's narrators, but their opposite.

Jorge Luis Borges has also invoked the spirit of Scheherazade, and Barth's admiration for Borges is worthy of note in this context. Barth is admiring a master of modern fiction who does not write novels but fables which allude to fictional works that may in turn represent reality, but which often depict invented worlds like Tlön, Uqbar, Orbis Tertius. Barth's images resemble Borges's familiar images of infinity. Mirrors, labyrinths, spirals, the Aleph and the Zahir, the garden of forking paths, and Scheherazade serve as vehicles for Borges's exploration of the metaphysics of infinite time and space, and for his exploration, furthermore, of the esthetics of embodying that infinity in necessarily finite fictions. In this regard, Borges compares himself to Whitman, setting down "a limited catalogue of endless things";[25] hence his use of outline, allusion, reference — forms which explicitly depend upon other forms, which are by definition incomplete. Even in Borges's conventional story structures, there characteristically exists a self-conscious tension between the brevity of their form and the immensity of their metaphysical speculations.

The Argentine writer does at times invoke apocalypse, but his vision, like Barth's, would appear more timeless than terminal. Borges's characters live in time, but when death overtakes them, time is abolished, and they are allowed to dream or imagine various versions of their own deaths, to relive their lives, to revise or amplify or modify them. So at first they seem to be relieved of the burden of historical identity which the characters of García Márquez, Faulkner, Pynchon, Cortázar must endure. In Borges's story, "The Life of Tadeo Isidoro Cruz (1829–1874)," Tadeo Isidoro transcends his historical limitations imaginatively. In a single lucid moment described in the last sentence of the story – the moment of his death – he recognizes his kinship to Martin Fierro, and hence to an ongoing tradition of literature and myth. But history reasserts itself. The metaphysics of fiction momentarily counterbalances the annihilation of time, but cannot undo it, as the parenthetical dates in the story's title remind us. And in "The Other Death," Borges's character Pedro Damián imagines a heroic death in order to counteract an ignominious one; but here again, just as the story seems ready to remove itself altogether from history, Borges reintroduces diachronicity and historical resolution. Pedro Damián has succeeded in wishing time to a standstill, but that timelessness is paradoxically temporary. His story ends: "Death carried him off at the age of twenty in a local battle of a sad and little-known war, but in the end he got what he longed for in his heart, and he was a long time in getting it, and perhaps there is no greater happiness."[26] This phrase gives to the story the same cadence of fictive finality as the more traditional "And he lived happily ever after," or the prayer for a happy end at the conclusion of *The Thousand and One Nights,* and sets in motion the same oscillation between closure in fiction and continuance in life. This oscillation between the finite and the infinite is epitomized in Borges's work by the title of his philosophical meditation on time, *Historia de la eternidad* (1953): The *history* and the *story* of eternity.

Barth comments that Borges's images of infinity – which include many of his *ficciones* per se – are "particularly pertinent to the literature of exhaustion." But it is not trivial to insist here that Borges does not offer them as a solution to the esthetic quandary of the writer in the late twentieth century. They are, rather, emblems of the permanent *human* contradiction of mortal creatures who are capable of imagining their immortality, and the permanent *narrative* contradiction of limited verbal structures which may nonetheless engender unlimited readings and ramifications. So Borges employs his images of infinity to explore the ironies of ends and endings, whereas Barth uses the same images in *Lost in the Funhouse* and *Chimera* to evade those ironies by evading endings altogether.

Barth's mistaken Scheherazadian equation between endless narration and endless life is evinced in *LETTERS,* where characters from his previous fictions reappear. The lives of Barth's characters are extended in their letters, but extension is not development. Our understanding of them from their first appearances is not enlarged, although complications of plot and circumstance are added in abundance. The author-as-fictional-character again serves to undermine the existence of a world outside the parameters of the literary field. This "author" writes two letters to a "reader," a device which might serve to unseal *LETTERS* by at least implying a world beyond the enclosed structure of the novel. However, these are precisely the letters with which Barth emphasizes its enclosure, using them to frame the other letters before and after. The final letter provides the formula whereby the reader may continue indefinitely to write letters in the style of *LETTERS*. Immediately following these formulaic directions, we come to the words, "the end." Whereas Barth omits the final word or final punctuation of several of the stories in *Lost in the Funhouse* and *Chimera,* here he tacks "the end" on self-consciously, but only after having carefully instructed the reader how to cancel that very end. The effect is to subvert the possibility of significant conclusion, and then to call attention to the need for such conclusion by its absence.

LETTERS reminds one of the English Puritan Thomas Beverley, who, having predicted the apocalypse in 1697, published in 1698 the explanation that the world had ended on schedule but that no one had noticed it.[27] Like Beverley, Barth's characters suggest that life is an illusion maintained by wraiths oblivious to the fact that they no longer exist. If the modernists viewed history as a procession of moments in which art might yet propose order, postmodernists such as Barth, Susan Sontag, Kurt Vonnegut, William Burroughs, and Joan Didion see history rather as "an aggregate of last moments," to use a phrase from Pynchon's *Gravity's Rainbow,* where one is more likely to glimpse annihilation than resolution. Much U.S. postmodern fiction is about nothingness, parodies of utopia, of nowhere, for which James Rother proposes the descriptive term, *holocaustic.*[28] The locus of such fiction has shifted to psychological fantasy, a shift which may partially explain the abnegations of minimalism and the aleatory elements in contemporary painting and music. It is precisely this shift that Barth addresses in his critical essay, "The Literature of Replenishment."

This essay is, as its title suggests, a kind of rebuttal of "The Literature of Exhaustion." Presented as an examination of the term postmodernism and of the literature that term represents, Barth uses the assessments of a number of literary critics as a point of departure.

> Now, for Professor Alter, Professor Hassan, and others, *post*modernist fiction merely emphasizes the "performing" self-consciousness and self-reflexiveness of modernism, in a spirit of cultural subversiveness and anarchy. With varying results, they maintain, postmodernist writers write a fiction that is more and more about itself and its processes, less and less about objective reality and life in the world. For Gerald Graff, too, postmodern fiction simply carries to its logical

and questionable extremes the anti-rationalist, anti-realist, anti-bourgeois program of modernism. . . ."[29]

However reductive Barth's description of these critics' work may be, it is impossible not to notice the applicability of the definition to much of Barth's own fiction, and impossible not to notice that Barth, too, is noticing. He nonetheless concedes that if this is all that can be said of postmodernism, then it "is indeed a kind of pallid, last ditch decadence, of no more than minor symptomatic interest" (69). Barth proceeds to recommend for the future something quite different, a synthesis of premodernist realism and modernist esthetics, "a fiction more democratic in its appeal than such late-modernist marvels . . . as Beckett's *Stories and Texts for Nothing* or Nabokov's *Pale Fire*," and, he reluctantly admits a little further on, "some of my own."

It is ironic that *One Hundred Years of Solitude,* published in the same year as Barth's earlier essay on literary exhaustion, should serve as his prime example of "literary replenishment." García Márquez provides for Barth the exemplary combination of "straightforwardness and artifice, realism and magic and myth, political passion and non-political artistry, characterization and caricature, humor and terror . . ." (71): Barth cites specifically the first sentence of *One Hundred Years of Solitude,* with its thoroughly historical perspective. In a paean to Cervantes, Borges, and García Márquez ("Praise be to the Spanish language and imagination!"), Barth recognizes each writer in turn as a quintessential exemplar of premodernism, modernism, and postmodernism, and each as a source of inspiration and renewal for the fictional tradition of our time. It would seem that in this essay, Barth is announcing the end of a stage in his own career, a shift away from his apocalyptic style back to his early preoccupation with the experience and expression of human temporality.

The novel that follows this essay, *Sabbatical: A Romance,* is a combination of the "straightforwardness and artifice" which Barth admires in García Márquez's work, and to some extent it does return to temporal concerns. Barth has commented that in *The Floating Opera,* Todd Andrews "wonders sentence by sentence whether his heart will carry him from subject to predicate; in *Sabbatical* . . . the background question is whether the world will end before the novel does."[30] He notes that the protagonists of *Sabbatical* are well-informed and conscientious people who know that "no degree of skill in navigation or of seaworthiness in the vessel guarantees that our destination will still be there at our Estimated Time of Arrival. This being the more or less apocalyptic case – the Sot-Weed Factor supplanted as it were by the Doomsday Factor – why set a course at all . . . ?" (37). The apocalyptic case is, as Barth says, "more or less": The significance of apocalyptic ends, whether individual or communal, is never really engaged in sabbatical, nor does one sense that the characters care enough about potential disaster for it to motivate their actions. Moreover, the novel's ending rivals those of *LETTERS, Chimera,* and the stories of *Lost in the Funhouse* in its circularity, its subversion of its own finality.

Sabbatical ends with the principal characters ready to repeat the novel which the reader has just finished reading. Playing with the conventional phrase of narrative closure, Barth's character says, "If that's going to be our story, then let's begin it at the end and end at the beginning, so we can go on forever. Begin with our living happily ever after."[31] But these characters subsequently agree that no story is "*ever* after," and they decide instead to adopt the modified form, "happily after." Whereas the phrase "happily ever after" promises continuance into a realm beyond the fiction even as it sounds its familiar final note of structural resolution, Barth's "happily after" remains self-consciously incomplete: Happily after what? the reader must wonder. Borges uses such formulaic concluding phrases to draw attention to the complex tensions between temporal ends and literary endings, as Barth does not. The last sentence of the novel is followed by an asterisk indicating a footnote which sends the reader back into the novel. *The Floating Opera* and Julio Cortázar's *A Manual for Manuel* also conclude by proposing to begin the story which we have just finished reading, but they differ from the self-reflexiveness of *Sabbatical* in their implied projection beyond the confines of the literary artifact into a potential future. Todd's future versions of his floating opera, and Andrés's future manual for Manuel, will result from temporal progression and narrative development, not from mere repetition. The conclusion of *Sabbatical* is subverted, as is continuance beyond, or even egress from, the fictional structure.

In my discussion of Cortázar's fiction in the preceding chapter, and of Barth's in this one, I have referred to two opposing types of narrative structures – the open and the closed – and to two very different attitudes toward ends and endings. Cortázar insists upon *disclosure,* upon open-ended structures that deny limitation, whereas Barth, after his first two novels, demands *enclosure,* limitation; Cortázar's fictional structures move centrifugally, Barth's centripetally; Cortázar speaks of his art in terms of explosion, whereas Barth's art might be characterized in terms of implosion. This distinction between open and closed fictional structures must remain to some extent theoretical and speculative, for no work of art that is made of words can be either entirely enclosed within its own stated boundaries or entirely without boundaries. Barth's narratives, while intentionally limited within their own particular fields, have implications which transcend their enclosed structures: One thinks, for example, of the discussion of mature love in *Chimera,* which has little to do with fives or sevens, circles or spirals. Similarly, Cortázar's novels, for all their technical devices aimed at creating fluid and indeterminate structures, must be enclosed between a front cover and a back, and codified in words which follow one after another on successive printed pages. Their experimentations with narrative endings allow both Barth and Cortázar to play upon the contradiction between life and its narrative embodiment, whether that contradiction is conceived as the brevity of the single life versus the ongoing life of a work of fiction or, conversely, as the inconclusive nature of human experience versus the inevitable ending of a work of fiction. Or in the case of some of Barth's stories, as the collapse of the distinction between the two. Although these novelists' apocalyptic sensibilities result in very different literary forms, they are united in their skepticism about endings, a creative skepticism which underlies and in some part explains the apocalyptic narrative structures of both Cortázar and Barth, however different those structures may be.

6

APOCALYPSE AND RENEWAL:
WALKER PERCY
AND THE U.S. SOUTH

Every moribund or sterile society attempts to save itself by creating a redemption myth which is also a fertility myth, a creation myth.

The Labyrinth of Solitude, Octavio Paz

IN MY INTRODUCTION, I argued for the importance of apocalyptic visions in both U.S. and Latin American fiction, but my discussion thus far would seem to suggest that such a vision, as it is traditionally understood, is more essentially Latin American than North American. Thomas Pynchon and John Barth are explicitly linked to the apocalyptic tradition, as I have shown, not because they use the conventional sense and structure of apocalypse, but because they react against them, Pynchon by substituting the metaphor of entropy for apocalypse, Barth by draining apocalyptic forms of their historical significance. Neither Pynchon nor Barth uses the myth of apocalypse for its eschatological narrative perspective, as does Gabriel García Márquez, or for its vision of radical political and esthetic renewal, as does Julio Cortázar. However, the case of Walker Percy, and of Southern U.S. fiction generally, is very different.

Percy writes from an avowedly Christian eschatological point of view. In his essay, "Notes for a Novel about the End of the World," he asserts that the subject of the postmodern novel is a man who has "very nearly come to the end of the line."[1] The "end of the line" is not heat death, as Pynchon would have it, or an esthetic that proposes the subversion of its own forms, as in Barth's fiction. Percy's sense of an ending is conditioned by the historical catastrophes and the "awesome new weapons" of the twentieth century, as well as by his view of the decay of values in contemporary U.S. culture. It leads him to portray "a new breed of person in whom the potential for catastrophe – and hope – has suddenly escalated" (9). Percy argues that if "we are living in eschatological times . . . times of enormous danger and commensurate hope, the prophetic–eschatological character of Christianity is no doubt peculiarly apposite" (9). The end of the world, seen in these terms, becomes a metaphor for Percy's "explicit and ultimate concern with the nature of man and the nature of reality where man finds himself" (6), as we have seen it to be in the work of García Márquez and Cortázar.

If Percy's eschatological orientation approaches the concerns of contemporary Latin American fiction more closely than those of his contemporaries in the United States, it may be that the historical experience of the U.S. South has more in common with that of Latin America than we usually recognize. I have already cited Carlos Fuentes on this point in my comparative discussion of Faulkner and García Márquez, and I want to use Fuentes's essays on William Faulkner and William Styron here to suggest the direction of my discussion of Percy's fiction.[2] Fuentes asserts that America was invented by Europe as a utopia; as such, it was doomed to be the land of the future and of happiness (an assertion which becomes the central theme of *Terra Nostra*). Because the South lost the Civil War and was until recently less affluent than the more industrialized areas of the United States, Fuentes argues that it was excluded from this American utopia, a fact which partially explains for him how Faulkner could write his "great fictional poems" about what it means to be a tragic being. Similarly, in the novels of Styron, the American dream disintegrates to re-emerge as universal tragedy. Referring to Styron's vision of the United States, Fuentes writes that the "land of choice designated by God to trample, humble and conquer in the name of 'Manifest Destiny,' that land of optimism and success, that land that had never known defeat, appears in the fictions of William Styron as a land devoured by its own secrets of loneliness, crime, corruption and dissatisfaction; and in the act of recognizing its dark mask, it recognizes that the mask is the shared face of all men."[3]

Beyond its exception from the U.S. ethic of progress and success, a sense of history as both compelling and oppressive links Southern U.S. fiction to Latin American fiction, as I have suggested in my comparative discussion of *Absalom, Absalom!* and *One Hundred Years of Solitude*. For many Southern writers, as for many Latin Americans (especially, perhaps, for Fuentes, as we will see), the source of their cultures' enduring irrationalities lies deep in the past, in memory, and the present can be understood only in its terms. That the aristocratic cultural tradition has ruptured and the past is separated by a chasm from the present is of course the point of Percy's title, *The Last Gentleman* (1966), as it is at least in part the point of Faulkner's title, *Absalom, Absalom!*. Their titles imply that the only remaining bridge between past and present, between fathers and sons, may be the novels themselves, though they stand, as it were, on opposite sides of the chasm, Percy's title expressing the son's perspective, Faulkner's that of the archetypal father, King David. In both cases, the novels' subject is loss: The past must be narrated, but it is nonetheless irrefutably gone. The title of another of

Percy's novels, *Lancelot* (1977), also points toward such cultural discontinuity, naming as it does the knight who destroyed the aristocratic tradition of the Round Table. As in *Lancelot,* at the heart of García Márquez's *Chronicle of a Death Foretold* lies the vestiges of a decaying tradition of honor. In short, much of the literature of both Latin America and the U.S. South is a product of traditional societies which share the knowledge that their traditions have been broken. It is perhaps for this reason that the past is so often depicted as an obsession and a trap for those who attempt to recuperate its forms in words.

If these writers portray the past as a burden, they do not look upon the present as boding any better. Modernity came late to the South, as it did to Latin America, and in both cases it irrupted violently into agrarian societies with feudal social structures. Large plantations (in Latin America, *latifundios*) had created sharply delineated social classes, divided according to landowners and laborers – that is, essentially according to the color of one's skin. Indentured labor, whether blacks or Indians, served as the basis of both feudal systems and continued to do so well into this century on both continents – indeed, the system still persists in parts of Latin America.[4] Modernity arrived late, and all at once. Cultural traditions were often discarded abruptly and wholesale, and the materialism of the new economic order embraced quickly and uncritically. So Faulkner, as his career advanced, became more preoccupied with the irresistible rise of the acquisitive Snopes than with the decline of the aristocratic Compsons; and Fuentes, in *Where the Air Is Clear,* records the inevitable foundering of traditions and values in the exponentially growing chaos of Mexico City. The conflict between the fatal flaws of the old order and the corrupt values of the new is constantly present in modern Southern fiction, as it is in Latin American fiction. Faulkner pays homage to the Old South even as he assaults it, and Percy's character, Will Barrett, must return to his father's world before he can live in his own; García Márquez's patriarch, José Arcadio Buendía, must find the Spanish galleon before founding Macondo; and in *Terra Nostra,* Fuentes returns to sixteenth-century Spain in order to portray twentieth-century Mexico.

If an ambiguous attachment to the historical past may be said to unite the literatures of the South and Latin America, so does an analogous vision of the future. García Márquez satirizes the "progress" imposed upon Macondo by U.S. enterprise with his image of *la hojarasca,* the leaf storm, the banana company hurricane; as we will see, Percy and Fuentes also offer radical critiques of the positivist doctrine of progress. They reject its primary effect, a naive apocalypticism which, like utopianism, focuses on a better future always beyond the reach of the present. Visions of the future must not diminish the present, but rather serve what Fuentes calls the "eternal present" and what Percy understands in terms of a "here and now" constantly in the process of becoming. Although their conception of temporal immediacy is rooted in different philosophical territory – Fuentes's in the historiography of Giambattista Vico, Percy's in an existential understanding of Christian eschatology – both are interested in the process of historical becoming, and how to embody that process in the novel.

Clearly then, there are comparable aspects of the engagement with history in Latin American literature and Southern U.S. literature. The two bodies of literature may be said to share the sense that contemporary culture has reached a crisis point – an end point – when the old forms are no longer sufficient and new forms are struggling to establish themselves. As I have proposed in my discussion of García Márquez and Faulkner, this intuition of the end often presupposes an intuition of historical decline based on a sense of the betrayal of the American Dream, that is, the betrayal of the hopes associated with the New World from its first settlement by Europeans. Furthermore, Latin American and Southern writers often share the conviction, inherent in apocalyptic narration, that one may understand and perhaps even shape the future by narrating the past. Literature may itself be the repository of historical consciousness, and thus, in turn, the impetus for an apocalyptic renovation of social and political forms – and in the case of Percy, a revitalization of belief.

This similarity of concerns in Latin American and Southern literature has been largely ignored with reference to Percy's fiction, perhaps because of the current critical emphasis on Percy's debt to the French existentialist writers Jean-Paul Sartre and Albert Camus.[5] However, the ahistoricism of these novelists – indeed, their contempt for historical consciousness, as Hayden White puts it[6] – seems to me to make their work less comparable to Percy's novels than is the Latin American fiction I have been discussing here. Though their novelistic emphases and, needless to say, their political contexts differ considerably, García Márquez, Cortázar, Fuentes, and Percy all address the movement of individual and cultural history, and the eschatological significance of that movement.[7]

Beyond their historical similarities, certain parallel cultural traits and habits of mind contribute to the suspicions of apocalypse which pervade the literature of both the Southern United States and Latin America. In the South, there still exists a dialectic of innocence and guilt, an "energy of opposition," as Ihab Hassan puts it, based on a sense of evil as present and active in history. This perennial sense of moral dualism exists, Hassan argues, because in the South the Protestant mind and the folk spirit have not succumbed entirely to a business ethic or to urban impersonality.[8] The biblical tradition in the South is unique in the United States in its literal reading of biblical images, events, prophecies, and in its literal application of that material to experienced reality. Though Southern Catholicism may differ in degree from fundamental Protestantism on this point, the two nonetheless approach each other precisely in their view of the end of time as justifying and redeeming the present. In its biblical understanding of the irrational forces operating in history, Southern literature shares a basic source of Latin American magic realism, which García Márquez epitomizes in *One Hundred Years of Solitude* when he has a character say, "If they believe it in the Bible, I don't see why they shouldn't believe it from me" (277). The grotesque and gothic elements that pervade modern Southern fiction link it to the magic realism of contemporary Latin American fiction, and to the visionary imagination of the apocalyptic biblical tradition in which they both participate.

As further examples of this Southern apocalypticism, besides Faulkner, Styron, and Percy, one thinks of the literary and literal uses of apocalypse in several Southern novels: Flannery O'Connor's *The Violent Bear It Away*, Katherine Anne Porter's *Pale Horse, Pale Rider*, William Goyen's underappreciated novel *Come, the Restorer* (1974), and James Baldwin's *The Fire Next Time*. Baldwin is not a Southerner, but his fiction addresses the tradition (and abuses) of Southern apocalypticism, as he makes clear in his discussion of *Uncle Tom's Cabin* in the opening pages of his autobiographical essay, *Notes of a Native Son*. Baldwin views racism as the primary condition and potential cause of apocalypse in America, a view that Percy shares in his essays, "Notes for a Novel about the End of the World," and "Stoicism in the South."

It is the late Texas writer, William Goyen, who summarizes the apocalyptic expectation inherent in so much Southern fiction. When asked in an interview whether his characters were always wounded or waiting for something, Goyen responded with a comment that describes the inhabitants of García Márquez's Macondo as clearly as it does Goyen's own in Charity or Trinity or Palestine, Texas:

> I think they're waiting for miracles, for wonderful visitations – they're waiting for the marvelous . . . for the wonderful surprise. It's probably the Second Coming, underneath. I'm sure that's all I've ever been writing about. Salvation, redemption, freedom from bondage, complete release. All those people from those little towns, that's what they were brought up to wait for: the end of the world, when the trumpets would sound. . . .[9]

Like Goyen, Walker Percy translates these abiding suspicions of apocalypse from their specific Southern landscape to the vaster region of universal myth. In all of his fiction, he is experimenting with a single central metaphor, the end of the world, to express his most basic cultural and spiritual concerns.

Apocalypse and Renewal

I.

Apocalypse is constantly invoked by Percy in order to suggest the necessity of ends, and the renewing effects those ends may have in the lives of alienated individuals. He places his protagonists at turning points, precipitated by personal or cultural crises, when they must evaluate their pasts and confront decisions about the new directions they wish their lives to take. Like the biblical apocalyptists, Percy and his characters construe the catastrophic end of the age as a positive event, for it serves as the symbolic precursor to spiritual and cultural renewal. Binx Bolling, in *The Moviegoer* (1961), wishes for the end of the world, and Will Barrett, protagonist of *The Last Gentleman* (1966) and *The Second Coming* (1980), finds that "It was not the prospect of the Last Day which depressed him but rather the prospect of living through an ordinary Wednesday morning."[10] Percy's least successful novel, *Love in the Ruins* (1971), is subtitled *The Adventures of a Bad Catholic at a Time Near the End of the World*. In that novel, Thomas More, narrator and protagonist, belies his namesake by describing not utopia but the "dread latter days" of contemporary American culture. He announces at the outset of his narration that the "center did not hold," an obvious reference to W. B. Yeats's poem, "The Second Coming," but Tom More's use of the past tense suggests that Yeats's sense of historical renewal ("Surely some revelation is at hand") no longer operates. More, however, does eventually leave off doomsaying and find self-renewal among the ruins, assuming Percy's prescribed attitude for the Catholic at the end of an era: a "wayfarer," patiently seeking a sign of God's grace.[11] The eponymous character of Percy's novel *Lancelot* (1977), unlike this author's other main characters, is an agent of destruction, a demonic figure who precipitates the violent end of his world. From his cell in a psychiatric hospital, Lancelot dreams of establishing a new world with a fellow patient in the woods of Virginia ("the new Adam and Eve of the new world"), but his choice of thanatos over eros in the past obviates renewal for him in the future.[12]

Toward the end of *The Moviegoer*, Binx Bolling makes a comment about apocalypse and renewal which all of Walker Percy's alienated protagonists reiterate in one way or another. He summarizes his view of society and himself in these terms: Contemporary humanity is "dead, dead, dead," and "malaise has settled like a fall-out and what people really fear is not that the bomb will fall but that the bomb will not fall."[13] Will Barrett also associates war and apocalypse at the beginning of *The Last Gentleman:* "If a man lives in the sphere of the possible and waits for something to happen, what he is waiting for is war – or the end of the world" (10). Lancelot, too, invokes the intensification of reality which war supposedly effects, and although the moral force of this character's statements is undermined by his psychotic behavior, his comments nonetheless contribute to the mythologizing of war. He recalls his great-great-grandfather, Manson Maury Lamar, whose infantry company provided reinforcements for Lee at the battle of Sharpsburg, and his uncle's participation in the battle of the Argonne ["He said it was too horrible. But he also said he never again felt real for the next forty years" (233)]. As if to contrast the diminished present to the heroic past, Lancelot notes with disgust that his son refused to go to Vietnam. Thus, war is repeatedly mentioned by Percy's protagonists as providing the antidote – and sometimes the *coup de grâce* – to their ennui. The idealization of military heroism was only strengthened in the South, it would seem, by losing the Civil War.

Lancelot's son has eschewed the supposed glories of the Southern martial tradition by refusing to go to war, but Lancelot cannot claim any medals either. Indeed, we may consider it a mark of Lancelot's sense of his own decline – his "slide into the future," as he puts it – that he must rely on weather, rather than war, to overcome the gulf between himself and the world. It takes a hurricane to blow him out of his alcoholic stupor. He does not, however, forsake military imagery in his discussion of his plan for historical renewal. He envisions his Third Revolution in the Shenandoah Valley as the modern continuation of the mythic warrior tradition: "We are the new Reformation. . . . We are going to set it out for you, what is good and what is bad, and no Jew–Christian waffling bullshit about it. What we are is the last of the West. . . . Lee and Richard and Saladin and Leonidas and Hector and Agamemnon and Richthofen and Charlemagne and Clovis and Martel" (190). Lancelot insists that he will establish his new world by means of the sword; to confirm this character's psychosis, he includes rape among the weapons in his arsenal. In *The Moviegoer,* Binx's cousin Kate – being a woman, and thus presumably without recourse to military remedies for her alienation – comments instead on her heightened consciousness of reality during the experience of a car accident in which her fiancé is killed. So disaster is constantly proposed as the antithesis of everydayness, that is, of existential alienation.

If we were to fail to understand these statements about the exhilarating effects of wars, natural disasters, acts of sexual violence, and fatal car accidents in terms of Percy's Christian eschatology, we would have to conclude that such statements serve little purpose other than to emphasize his characters' radical estrangement from meaningful social relations or moral systems. Obviously, such catastrophes in themselves can hardly be a viable source of either communal or individual integration. On the contrary, their comments would have to be taken as indications of their brutish insensitivity to the horrifying consequences of such catastrophes for both individuals and the human community at large. Percy seems to have anticipated this incomplete interpretation, for in several of his essays he outlines the mythic context in which catastrophe must be understood.[14] He repeatedly reminds his reader that apocalypse is not merely the wish for destruction, but also for radical reconstruction. This paradox of the creative force of destruction lies at the heart of Christian eschatology, which presupposes the more basic soteriological paradox of Christ's death as the source of eternal life, is incorporated into each of Percy's novels. Catastrophe contains the seeds of revitalization, and what may seem to be a dead end to Percy's characters is likely to prove itself instead a stage on the road to their social, psychological, and spiritual integration. Only Lancelot dramatizes an exception to this generalization, but this novel too presents an instance of the potentially positive effects of destruction, however mistaken the character's emphasis and the means to his end. Lancelot is the mirror image of the other characters, and is offered as one more confirming example of Percy's apocalyptic faith.

The Book of Revelation may be considered a forerunner of modern existentialist narration. It is the quintessential cri de coeur of the underground man. Percy's alienated characters are by definition apocalyptists, outsiders who yearn for the destruction of the world which they no longer find acceptable. They are exiles, though we should not exaggerate the analogy to their biblical forerunners. Their exile is a matter of degree and self-designation rather than of political or religious persecution. Nevertheless, they are apocalyptists in their desire for social and psychic disruption and renewal and, in Lancelot's case, in his understanding of himself as both outlaw and saint.

To say that Percy's protagonists are outsiders is not to minimize their moral stake in the world which they conceive of as collapsing around them. Their awareness of the approaching end is tempered by the insight, at which each of them arrives, that there is time to begin again. This tension is typical of the apocalyptic vision. The apocalyptist teeters between the conviction that moral corruption and social chaos have progressed beyond the point of reform, and the hope that it isn't too late after all. His rhetoric depends upon this strategy of balancing the terror of doom against the hope of millennium, upon the palpable tension between anxiety and assurance, divine wrath and divine mercy. The urgent tone of apocalyptic narration, the rush of its syntax and the rapid accumulation of its images, are the effects of this tension. Percy's characters feel the weight of time upon them. Like Shreve in *Absalom, Absalom!,* Will Barrett in *The Last Gentleman* repeatedly interjects the word "Wait!" as time appears to race just beyond his reach toward its conclusion. And Lancelot frenetically multiplies theories of history as he senses his own history closing in upon him. Nevertheless, these characters' consciousness of the shortness of time is mitigated by their assumption, also conventionally apocalyptic, that they will survive the end to participate in the rejuvenation they envision. This assumption is rooted precisely in their position of alienation. Their distance from the mainstream of their society gives them, they are convinced, the perspective necessary to understand and judge society, and to see beyond its end to something better.

The apocalyptist is both a decipherer and a cipherer, seeking in historical events and patterns an understanding of the future while at the same time expressing that understanding in ambiguous images and coded numerical configurations. His sense of divinely accorded clairvoyance, combined with his acute awareness of his own humanly limited vision, leads, I have suggested, to the unexpected mixture of tones in Revelation, from authoritative to abjectly obedient. This combination may also lead, as it does in related ways in Thomas Pynchon's fiction, to an intense paranoia based on the apocalyptist's conviction that *everything* possesses hidden meaning, and that *every* meaning is by definition hidden. While all of Percy's protagonists except Lancelot escape paranoia as such, they nonetheless initially need to view reality through some kind of screen or lens in order to focus and certify historical experience, at the same time that it distances it and gives them a special perspective on it. Lewis A. Lawson has noted the impulse of Percy's alienated characters to use some "scientific–empirical apparatus" to mediate between them and the world.[15] Binx goes to the movies; Tom More uses a "lapsometer"; Lancelot peers through binoculars, makes home movies, and fanatically watches the TV news. With the exception of Lancelot, Percy's characters manage to overcome their need for a distancing apparatus, but not until they have stood apart and searched for signs which will allow them insight into what otherwise resists their best efforts at understanding. The appeal of the apocalyptic perspective – removed from, and, as it were, looking down upon a corrupt society – is strong, not only for Percy's characters but also for Percy himself, who describes his own literary function in apocalyptic terms.

In "Notes for a Novel about the End of the World," Percy argues that the novelist may perform a "quasi-prophetic function," and insists on his or her responsibility to overcome the existential complacency of the reader. In this context, he compares his own use of cataclysmic events and images to Flannery O'Connor's use of the grotesque: O'Connor makes alienation dramatic by posing monstrousness – as Percy poses catastrophe – against implied norms of behavior and belief. Percy's aim is to "shock and therefore warn his readers by speaking of last things, if not the Last Days of the Gospels, then of a possible coming destruction, of a laying waste of cities, of vineyards reverting to the wilderness. Like the prophet he may find himself in radical disagreement with his fellow countrymen. Unlike the prophet, he does not generally get killed. More often he is ignored."[16] In his reference here to both prophecy and apocalypse, and in his biblical tone and imagery, Percy emphasizes the connection he wishes to establish between his own novelistic enterprise and the Judeo-Christian hortatory tradition.

I have already noted, in my discussion of William Faulkner's fiction, the vestigial awareness of paradise upon which the apocalyptic vision depends. This sense of paradise, and paradise lost, exists as well in Percy's fiction. In "Notes for a Novel about the End of the World," Percy asks his reader, "Is it too much to say that the novelist, unlike the new theologian, is one of the few remaining witnesses to the doctrine of original sin, the imminence of catastrophe in paradise?" (7). In contemporary America, physical well-being and metaphysical well-being are easily confused, so the novelist must make clear the difference between the "paradise" of the Paradise Estates of Covington, Louisiana, in *Love in the Ruins,* or the Elysian Fields of suburban New Orleans in *The Moviegoer,* and the transcendent realm which Christianity locates at the end of human time. Furthermore, the novelist must heighten the reader's sense of the urgency of time's movement toward that end. Like the biblical apocalyptist, Percy argues that contemporary novelists must fulfill two seemingly contradictory functions. First, they must describe and hence in some sense expedite the end with the urgency of language and images; and second, they must reverse the finality of that end by presenting it in eschatological terms, that is, in terms of individual and collective salvation. They will, in the process, create a symbolic narration that serves an apocalyptic (regenerative) function.

Walker Percy has written substantially about semiotics, the study of sign systems and symbolic discourse.[17] While the specifics of his semiotic writings are tangential to my discussion, their relation to his understanding of the novelist-as-apocalyptist is not. Apocalyptic narrative is above all symbolic, and self-consciously so. It questions the relation of the reader/believer to the world and to history, and encodes the evidence of that relation in highly symbolic structures. Eschatological novelists must read and interpret the signs of the times, and then re-interpret them for their audience in ways that are consonant with the meaning they understand to be latent in history itself. Percy refers to himself as an eschatological novelist, then asks, "Is there any other way to understand why people feel so bad in the twentieth century and writers feel so good writing about people feeling bad than in terms of the peculiar parameters, the joys and sorrows of symbol-mongering?"[18] The novel, as Percy conceives of it, must be a revelation in the biblical sense of the word, that is, a disclosure of God's signs about time and time's end.

II.

I have said that Percy's character Lancelot represents eschatological insight gone wrong. He understands perfectly the possibility of exchanging old worlds for new, but he does not accept any moral limitations on the means of enacting the exchange. He takes the idea of apocalypse literally as a license for violence. He murders his wife and several others by setting fire to his antebellum mansion; the holocaust symbolizes the destruction of the Southern aristocratic past as well. (There is here an obvious analogy with the conflagration of Sutpen's mansion in *Absalom, Absalom!*, also the end of a uniquely Southern world.) Lancelot speaks constantly of a broadsword, that symbolic apocalyptic instrument with which he will purge those who do not agree with his plan for the future. Violence is an essential element of apocalytic narration, but it is orchestrated by God, not the apocalyptist. When Lancelot sets fire to his mansion for the purpose of murder, he arrogates to himself supernatural power. He plays at once a combination of Christ and Antichrist, fallen angel and apocalyptic avenger. So he speaks of himself, when he is blown clear of the flames by an explosion, as "Lucifer blown out of hell, great wings spread against the starlight" (266). As far as he is concerned, the fire effaces the past, and the present is so corrupt that it cannot be salvaged. Time must be violently truncated. Lancelot's martial vision of an abrupt and violent end is consonant with biblical apocalypse, though Percy makes it clear that his character is sadly mistaken about the source of command.[19]

I have noted, in Percy's *Love in the Ruins,* that the character Tom More reworks Yeats's famous line, "Things fall apart; the center cannot hold." It is Lancelot, however, whose understanding of the relation of violence to apocalypse more closely resembles Yeats's.[20] Frank Kermode's discussion of Yeats in *The Sense of an Ending* focuses above all on the poet's sense of the reciprocal relation of violence to vision ("thunder of feet, tumult of images").[21] For Yeats, violence was indicative of the extreme psychological situation at the end of an era. Social anarchy was paralleled on the personal level by rape, murder, moral collapse, all necessary "to break the teeth of time." Of course the purgation effected by violence is also basic to tragedy, but here, violence is tied specifically to time – to historical movement and historical vision: The "blood dimmed tide" was to precede and in some sense cause the new annunciation, the new gyre. Lancelot totally misuses this idea, as I have said, but his relation to Yeats's thought is nonetheless clear. Percy is hardly alone among recent U.S. novelists to exploit the metaphysics of apocalyptic violence and renewal. Recall the final scene of communal violence in Nathanael West's *The Day of the Locust,* the sexual aggression in Norman Mailer's *An American Dream,* or the symbolism of judgment in Flannery O'Connor's *The Violent Bear It Away.*[22]

Lancelot's violent apocalypticism has strong political implications. Both Cleanth Brooks and Lewis A. Lawson have argued convincingly for the importance of the political philosophy of Eric Voegelin in understanding Lancelot's false conception of history.[23] Voegelin began his academic career as a young man in Austria during the late 1920s; his experience of watching Hitler's rise to power, his refusal to play his designated role in the Third

Reich as the political philosopher who would make Nazi racism the-oretically respectable, and his emigration to the United States in 1939 pro-vided the early context for what one commentator has called Voegelin's lifelong concern to understand "the demonism of the age."[24] Voegelin explores in a variety of works the subject of civil theology, particularly the secular messianism of modern ideological movements which promise an earthly paradise and which therefore both depend upon and seek to displace Christian apocalyptic archetypes with their own secular ideals. (We have seen this idea dramatized by Cortázar, and will see it again in Fuentes's fiction, though their purpose is not to revalidate a Christian eschatological understanding of history, as is Percy's and Voegelin's, but rather to indict political repression.) The source of the secularized apocalypticism which in Voegelin's opinion has led to modern totalitarian movements such as Nazism and Stalinism is located in the writings of an Italian abbot, Joachim de Fiore (ca. 1135–1202).[25]

Joachim was a central figure in the apocalyptic thought of the Middle Ages. In fact, Norman Cohn has suggested in his seminal book on medieval apocalypticism that Joachim's prophetic system was the most influential in Europe until the appearance of Marxism.[26] A complete discussion of Joachim's visionary system is beyond the scope of my chapter, and Lewis A. Lawson has already called attention to the specific parallels between Joachim's system and Lancelot's various tripartite historical summaries and projections.[27] I want here only to make some general comparative observa-tions about Joachim and Percy's character Lancelot, observations that will be relevant in the following chapter on Fuentes's fiction, as well as serving to further my definition of Percy's apocalyptic vision.

Joachim was inspired by what he conceived of as the ordering patterns of history. In his *Expositio in Apocalypsim,* and in his idiosyncratic mixture of theological concept and artistic imagery in the *Liber Figurarum (Book of Figures),* he presented his vision of the symbolic structures of temporal reality. Joachim found in the historical events and institutions of his own time the fulfillment of God's apocalyptic plan. He divided history into three stages, predicting that the third and last stage of history was about to begin under the earthly leadership of an angelic pope (whom he identified as Frederick II) and a religious order of spiritual men (whom he identified as the spiritual Franciscans).[28] Joachim's imputation of apocalyptic signifi-cance to specific historical personages and groups – his "immanentization of the Christian eschaton," as Voegelin terms it – challenged and ultimately replaced the Augustinian separation of secular and sacred histories, which had been maintained for almost a millennium. According to Voegelin, this Joachimite confusion of the immanent and the transcendent also charac-terized Hitler's vision of earthly perfection under a secular messiah. That Hitler's regime was called the Third Reich suggests Joachim's legacy.

Lancelot implicitly associates himself with Joachim's potent myth of the leaders of the third age, the spiritual virtuosi who see themselves as harbingers of the future. In his messianic image of himself, Lancelot finds the transcendental justification for his own historical importance, and the mechanism by which he convinces himself he can control his future and dismiss his past. That Percy's character explains his violent crimes in terms of a coherent apocalyptic program of retribution and ultimate historical renewal clearly links him to the ethical abuses Voegelin traces back to Joachim of Fiore.

Apocalyptic visions are inspired by the desire to impose order on time and, thus, to control the future, to make it less threatening because it is less unknown. In Joachim's intricate historical patterns, as in Lancelot's proliferating systems of temporal ages and stages, this relation of historical explanation to psychological consolation is basic. In fact, it may be argued that Lancelot commits murder for the very purpose of reactivating a meaningful historical system of "great events." As he cuts the throat of his wife's lover, he casts about, as he says, for the feeling to match the deed: "Weren't we raised to believe that 'great deeds' were performed with great feelings . . . ?" (262) And as he is blown sky high by the explosion he has caused, he reassures himself that "there are still great moments" (266). So he imagines that he has acted to reinstate a system of historical events weighted with interpretable significance: It is this system which he later, in his psychiatric cell, busies himself inventing. Lancelot's apocalyptic plan for a "new order" provides him with comfortingly absolute answers to ultimate theological and philosophical questions, as well as with the justification for murder.

This confusion between universal history and individual desire is addressed by Marjorie Reeves, whose scholarly studies provide modern readers with a complex portrait of Joachim of Fiore. Reeves examines Joachim's search for symbolic significance in biblical, ecclesiastical, and secular history, noting that in each event and episode, he found "an inner meaning which linked it by concord with events of another era. . . . Joachim – like so many other medieval thinkers – rejoiced in looking for these inner meanings, but interpreted them, not so much in terms of the individual Christian's salvation, as in those of the destiny of the whole human race."[29] Lancelot, on the contrary, is not interested in the destiny of the whole human race except as it relates to his own vindication. He is absorbed not by metaphysical truths but by the effort to force events one after another into his own apocalyptic system. God and the human community have been replaced by the narcissistic self who seeks gratification in the system which he has invented for that sole purpose.

Like Lancelot, the narrator of *Love in the Ruins* also conjures up historical schemata in Joachimite fashion. Tom More refers to the three stages of

American history, counting backward from 1983, the year in which the novel is set and, he notes, the year before the *annus apocalypsis* prophesied by George Orwell. He too hopes to make history comprehensible and meaningful by breaking it into predictable pieces. However, he learns during the course of the novel, as Lancelot never does, that the ultimate questions concerning first and last things remain significant precisely because no single answer or system can exhaust them. He understands, furthermore, that there would be no search for the meaning of history if its meaning were easily or entirely manifest in historical events. But even though Tom More reaches the proper existential conclusions in terms of Percy's Christian eschatology, *Love in the Ruins* is unsuccessful in my opinion because the author chooses to portray not only the crisis preceding the advent of a new world, but also the new world itself.

The new world described in the epilogue to *Love in the Ruins* is a suburban utopia which serves only to trivialize the apocalyptic aspirations described in the body of the novel. We see Tom More cultivating his Southern garden (collard greens), basting his Christmas turkey, holding his wife on his lap, fishing – activities meant to figure More's reconciliation to the present but which instead suggest no more than his well-adjusted affluence. In his other novels, Percy recognizes that perfection stales when it is rendered too explicitly, and that material well-being does not necessarily figure spiritual health; he therefore wisely leaves the characters in his other novels just on the verge of the new worlds which they have imagined and will attempt to enact. Effective apocalyptic literature has always focused its descriptive powers on the imperfect old world rather than the perfect new world, leaving the contours of the ideal future indistinct. Its focus on the "before" rather than the "after" is, as I have said, the factor that distinguishes apocalyptic from utopian literature. *Love in the Ruins* banalizes the apocalyptic experience of its protagonist by describing too specifically its end.

In *Lancelot,* on the other hand, Percy emphasizes the apocalyptic urge to depreciate this world in favor of the next. Lancelot's apocalyptic vision – what I call his desperate apocalypticism – is based on a horror of existence and a desire to escape from it by positing an ideal realm which totally discredits the world of his present experience. Although Lancelot's extreme position is condemned in the novel, the question has nonetheless been raised about the extent to which Percy's fiction generally appears to eschew political engagement in favor of waiting for a future, supernatural solution. Cecil L. Eubanks observes in Percy's work a certain philosophical turning away from the world, a refusal "to recognize the dialectical tension between grace as 'the Word' and grace as 'the Word made flesh.' "[30] Eubanks further notes that Percy's dependence on Eric Voegelin, with Voegelin's emphasis on the Augustinian separation of sacred transcendence from secular history, might be considered to constitute a rejection of political or social action. While this seems to me a suggestion worth entertaining, Voegelin's political philosophy does not necessarily lead to a withdrawal from the processes of secular history. In the following chapter, we will see that Fuentes uses Voegelin's insights about Joachim not only to understand the totalitarian perversions of secular apocalypticism but also to dramatize the positive effects of Joachimism in inspiring the revolutionary millenarian groups in medieval and renaissance Europe. And Yeats – whose apocalyptic vision coincides with Percy's in ways I have already suggested, and whose poems are cited in Fuentes's *Terra Nostra* – refers to Joachim's *Expositio in apocalypsim* as "that terrible book in which the freedom of the Renaissance lay hidden."[31] By no means does Joachimism *necessarily* lead either to historical aggression or historical withdrawal, as the character of Lancelot might seem to suggest.

Although it is true that Percy's alienated characters are tempted to dismiss this world, they ultimately manage, with the exception of Lancelot, to escape the rejection of the present that total alienation implies. Percy is very aware of the dissociation resulting from the radical disenchantment with the world as it is, and he dramatizes the necessity of existential engagement in all of his novels. Even Lancelot, in a moment of honesty, acknowledges that his apocalyptic systems are escapist. Toward the end of the novel, he admits that "The present is something else. To live in the past and the future is easy. To live in the present is like threading a needle" (253). Binx Bolling, at the end of *The Moviegoer,* does decide to "listen to people, see how they stick themselves into the world, hand them along a ways in their dark journey and be handed along. . . " (184). At the end of *Love in the Ruins,* Tom More's priest tells him what he already knows, that there are things more important than "middle-aged daydreams," and among them are "doing our jobs, you being a better doctor, I being a better priest, showing a bit of ordinary kindness to people, particularly our own families . . . doing what we can for our poor unhappy country. . . " (376). And Will Barrett also comes to an understanding of the present that validates this world as well as the next. He knows that the perfection envisioned by the Christian apocalyptist is not to be had in this world, but he also knows that that is not sufficient reason to dismiss this world or the present moment.

III.

It is Will Barrett who best illustrates the apocalyptic conviction that impels Walker Percy's fiction. This character is developed over the course of two novels, *The Last Gentleman* and *The Second Coming.* Barrett's sense of the future, his preoccupation with his own end and the end of the age in which he lives as a middle-aged man in *The Second Coming,* is apparent in the youthful Will of *The Last Gentleman,* some thirty years earlier. At the begin-

ning of *The Last Gentleman,* the narrator describes the young Will's eschatological obsession and relates it to the South and to what Percy elsewhere calls Southern stoicism: "Like many young men in the South, he
became overly subtle and had trouble ruling out the possible. They are not
like an immigrant's son in Passaic who decides to become a dentist and that
is that" (10). The temporal attitude implied by Will's absolute openness to
the future would seem to be the obverse of Pynchon's entropic vision,
which dismisses all futures but one, or of Barth's enclosed narrative structures, which admit no temporal development at all. Will's stance is in part
the result of disappointed expectations, for his ideas about his future have
gradually been falsified: "When he was a youth he had lived his life in a state
of the liveliest expectation, thinking to himself: what a fine thing it will be
to become a man and to know what to do – like an Apache youth who at
the right time goes out into the plains alone, dreams dreams, sees visions,
returns and knows he is a man. But no such time had come and he still
didn't know how to live" (11). Will's temporal openness and his alienation
are clearly related.

Visions of Apache youths and ritual initiations are romantic delusions for
the young Will. In fact, the narrator states, it is living "from one ordinary
minute to the next on a Wednesday afternoon" which he must eventually
confront and master. Wednesday, the middle of the week, is used repeatedly by Percy to signal Will's temporal anxiety, a point which recalls Frank
Kermode's discussion of the modern predicament "in the midst" of history,
without relation to a beginning or an end that would give meaning to the
middle.[32] Even in his confusion, however, Will has a strong sense that
something "was going to happen and when it did he would know the secret
of his own life" (11). For Will, the end of the world becomes the symbol of
that awaited moment when he imagines that the secret of his life will be
revealed: Apocalypse here takes on its original etymological significance of
revelation. We are not surprised that Will's apocalypse/revelation is not
immediately forthcoming. Neither war nor the end of the world – nor
anything else, for that matter – occurs forthwith to clarify for him the
meaning of his life. However, at the end of this novel, we understand that a
transcendent reality has begun to reveal itself. When Will appears in *The
Second Coming,* his longing for revelation is in fact satisfied. Chronos is
interrupted by *kairos,* and apocalypse becomes the figure for the end of
Will's merely successive Wednesdays.[33]

One of the epigraphs to *The Last Gentleman* provides an insight into the
historical situation of Percy's character. This epigraph is from *The End of the
Modern World,* by the German theologian Romano Guardini:

We know now that the modern world is coming to an end . . . at the
same time, the unbeliever will emerge from the fogs of secularism. He

will cease to reap benefit from the values and forces developed by the very Revelation he denies . . . Loneliness and faith will be terrible. Love will disappear from the face of the public world, but the more precious will be that love which flows from one lonely person to another . . . the world to come will be filled with animosity and danger, but it will be a world open and clean.

Guardini presents a radical critique of the modern secularization of the Christian church and Christian values. He calls for a moment of decision (it is in this decisive moment that Guardini locates "the essence of the end") when both Christians and non-Christians will reject the secularized aspects of Christianity as hypocritical sentimentalities. Christians will return to a more rigorous metaphysics and non-Christians will decide that they will live "honestly without Christ and without the God revealed through Him."[34] Guardini reiterates Nietzsche's warning that non-Christians in the modern world have no realization of what it truly means to be without Christ, and deplores the modern cultural hypocrisy which "denies Christian doctrine and a Christian order of life even as it usurps its human and cultural effects" (128). In *The Last Gentleman,* Will initially represents the atomized "mass man" whom Guardini describes as "absorbed by technology and rational abstraction."[35] But despite his "abstraction" as a young man, Will does reach a decisive moment, though he manages to do so only thirty years later, in *The Second Coming.*

If Will eventually approximates Guardini's Christian in a post-Christian age, it is the character Dr. Sutter Vaught in *The Last Gentleman* who embodies the attitudes proper to Guardini's nonbeliever. Vaught is a discredited and disillusioned physician who rejects secularized Christian values, but who recognizes that a strictly scientific understanding of human beings abstracts them from nature and from themselves. Vaught proposes that the only means of overcoming this dissociation is sex, that the only viable contemporary alternative to Christianity is pornography. His notebooks are interpolated into the narration of the novel, and, in one entry, he writes: "Lewdness – sole concrete metaphysic of layman in age of science – sacrament of the dispossessed . . ." (279). Sutter announces himself as the perfect pornographer, "a man who lives both in anteroom of science . . . and who also lives in twilight of Christianity, *e.g.,* a technician. The perfect pornographer = lapsed Christian Southerner (who retains the memory not merely of Christianity but of a region immersed in place and time) who presently lives in Berkeley or Ann Arbor, which are not true places but sites of abstract activity . . ." (280). Vaught's search for pleasure without ethical reference is discredited in the novel [he is, in the narrator's judgment, "the dismalest failure, a man who had thrown himself away" (381)], but his self-conscious rejection of Christian morality in an amoral culture is'nonetheless perfectly congruent with Guardini's vision of the new age.

Sutter's sister dramatizes – even more clearly than Will at this point in his development – Guardini's prescribed stance of the believer at the end of the modern age. Val, a nun who runs a Catholic school in rural Alabama, is described sarcastically by Sutter in an odd but expressive mixture of the phrases from Romano Guardini and the Book of Revelation. He says that she conceives of herself as "the surviving remnant of her Catholic Thing," and that she hopes believers and nonbelievers will declare themselves as such:

> She believes that then, if we go the route and run out of Christendom, that the air would be cleared and even that God might give us a sign. . . . Did you notice how much it looked like one of those surviving enclaves after the Final War, and she's probably right: I mean, who in hell would want to bomb South Alabama? . . .
>
> Don't you see? Nothing happened. She got all dressed up for the bridegroom and the bridegroom didn't come. There she sits in the woods as if the world had ended and she was one of the Elected ones Left to keep the Thing going, but the world has not ended, in fact is more the same than usual (377–8).

It is relevant in this context that Val, who is clearly Percy's spokesperson on the subject of contemporary moral failure, should specifically reject entropy as a metaphor for human history, claiming instead, according to her dying brother Jamie, "a historical movement in the direction of negative entropy" (370). Val asks Will to see that Jamie is baptized before he dies; it is through Jamie's death that Will manages to begin to participate once again in historical reality. As for Sutter, he maintains his position as a "spiritual Swede" who will "die like an honest man" (379).

The substitution of sex for belief which characterizes Sutter Vaught in *The Last Gentleman* also characterizes Lancelot. Of course, Vaught has consciously chosen his role as "pornographer" in ways that Lancelot, with his lack of self-awareness and psychic self-control, is quite incapable of doing. Lancelot's flashbacks to his youth suggest that he has always substituted the physical for the metaphysical, and that such a substitution is an unavoidable aspect of the decadent aristocratic culture in which he was reared. Lancelot cannot dissociate the secular from the sacred, as Sutter does, but continually images his sexual relations in Christian terms. Speaking of his beautiful and unfaithful wife, he tells the priest who listens to his story in the psychiatric hospital, "That was my communion, Father . . . that sweet dark sanctuary guarded by the heavy gold columns of her thighs, the ark of her covenant"

(181). When he learns of his wife's infidelity, Lancelot's mélange of sex and salvation veers sharply into psychosis. If his paradise with his wife was lost because of sex, then it is by sex that he thinks he can regain it. He vows to base his new world on a sexual regime that is at once repressive and promiscuous. Lancelot assures his listener that "The secret of life is violence and rape, and its gospel is pornography" (241), and uses an apocalyptic image – "the omega point" – to argue that the culmination of evolution is sexual aggression. Lancelot's psychotic sexual behavior is associated with temporal dislocation, an association summarized by Lancelot's observation that jealousy makes time stretch and warp, that it alters the very shape of time itself.

We know that apocalyptic visions incorporate sexual imagery: Revelation images the most opprobrious of spiritual and social offenses in lurid sexual terms. The result of such imagery is not a sense of sexual license so much as a palpable undercurrent of repressed sexuality, the psychological analogue to the political impotence of the apocalyptist. Lancelot's phallic bombast must be understood in terms of impotence, in his case actual rather than figurative. His use of the apocalyptic image of the omega point, and his reference to the "kingdom of heaven" just before he begins to rant about his sexual theory of history, connect his narrative to the conventional apocalyptic use of sexual imagery to figure a range of abuses. Indeed, in his novelistic epitomizing of the spiritual ills of contemporary culture in sexual terms, Walker Percy himself, not just his narrators, would seem to participate in and extend this characteristic apocalyptic narrative device.

I do not mean to suggest that Percy's use of the imagery of sexual corruption is merely rhetorical. On the contrary, it seems clear to me that Percy is troubled – too troubled, perhaps – by the changing sexual mores of the contemporary American culture he depicts in his fiction. One even detects occasionally in Percy's novels the false dichotomy between asceticism and promiscuity, an extention of Pauline theology which Carlos Fuentes explicitly rejects in *Terra Nostra*. Though I have argued that Percy's fiction is similar to Latin American fiction in several respects, on this point it would seem to be very different. We have only to think of the ebullient sex in García Márquez's fiction, its regenerative potential in Fuentes's fiction, or Cortázar's paralleling of sexual and visionary energies, to recognize the contrast. We must wait until the end of *The Second Coming* for sex to be treated by Percy as anything other than a source of anxiety, even of psychopathology. Of course, the English Puritan and Hispanic Catholic traditions have always differed in their cultural attitudes toward sexuality, and it is therefore no wonder, we may conclude, that Percy departs from Latin American writers in this regard. But before we reach a conclusion which might itself present a false dichotomy, we should take note of a Latin American writer who in fact shares Percy's sense of the coincidence of cultural decadence and contemporary sexual behavior.

Octavio Paz, at the end of a comparative discussion of the United States and Mexico, expresses his radical skepticism about several cultural practices – what he calls "inferior forms of credulity": "The hedonism of the West is the other face of desperation; its skepticism is not wisdom but renunciation; its nihilism ends in suicide and in inferior forms of credulity, such as political fanaticism and magical chimeras. The empty place left by Christianity in the modern soul is filled not by philosophy but by the crudest superstitions. Our eroticism is a technique, not an art or a passion."[36] Paz, like Percy, links hedonism to the loss of meaningful institutions and beliefs and, furthermore, to the loss of an eschatological sense of history: "The liberal societies spin tirelessly, not forward, but round and round. If they change, they are not transfigured" (152). Paz's comment is useful in relativizing the opposition that may seem to exist between Percy's characteristic treatment of sexual relations and that found in Latin American fiction. Paz's context is international, his concern is the crisis of "modern" culture on the broad geographical scale implied by the word "Western." His observations may thus complement and enlarge the relevance of Percy's Southern setting.

Unlike Sutter Vaught and Lancelot, Will Barrett is not looking for sex but for signs. He is, throughout most of *The Last Gentleman,* an observer, or at most, a passive seeker. Although the narrator refers to him as "the engineer," Will is not an engineer but a technician, operating the air-conditioning system on the night shift in the sub-basement of Macy's in New York as the novel opens. At this point, as I have said, Will corresponds to Romano Guardini's definition of "mass man," distanced from a subjective or symbolic understanding of the world by technology and by his lack of purpose.[37] He eventually leaves New York, returns to the South, and then continues on to New Mexico; his itinerary is determined not by his own plans or desires but by accident, coincidence, and the needs of other characters, namely the Vaughts, whom he encounters along the way. Sutter and Val Vaught's assertively stated philosophical and sociological formulations contrast to Will's lack of any clear system of values, or indeed, his lack of any clear understanding of the culture in which he is caught. His utter detachment from historical reality is most obvious when he sleeps through the violence on the campus of Ole Miss, a novelistic incident closely based on the forced integration in 1962 of the University of Mississippi by National Guard troops. It is only in the final two scenes of the novel that Will is able to insert himself back into time in a meaningful way.

Will Barrett's problem is figured in psychological terms. The young Will suffers from "fugues" – amnesia and a strong and recurring sense of déjà vu. These are temporal dysfunctions. Both amnesia and the sense of déjà vu create gaps or other distortions in time, and hence confuse the character's sense of his relation to duration. Percy has commented that Will's disorientation suggests "a post-Christian shakiness about historic time," a comment that he elaborates in terms of the two temporal systems discussed by Eric Voegelin. Referring to Voegelin's *The New Science of Politics,* Percy says, "In his book, Voegelin contrasts the unhistoric cyclical time of the Greeks and Orientals with historic linear time of Israel – historical time began when Israel emerged."[38] Will's ailments would seem emblematic of his unwitting and unwilled relation to these contradictory temporal movements. His amnesia suggests a linear system gone awry as random portions of his past are left irretrievably behind, and his sense of déjà vu suggests a cyclical system out of control as random portions of his past return unbidden. This welling up of repeated images is not like Barth's repeated patterns of events and characters, which are essentially esthetic and structural in purpose; nor are they like Cortázar's *figuras,* which are meant to suggest the complex multiplicity of experience and its fictional embodiments. Here, repetition is an indication of temporal and psychic dislocation: Will's problem is to begin to understand and participate in the forward-moving present of his own life.

Repetition thus becomes a philosophical index in *The Last Gentleman.* Voegelin locates the essential difference between the temporal systems he describes in their different understanding of the movement of time toward its perceived goal. Whereas the Greek cyclical system conceives of history as an immanent process enacted entirely and repeatedly within this world, Judeo-Christian history proposes a realm that transcends this world and is based on an apocalyptic vision of ultimate and eternal fulfillment. Voegelin emphasizes the unique and unrepeatable end toward which Judeo-Christian history moves, an end that imparts a direction and a destination to time's movement. The opposition between repetition and uniqueness, between immanence and transcendence is constantly drawn in Sutter's notebooks, but it is particularly to Will that Voegelin's discussion pertains. Until Will achieves an understanding of the historical nature and significance of his own life, his relation to his future will be as random as is his relation to his own past.

Voegelin's *Order and History* is particularly useful in understanding Will Barrett's "post-Christian shakiness about historic time." In the first volume of this work, entitled *Israel and Revelation,* Voegelin discusses divine revelation and the symbolic interpretation of revelation upon which humanity's historical existence depends. He argues that humanity has knowledge of itself "as a part of being, capable of experiencing itself as such, of using language and calling that experience 'man'."[39] This knowledge is precarious, and in the face of the mystery of existence, symbols arise by which we attempt to make our existence intelligible, that is, by which we express our intimations of order. Symbolization is linguistic and communal: Symbolic language expresses society's common understanding of order. According to Voegelin, humanity does not create this order. Rather, it is through revelation – what Voegelin calls "leaps upward in being" – that humanity intimates a "world-transcendent order," a spiritual reality. Speaking of Judeo-Christian culture, Voegelin asserts that the revelation on Mount Sinai was given by a transcendent God who imposed on his chosen people an existence in historical form. Divine revelation broke into the repetitive cycle of past, present, and future, creating the experience of a before and an after, that is, creating the experience of history. For Voegelin, history is the movement of divine reality through a complex of meaningful events toward a transcendent end. These ideas underlie the behavior of Percy's character and suggest the context in which the conclusion of *The Last Gentleman* must be interpreted.

Will's peripatetic journey at last assumes a direction at the deathbed of Jamie Vaught, the younger brother of Sutter and Val, where Will plays the role of interpreter between Jamie and an attendant priest. Jamie is so weak from the final ravages of leukemia that he cannot speak clearly enough to be understood by the priest. Will therefore finds himself deciphering Jamie's last words for the priest, who in turn enacts the symbolic rite which serves as both Jamie's baptism and extreme unction. In the specificity of the physical details of Jamie's death, Percy makes effective use of his physcian's knowledge. His painfully precise description seems aimed at heightening our awareness of our mortal human condition, and our awareness, furthermore, of our human relation to both immanent and transcendent realms. For Percy, as for Voegelin, the secular and the sacred are separate orders, but there are nevertheless moments when the transcendent breaks into the immanent, when *kairos* invades chronology and time is fulfilled. Jamie's end inspires in Will a moment of eschatological insight when, as Voegelin would put it, the "World-transcendent order" reveals itself in time. It is the revelatory sign Will has been seeking. Though the novel concludes before we can be certain whether he is capable of interpreting it and acting upon it, there is the strong suggestion that something significant has occurred and that it will permanently affect Will's future.

Immediately after Jamie's death, Will leaves the hospital in pursuit of Sutter Vaught, who has also been there with Jamie, because he wants to ask him what happened in the hospital room. When he is within shouting distance, he calls to Sutter to wait. When he emphatically repeats the word "wait," we see that his temporal confusion has begun to dissipate. Instead of floating through a temporal medium, as he has done during the entire course of the novel, Will begins to understand time in eschatological terms. We remember at the end of *Absalom, Absalom!* Shreve's repeated plea to Quentin to wait. Like Shreve and Quentin, Will feels the pressure of an end bearing down upon him, and he suddenly and purposefully pursues a direction. When Sutter gets into his car and begins to drive away, Will runs after him "with great joyous ten-foot antelope bounds" in order to ask "a final question." Though we do not learn what that last question is, we *do* know with certainty that, for Will, time's movement has become weighted with significance and presses on, if not to the world's end, then to his own. Jamie's baptism and death provide the means by which Will sets his relations with the infinite, and the means by which he can reconcile everydayness with significant historical existence. When we read the sequel to this novel, we find that Will asks his final question not of Sutter Vaught, but of God.

IV.

What we may predict about Will's evolving sense of time at the end of *The Last Gentleman* is necessarily conditioned by the character's reappearance in *The Second Coming*. We are used to the reappearance of characters in two or more works by a given writer. The great practitioners of this fictional strategy in U.S. and Latin American fiction are Faulkner and García Márquez, and I have also mentioned John Barth's resurrection of characters from one novel to another. However, I would propose that Percy's motives for the fictional reincarnation of his character differ from those of Barth or Faulkner or García Márquez. Faulkner and García Márquez, in various of their novels and short stories, contribute the parts of what are offered as complete and coherent worlds – Yoknapatawpha County and Macondo. Like any real county or town, they are populated with a set of characters who appear and reappear in different times and places. Barth's purpose inverts Faulkner's and García Márquez's. Instead of reintroducing characters for realistic effect, he does so to point up their fictionality, placing them in different narrative settings in order to draw attention to his own verbal forms. In Percy's case, the reappearance of Will Barrett and several other characters is calculated to dramatize their historical development over a substantial period of time (indeed, a lifetime), and to emphasize their temporal condition per se. By presenting them twice, first young and then old, Percy seems to afford his characters a life outside and independent of the novels in which the reader knows them, living and aging offstage, as it were, between appearances. In making them age thirty years between novels, Percy emphasizes their status as beings to whom the passage of time matters and for whom change is as undeniable as the death toward which each of them moves. Furthermore, the characters' reappearance seems to reiterate symbolically Percy's theme of apocalyptic renewal, the end in *The Last Gentleman* serving as a new beginning in *The Second Coming*.

I have said that at the end of *The Last Gentleman*, Will begins to understand the eschatological nature of time and his own existence. As *The Second Coming* begins, he is still working on that understanding, still interpreting potential signs of the approaching apocalypse. It is one sign in particular, the absence of Jews in North Carolina, which obsesses him. This fact (if it is a fact) indicates to Will the fulfillment of one of the biblical prerequisites for the Second Coming of Christ, the return of the Jews to their homeland. So he descends into a cave near his property, where either he will receive a confirming sign from God or he will die. If, as we will see, Will's father spent his life looking back toward a mythical past which he considered preferable to his present, here Will commits a related error: He looks forward toward the promised future, denying his present and almost opting, as did his father, for suicide rather than continue living in the present. So he hurls his challenge:

> Speak, God, and let me know if the Jews are a sign and the Last Days are at hand.
> If the Last Days are at hand, one shall know what to do. I shall go to Megiddo with Sutter and wait for the Stranger from the East.
> If you do not speak and the Jews are not a sign, then that too is an answer of sorts. It means that what is at hand are not the Last Days, but only the last days, my last days, a minor event, to be sure, but an event of importance to me (212–13).

Megiddo, the supposed site of Armageddon, will be the "ring-side seat" if indeed the Last Days are at hand, and it is there that Will has asked his old acquaintaince, Sutter Vaught, to go and wait for his arrival or the end of the world, whichever comes first. "So it was," comments the narrator, "that Will Barrett went mad." Describing his "madness," the narrator notes ironically, "He had become convinced that the Last Days were at hand, that the world had fallen into the hands of the only species which knows how to destroy itself along with all other living creatures on earth . . ." (197). No Armageddon occurs, and Will must act before he is acted upon. Because of a violent illness, he leaves the cave, and on his way out he falls into a new world. He finds himself on the floor of the primitive dwelling of a young woman named Allie Huger, who becomes the agent of his regeneration. Percy makes it clear that apocalypse is an existential matter, a figure for the necessity of personal commitment, for acts of faith.

As in *The Last Gentleman,* the crux of evaluating Will's experience in *The Second Coming* lies in evaluating his relation to time. The new life that he wills into existence in the latter novel is dependent upon his bringing about the end of his old life, or, at least, upon successfully integrating it into his present. Although Will's fugues have by this time been diagnosed as a physiological rather than a psychological problem, he does not have his past under control yet. The central event of that past is a hunting accident when his father tried to kill both himself and Will.[40] The memory of the accident wells up involuntarily, but fortunately so, for, once recalled, Will begins at this late stage in his life to understand his father's philosophical pessimism and his culture's. Percy's essay, "Stoicism in the South," describes the sense of doom which haunts Will's father: "Its most characteristic mood was a poetic pessimism which took a grim satisfaction in the dissolution of its values – because social decay confirmed one in his original choice of the wintry kingdom of the self. . . . for the Stoic there is no real hope. His finest hour is to sit tight-lipped and ironic while the world comes crashing down around him."[41] In this essay, Percy comments that this was an attitude well suited to the hierarchical society of the nineteenth-century South, and he uses Faulkner's aristocratic character, Sartoris, to illustrate the concept of honor inherent in the Stoic's stance. But Percy also notes that this attitude is not confined to the South: "It is not just Faulkner who bears witness to the coming of the mass man, to the alienation and vulgarization of the urban consumer. Ortega and Marcel are neither Southern nor Stoic" (343). Percy rejects the disengaged stance of the alienated stoic, arguing for a Christian commitment to political and social issues, a commitment that is both personal and institutional.

It is, then, Will's father who is the last gentleman in the novel by that name. It is he rather than Will who is portrayed as a Southern stoic according to Percy's definition, a man "killed by his own irony and sadness and by the strain of living out an ordinary day in a perfect dance of honor." This description also fits Quentin in *Absalom, Absalom!*, who, like Will's father, is burdened by the Southern aristocratic imperative of honor and who also eventually commits suicide. However, it is a mark of Percy's greater optimism when compared to Faulkner that he allows his sons an egress from the sins of their fathers as Faulkner does not. And as García Márquez does not: Aureliano Babilonia is also a last gentleman, trapped by a family tradition of historical fatalism he can no more escape than Quentin can. That the false morality of the old world is not easily sloughed off is as much the point of apocalyptic narration as its vision of renewal, and, in fact, the point which Faulkner and García Márquez, and Percy in *Lancelot*, choose to emphasize. We know that neither Quentin nor Aureliano nor Lancelot manages to free himself from his past. In *The Second Coming*, however, Will Barrett does escape from the curse under which his father lived and died.

Will's struggle to confront and overcome his Southern stoic heritage is one of the principal sources of dramatic tension in *The Second Coming*. Percy repeatedly emphasizes the psychological price the process exacts. I have said that Will manages to free himself from the doomed world of his past and establish his own identity in the present, but he is nonetheless sorely tempted by the siren's song he hears his father singing. Even though his father has been dead for years, he imagines his call: "Come, what else is there? What other end if you don't make the end? Make your own bright end in the darkness of this dying world, this foul and feckless place. . . . Close it out.

At least you can do that, not only not lose but win, with one last splendid gesture defeat the whole foul feckless world" (337). This death wish in some measure impels Will to enter the cave and challenge God to end the world. By the conclusion of the novel, however, Will has dealt with his past: In the terms of Percy's essay on Southern stoicism, we may say that Will moves from Stoic pessimism to a Christian existential engagement of the present.

Percy's reference to the Spanish philosopher José Ortega y Gasset offers an additional means of understanding the temporal dislocation Will must overcome. I have already speculated that Ortega's ideas are related to Jorge Luis Borges's on the exhaustion of literary forms and, indirectly, to John Barth's. Relevant to Percy's fiction are not only Ortega's pervasive sense of living at the end of a cultural era, and his concomitant sense of esthetic exhaustion, but also his interest in the temporal disposition of the romantic.

In an important essay, Percy associates Ortega with one of his own epigrammatic images of cultural decadence: "Like Ortega's romantic, the heart's desire of the alienated man is to see vines sprouting through the masonry."[42] Ortega suggests to Percy that the tendency to lament a lost past (the image of the viney masonry) often blends with the longing for an ideal future. This combination of nostalgia and idealism is symbolized for Ortega (as it is for Carlos Fuentes) by Don Quixote, who looks simultaneously back to the Golden Age and forward to utopia. Don Quixote always places "just beyond his reach the very thing he prizes."[43] The phrase is neither Don Quixote's nor Ortega's, but that of Percy's character Binx Bolling, and it epitomizes the Ortegan romantic dilemma of how to live an authentic existence in the present when both past and future are held up as being what the present can never be. Like the characters in *One Hundred Years of Solitude,* who are continually torn between future and past by presentiment and memory, Percy's main characters all suffer this temporal tearing of the self. The narrator of *The Second Coming* states what Will knows about himself: "Not once in this entire life had he allowed himself to come to rest in the quiet center of himself but had forever cast himself forward from some dark past he could not remember to a future which did not exist. Not once had he been present for his life" (123–4). It is the character Allie who acts to close the gap between identity and desire, she who dramatizes Will's need to regain the present in order to have any future at all.

Allie lives with childlike simplicity in the present. While she may be a little too childlike for some readers, and her idiosyncratic speech annoying rather than ingratiating, it is clear that, in the context of the temporal understanding Percy is evolving for Will, Allie is meant to serve as the locus of the present tense. She has herself just begun a new existence, and the newness of her language figures her utter receptivity to the richness and immediacy of experience. The ideal of a second chance inherent in the image of Christ's return is made specific in Will's revitalization by his love for Allie: The novel's title takes on sexual as well as eschatological implications in its final pages. Will correctly suspects that Allie herself is a sign of God's presence: "Is she a gift and therefore a sign of a giver?" (360). The answer is implied in Will's question. It is she who inspires Will's second coming, she who activates the various levels of meaning of that phrase.

The Greek word *parousia* is most often translated in English as "coming," but its etymological meaning (the root of the word is the present participle of the verb to be) is "presence" or "being present." From a Christian existential point of view, Christ's Second Coming is not to be construed as an event to be awaited in the future, but as the future coming into and constantly renewing the present. I have referred to Guardini, Voegelin, and Ortega primarily to define the temporal *maladies* of Percy's characters. To understand the *proper* relation of the future to the present – the existential integration of the future into the present suggested in the etymology of the word *parousia* – I will refer to one more philosophical basis of Percy's fiction. That is Martin Heidegger's *Being and Time*.

Everydayness, the term so often used by Percy to suggest his characters' essential temporality, is of course Heidegger's term, and the dramatized realization of Will's own particular potential at the end of the novel is also informed by Heidegger.[44] According to Heidegger, "the conceptions of 'future,' 'past' and 'Present' have first arisen [as an] inauthentic way of understanding time" (¶65, p. 374). Heidegger prefers the terms "no longer" and "not yet" for their inherent suggestion of the necessary relation of "before" and "after" to "now." Heidegger defines the future as a *"coming towards,"* a *"being towards"* one's ownmost, distinctive potentiality-for-Being. . . . By the term 'futural,' we do not here have in view a 'now' which has *not yet* become 'actual' and which sometime *will be* for the first time. We have in view the coming in which Dasein [the experiencing self], in its ownmost potentiality-for-Being, comes towards itself" (¶65, pp. 372–3, Heidegger's emphasis). The self must be aware of itself as an anticipating being, as looking forward to, as going toward, and for Heidegger, the most compelling form of this awareness is the comprehension that one is going to *"not-be,"* that one will die.

Heidegger's concern is what impending death can mean to an individual in the fullness of life. Authentic existence in the present depends upon grasping the fact of an end. So Heidegger explores *"Being-towards-death"*: "With death, Dasein stands before itself in its own most potentiality-for-Being" (¶50, p. 294). The individual's consciousness of death creates a comprehensive perspective on life and, hence, a potentially authentic *Being-a-whole;* for Heidegger, the existential meaning of the Christian eschaton resides precisely in such potentiality.[45] Death shifts questions about modes of existence to the essential question of what it means to be.

Percy dramatizes Heidegger's argument by placing his characters in situutations where they must confront the end of life as an existential issue. Sutter Vaught recognizes this in *The Last Gentleman* when he says, "The certain availability of death is the very condition of recovering oneself" (291); and Will, even before he decides to challenge death in *The Second Coming,* understands its importance in the unfolding life of the self: "Why is it that without death one misses his life?" (124). When he enters the cave, he does so to face the fact of his own death. The perspective Will acquires in the cave and in his subsequent love for Allie allows him to re-enter a temporal medium which integrates the "not yet" and the "no longer." He begins to understand that the present is not a diminishing of the aristocratic past, nor is it a straining forward toward some luminous and unattainable future. That Will explicitly connects his possession of both Allie and God ["Am I crazy to want both, her and him? No, not want, must have. And will have." (360)] confirms this understanding and confirms as well an existential definition of *parousia.* Christ's coming is not an event which *will* happen, but one which *is* happening: The eschatological event is to be experienced rather than awaited. So Will's attempt to transcend the world becomes the means of his reconciliation with the world. The immanent and transcendent are no longer contradictory but complementary.

In "Notes for a Novel about the End of the World," Percy writes, "A serious novel about the destruction of the United States and the end of the world should perform the function of prophecy in reverse. The novelist writes about the coming end in order to warn about present ills and so avert the end" (5). If science and secular humanism have ignored humanity's place in the world, then, for Percy, the novel is the vehicle which remains, and his own novels are offered as examples of his thesis. In the next chapter, we will see that this optimism about the regenerative function of fiction also inheres in the work of Carlos Fuentes, for whom literature is the only utopia possible in a world which exists in the present, not the future, tense.

7

BEYOND APOCALYPSE:
CARLOS FUENTES'S
TERRA NOSTRA

down the gullies of the era we may catch ourselves looking forward to what will in no
time be staring you larrikins on the postface in that multimirror megaron of return-
ingties, whirled without end to end.

Finnigans Wake, James Joyce

T HE WORK OF CARLOS FUENTES provides an appropri-
ately open-ended ending for this study of apocalyptic historicism.
Fuentes self-consciously and explicitly invokes the historical patterns of apocalypse, as well as particular apocalyptic thinkers, sects, and
works of art, then calls into question their future-oriented linearity, their
temporal and textual finality. He has often remarked that history must be
written by novelists, and his own literary production is profoundly rooted
in Mexican history, whether the political and social history of this century
in *The Death of Artemio Cruz* (1962), the historical layers of Tenochtitlán/
Mexico City in *Where the Air Is Clear* (1958) and *Burnt Water* (1981), or the
history of literary relations between the Old and New Worlds in *Distant
Relations* (1980). Like his fiction, his essays are unified by their consideration
of the nature of temporal movement, despite the diversity of their subject
matter: The title of an untranslated volume of essays, *Tiempo mexicano
(Mexican Time,* 1971), is emblematic of Fuentes's multifaceted exploration
of the nature of Mexican historical reality. Of the authors I discuss in this
study, Fuentes is perhaps the most self-conscious in his use of spatial metaphors and poetic images to describe the movement of history and the shape
of time itself.

In foregoing chapters, I have aimed to give an overview of the work of
the writers under consideration because I have argued that the historical and
narrative concerns which comprise an apocalyptic vision are basic and integral to their entire corpus. This is also true of Fuentes's literary production.
The deathbed narration of *The Death of Artemio Cruz* (1962), the decadent,
otherworldly setting of *Aura* (1962), the abstract, Borgesian meditation on
death and rebirth in *Birthday* (1969), the global stakes of the international

spy novel, *Hydra Head* (1978) – all would lend themselves to a discussion of apocalyptic issues such as I have been raising here. However, my discussion in this chapter will be limited to *Terra Nostra* (1975) because of the complexity and sheer magnitude of its historical and literary subject matter.

I have already mentioned Fuentes's sense of the affinity of Latin American and U.S. Southern literature, based on their common exclusion from the prevailing American ethic of success and progress. This view is clearly related to Fuentes's abiding conviction that the linear, progressive time of Europe has been indiscriminately imposed on Latin America, that the mythic, cyclical vision of Latin America's indigenous history has been suppressed by scientific positivism and its consequence, the doctrine of progress. He defines Mexican time by opposing it to the future-oriented time of the industrialized West: It is

> time which conceives itself in a perpetual present, one that is not alienated by the pursuit of the future, a future that we can never reach. . . . This bastardization of the philosophy of the Enlightenment is common to both the capitalist and the socialist bureaucratic systems – the promise of the future, of the paradise on earth. The mythical time, which as I say is a present, does not admit the past as such. It considers what we call the past – in the Western linear system – as a present which is accreting, which is constantly enriching the moment, the instant. The past is never condemned to the past in a mythical system.[1]

Fuentes's mythical time is synchronic rather than diachronic ("a time in spirals, in mandalas . . ."), a medium which allows the recuperation of epochs buried alive by successive cultural and political invasions, but which survive nonetheless beneath the surface of the present. The Spanish conquest denied the existence of the indigenous Mexican world, independence denied the colonial world, the revolution rejected nineteenth-century rationalism. Fuentes insists that although (and because) Mexico has attempted to cancel its history at every stage, each of these unfinished histories is latent in contemporary culture, coexisting and interpenetrating in "an irrationality which, near though invisible, accompanies . . . the visible factualness of our history."[2] Thus Mexican history, and Latin American history generally, is seen as series of ruptures, discontinuous fragments which can only be integrated by an inclusive mythic temporal vision and its consequent narrative modes. Latin America's future lies in responsible memories of its own past rather than in imported dreams of future progress.

In a 1981 *Paris Review* interview, Fuentes stated that *Terra Nostra* represents "a vain attempt to absorb and express a total history," a motivating impulse clearly related to that of traditional apocalyptic narration. But he also says that his novel deals with origins – the Mediterranean and Spanish sources of Spanish American culture.[3] This second statement would seem to remove it from the explicit apocalyptic concern of ends and endings, but Fuentes argues that origins and ends are never distinct or separate, that to return is to advance. In the circular myths of pre–Cortesian Mexico, the past is united to the future: "each stone, each temple, each sculpture of ancient Mexico is . . . a receptacle of desperate expectation: the return of [the Aztec god] Quetzalcoatl, a return to the origin without separation, identical to the meeting with a beneficent future."[4] This movement of mythic time has taken some ironic turns: Fuentes describes the moment when the linear time of European history collided with Mexican myth, when Hernán Cortés disembarked in Mexico at the time predicted by the Aztecs' omens for Quezalcoatl's coming, thus keeping the promise of the god's return and also breaking it forever. Since then, according to Fuentes, the history of Mexico has been a history of absence and waiting, a second search for identity. This sense of historical expectancy resembles apocalyptic eschatology and, indeed, Mircea Eliade has shown us that societies may displace the return to sacred origins into the future.[5] However, Fuentes rejects visionary histories which focus on a single promised end. Precisely because Mexico's history has been a series of "subverted Edens," of unfulfilled dreams of future perfection, the novelist must return to the past and incorporate it into his narrative structures, into the "eternal present" which Fuentes announces as his subject in the final pages of *Terra Nostra*.

The imposition of a European temporal mode on the mythic American realm began, Fuentes would have it, with the utopianism projected by the Old World upon the New World. America was immediately conceived by Europe as a utopia so that it could wash its sins there. This, Fuentes asserts, is the very meaning of the discovery of the New World. Catholic Europe no longer had to relegate paradise to an Edenic realm in the distant past or postpone the millennium into the distant future. Paradise could be realized immediately, it seemed, in America. Citing a phrase from Octavio Paz, Fuentes writes: "We are 'a chapter in the history of utopias'; that is, we are children of the word: we were imagined (desired) before we existed."[6] If Fuentes rejects this utopianism, it is not because he rejects the possibility of a better world. What he does reject is the idea that a better world can be achieved by discarding the past in the name of the future.[7]

Fuentes directly addresses this point in a recent essay on the fiction of the Czech writer, Milan Kundera.[8] He argues that utopianism and totalitarianism are two sides of a single coin because both are careless of the past. Totalitarianism exploits the archetypes of paradise, promising a perfect society in the future. It sells people a future in exchange for their past, which will be revised and rewritten to suit the vision of the future held by those in power. Such exploitation of utopian and apocalyptic idealism is illustrated aplenty in *Terra Nostra*, as it is in Kundera's fiction. Yet, despite Fuentes's suspicion of future-oriented historical visions, he also recognizes that constructive social change may be their product. If the ideal of social perfection has impelled some of this century's most horrible social and political abuses (the proposition at the heart of Percy's *Lancelot* and Cortázar's "We Love Glenda So Much"), it may also inspire us to our best selves. Fuentes allows that community interests and values may be placed above the interests of power in the "tradition of communal and revolutionary utopianism."[9] Just such a tradition – medieval millenarianism – is invoked in *Terra Nostra*.

In the preface to *Terra Nostra*, Fuentes cites Norman Cohn's study, *The Pursuit of the Millennium*, as an important basis of his novel. Cohn's work deals with the various millenarian movements in Western Europe between the eleventh and sixteenth centuries which pictured salvation as collective, terrestrial, imminent, total, and miraculous.[10] Fuentes introduces a number of such Edenic, utopian, and apocalyptic projections into his novel: Although they differ in important respects, they are similar in proposing idealized realms which will put a stop to time. In *Terra Nostra*, these idealized visions overlap and easily convert into one another; indeed, the unity of *Terra Nostra* stems not from plot structure or point of view but from this complex thematic treatment of the visionary future. Fuentes constantly juxtaposes dreams of paradise with real historical time in order to investigate the nature of both.

I.

Terra Nostra, a novel about the sixteenth-century Spanish Catholic origins of Mexico, is set in the future, between June and December, 1999, and ends on January 1, 2000. Hence, unlike most historical fiction, it is not designed to suggest that the text is contemporaneous with the historical period it depicts; instead, it is narrated from a perspective that is already the future of that history, and of the reader's history as well. Past and future are thus integrated into and mediated by the novel itself, which moves toward its apocalyptic ending not to portray the destruction of a fictional world, as in *One Hundred Years of Solitude*, but rather to evoke the mythic moment when history, the grounding fact of the narration, and the novel, its outcome, are one.

Fuentes's historically integrative narration is rooted in the work of the eighteenth-century historiographer, Giambattista Vico, whose theory of cyclically recurring stages of civilization provides a complementary structure to apocalyptic historicism. Vico's *New Science* (1744) suggests, in its own investigation and presentation of the "poetic" origins of human history, the philosophical framework and method for Fuentes's reconstruction of Mexico's political and literary origins. In Vico's vision of history as a spiral, Fuentes finds the historiographic mode by which to integrate the linear and circular times that meet in Mexico. When asked about the mixture of fact and fiction in *Terra Nostra,* its author commented, "After all, history is only what we remember of history. What is fact in history? The novel asks this question. We made history. But history doesn't exist if we don't remember it. That is, if we don't imagine it, finally."[11] Fuentes continues to say that he has long been impressed with the writings of Vico, because Vico is "probably the first philosopher who says we create history. Men and women, we create history, it is *our* creation, it is not the creation of God. But this throws a certain burden on us. Since we made history, we have to imagine history. We have to imagine the past . . ." (106). For Vico as for Fuentes, historical reality is indissoluably linked to human creation and recreation.[12] Vico's new science is a science of humanity. It constitutes a rejection of the scientific positivism of his own century and a rejection as well of the Cartesian concept that the intellect can apprehend first principles intuitively, without reference to concrete historical experience. In his effort to give substance to the otherwise banished beginnings of history, Vico maintains that the writer must recognize his or her obligation to practical reality *and* to the sympathetic imagination. The obligation to practical reality will remind one that there is no schematic method by which to understand the origins of history, and the obligation to the sympathetic imagination will allow one to intuit what cannot be known *except* by inventing it.

Vico's effort to recapture what he called the "poetic wisdom" of the ancients for his own postpoetic age is grounded in philological and literary reconstruction, and its greatest challenge for Vico lay in the separation of the modern mind from the *"universali fantastici"* – the "fantastic (or imaginative) universals" of poetic expression. The ancients spoke, and hence thought, metaphorically, hieroglyphically, whereas subsequent ages have modified the linguistic tropes, employing successively metonymic and descriptive modes. To accomplish his task of historical recuperation, Vico goes back to the Greek fables, and to Homer, to whom he devotes one entire section of the five of the *New Science.* Vico sees the fable and the Homeric epic as recapitulations by the Greeks themselves of their own history, as linguistic models of the age (¶ 679). They contain figurative language which is communal, autochthonous, set in a specific historical context, and yet is also generally suggestive of the movement of history through its stages. For Vico, the fables are original creations, yet do not have a particular author; they possess a specific narrative logic, yet suggest a more general historical context; they are products of the beginning of history, yet recapitulate it in a final sense. They are privileged historical documents, even if they are not historically true.

Like Vico, Fuentes constructs his history in *Terra Nostra* out of the *"universali fantastici"* which he finds at the beginning of his own cultural tradition, concurring in Vico's belief that the most imaginative texts are also the most real, and that history is to be heard in the voices of the poets. Fuentes uses characters and narrators from three of the most important literary texts of the Spanish Renaissance, *La Celestina* (1499), by Fernando de Rojas; *El burlador de Sevilla* (ca. 1620), Tirso de Molina's play about Don Juan; and, of course, *Don Quixote* (1605 and 1615), by Miguel de Cervantes; as well as a multitude of other cultural texts from the European Renaissance and the more recent past. The densely allusive fabric of *Terra Nostra* dramatizes the Vichian process of historical recuperation on the level of the literary text. It also dramatizes Fuentes's sense that it is the communal and historical nature of language and the literary tradition, rather than the individual author, which speaks in the work of literature.

Fuentes's Vichian aesthetic is presented in his extended theoretical essay, *Cervantes, or The Critique of Reading* (1976). Based on a series of lectures given the year after the publication of *Terra Nostra,* the essay is explicitly intended as a commentary on the novel.[13] The two complementary Vichian questions implicit throughout the essay are how to embody the past in the literary text, and how to recover the past from the literary texts that contain it. For Fuentes as for Vico, the language of the past provides a mythic infusion into contemporary forms: Fuentes writes that "every word of man, however banal, corrupt or insignificant it may seem, contains behind its exhausted appearance and within its slender syllables all the cements of renovation and also all the echoes of an ancestral, original, founding memory."[14] Literature can never be exhausted because of the intrinsic historicity of language, an idea which contradicts John Barth's sense of literary exhaustion and extends Jorge Luis Borges's conception of the literary tradition. Fuentes rejects the contemporary sense of the word "original" as meaning "without precursors" or "individual innovation," insisting instead on the restoration of the etymological link between "origin" and "original," that is, on the complex contemporaneity of past, present, and future, in literature and in life.

In *Cervantes, or The Critique of Reading,* Fuentes discusses the sixteenth-century setting of *Terra Nostra.* He uses the events of 1492, 1521, and 1598 to symbolize the unification, centralization, and homogenization which ended a 700-year alliance of three cultures in Spain – the Christian, Jewish, and Moorish. These dates epitomize the constrictive spirit of Spain under the Hapsburg monarchy, and especially under Felipe II, designated "El Señor" in *Terra Nostra,* who reigned from 1556 to 1598 and whose architectural monument and royal mausoleum, the Escorial, "the necropolis," becomes the emblematic locus of Fuentes's novel.

In 1492, the conquest of Granada unified for the first time the *civitas espanola;* in the same year, the edict of expulsion of the Jews deprived Spanish society of those members most able to move Spain into modernity; and Columbus landed on territory that he labeled Hispaniola. The first two events were part of the exclusionary politics begun by the Catholic Kings who preceded the Hapsburgs; the third might have counteracted those policies but for the events of 1521, which definitively sealed off the country for centuries to come.

In 1521, the first Hapsburg in Spain, Carlos V, defeated a communitarian rebellion in Villalar, Castille, an event which signals for Fuentes the defeat of nascent democratic tendencies in Spain and a victory for medievalism, that is, for the preservation of the ideal of a monolithic and centralized Holy Roman Empire. In the same year, Cortés conquered Tenochtitlán, the great capital of the Aztec empire in the New World. Fuentes links this conquest to the defeat of the *comuneros* at Villalar, saying that it assured in advance that Hispanic America would be overwhelmed by and incorporated into the totalitarian world of the Spanish Catholic monarchy.

Fuentes's third date is 1598, the death of Felipe II, who leaves behind him the mechanisms to maintain the political structure of medieval empire and to impose religious and intellectual blinders on Spain and Spanish America. The expulsion of the Moslems from Spain in 1609, the Counter-Reformation and Inquisition by which Spain established itself as *defensor fides* and the reactionary center of Europe, are Felipe's legacy. So, Fuentes observes, the culmination of Spain's power coincides with the onset of its decline; beginnings and ends are never separate.

That these crucial dates and the politics they represent have continued to cycle in Hispanic America is confirmed near the end of *Terra Nostra,* where Fuentes associates them with the linear chronology imposed by the Old World on the New. Referring to Spanish America, he writes, "history has had its second chance . . . everything has ended, it was all a lie, the same crimes were repeated, the same errors, the same madness, the same omissions as on any other of the true days of that linear, implacable, exhaustible chronology: 1492, 1521, 1598. . . ."[15] This chronology is mitigated, however, by Fuentes's Vichian belief that another, counterbalancing history is to be read in the literature of the period. If, as we will see, the novel ends with a tenuous vision of renewal, it is due in part to the inexhaustible nature of literature and language.

Fuentes notes the paradox of the incredible literary productivity during the period when Felipe's exclusionary policies were undoing a pluralistic culture and creating a monolithic Spain incapable of institutional self-criticism. This was the Golden Age of Spanish literature, which saw the masterpieces of Lope de Vega, Quevedo, Góngora, Calderón, as well as those by Rojas, Tirso, and Cervantes which figure so centrally in *Terra Nostra*. Extending the well-known observations of Spanish historian Américo Castro, Fuentes asserts that Spanish art has always responded to apocalyptic times, to times of turmoil and transition when old forms no longer suffice and new forms have not yet been established. He cites the work of the

Generations of 1898 and 1927 in Spanish literature as recent examples of art that has responded creatively to the exhaustion of social and political institutions, and he implicitly extends his argument to include contemporary Latin American literature as well. Literature would seem to exist in a dialectical relation to history, incorporating it, transforming it, renewing it.

In his discussion of *La Celestina, Don Juan,* and *Don Quixote* in *Cervantes, or The Critique of Reading,* Fuentes emphasizes their rejection of a singular linear chronology, their dual backward and forward temporal perspective, their fusion of myth and history. *La Celestina* was written by a Jewish convert after the expulsion of the Jews from Spain and during the period of persecution of Jews like Rojas, who had not left but had chosen to remain in Spain and convert to Catholicism. *La Celestina* is thus paradoxically the masterpiece of Jewish Spain, a cultural entity which had officially ceased to exist by the time the work was written. As such, it provides a final monument to the brilliant age of Jewish coexistence in Islamic and Christian Spain, a period surpassed in European Jewish history only by the cultural wealth of the century that ended at Auschwitz. Fuentes notes that *La Celestina* is a literary as well as a cultural turning point. It marks simultaneously the end of medieval Spanish literature and the beginning of Renaissance literature; it self-consciously and self-critically parodies medieval literary conventions even as it uses them; and in its self-reflexive consideration of the nature of writing per se, it anticipates Cervantes's major works by over 100 years. Celestina, who becomes Fuentes's protean female figure with the tattooed lips in *Terra Nostra,* is described as "the woman who goes between two worlds, one of the most punctual reality, the other of the most intangible magic," and "the image of origin, the mythic, founding vision, from the dawn of history" (51). This character (whose name has come to mean "go-between" in Spanish) looks backward to the dawn of history and also forward, to its end. In his essay, Fuentes adds to his list of Celestina's attributes her sacred function as "secret sibyl." In *Terra Nostra,* she is repeatedly associated with the oracles of the medieval sibyls, prophetesses whose apocalyptic utterances derived from Joachim of Fiore and the Book of Revelation and were among the heterodoxies which, like literature itself, eluded Felipe II's centralizing policies.[16]

The importance of Joachimite thought and its modern political implications were early impressed upon Fuentes, as they were on Walker Percy, by Eric Voegelin's study of the origins of twentieth-century totalitarianism, *The New Science of Politics.*[17] Fuentes makes fictional use of Joachimite apocalypticism throughout *Terra Nostra.* The Sibylline oracles with which Celestina is associated in the novel follow Joachim in foreseeing the coming of a third age when an earthly ruler, whether an angelic pope or a last emperor, will unite the world, politically and spiritually; the Antichrist will be overcome; and the Kingdom of God will be initiated on earth. This vision of the future is explicitly invoked in two chapters of *Terra Nostra*, "The Palace of Diocletian" and "The Prophecy of the Third Age," only to be discredited, along with nostalgia for a perfect past, by a "magus" who may represent Joachim himself. He says to Celestina, "we shall not return to the original age of gold, nor shall we find it at the end of history, the age of gold is within history, it is called the future, but the future is today, not tomorrow, the future is present, the future is immediate, or it is nothing; the future is here, or there is no such time . . ." (550). The Joachimite apocalyptic vision is thus enlarged by its association with the literary go-between, Celestina. It is no longer primarily a vision of a unique culminating event of history, but rather a vision of the necessary condition of historical change in a present which stretches eternally between past and future.

Don Juan, Tirso's character in *El burlador de Sevilla*, also goes between this world and the underworld, between life and death, a voice from the past who generates a future in the many Don Juans who will follow his lead. But it is *Don Quixote* which serves as the principal literary landmark in *Terra Nostra*. As Cervantes's novel reaches back ironically to the chivalric dreams of a medieval world, it both criticizes and integrates the modes and values of that past world into its own historical and literary present. It is just such integration that Vico finds in Homer and the Greek fables, and that Rojas and Tirso also achieve, according to Fuentes. When, at the end of *Terra Nostra*, the character Ludovico tells the dying despot, El Señor, that he has opened his eyes to read the only thing that will be saved from "our terrible time," Felipe thinks that he means the millennium. Ludovico responds, "I was more modest, my friend. I opened them to read three books: that of the Convent Trotter, that of the Knight of the Sorrowful Countenance, and that of the deceiver Don Juan. Believe me, Felipe: only there in those three books did I truly find the destiny of our history" (741). It is for this visionary fusion of history and destiny, past and future, that Fuentes also aims in *Terra Nostra*.

That the process of literary remembering and recuperating is endless and communal is made explicit by a character in *Terra Nostra* who tells Felipe that the story of the mad knight of La Mancha will never be completed, that it belongs to everyone. The adventures of Don Quixote are multiplied by the number of readers they will have, a number that will proliferate beyond measure thanks to printing (an intolerable invention to the monarch for this reason.) Because Felipe abuses language politically, to impose his own individual will, and ethically, to limit the world within its medieval Catholic boundaries and hence circumscribe its dynamic historical character, he rejects the poetic universality of Don Quixote, arguing instead that "The only legitimacy is the reflection of one's possession of the unique text" (605). It is, of course, precisely this "uniqueness" (based on the misconception of

"originality") which Fuentes opposes in his multivocal and historically integrative novel.

This symbolic counterbalancing of Felipe II and Don Quixote in *Terra
Nostra* is on one level ironic, for Don Quixote is not only Felipe's opposite
but also his reflection. Like Don Quixote, Fuentes's monarch lives in a
dream whose illusory fabric keeps tearing. He burns heretics, but it is often
as problematic to tell a heretic from a saint as to tell a windmill from a giant,
or a sheep from a Moor. Both Felipe and Don Quixote are made to assume
the anxieties of the age, when for the first time identity and truth and
history became matters of opinion and narrative invention. If, however,
these characters confuse reality and fiction, their creators certainly do not:
Both *Don Quixote* and *Terra Nostra* are extended considerations of the
nature of the two. Commenting on Cervantes's distinction between literary
narration and historical reality, Fuentes writes in *Cervantes, or The Critique
of Reading* that "literature creates reality, adds to reality, is not merely a
verbal correspondence to immutable or anterior truths. A new reality in
paper, literature tells of the things of the world, but is *itself a new thing* in the
world" (93, Fuentes's emphasis). The Knight's existence, Fuentes insists,
will not be found in the single reading of his life, but in the manifold
readings granted him in literature (81).

Fuentes's Borgesian sense of the endlessness of the literary present tense,
as opposed to the limited span – and the inevitable eventual past tense – of a
single life, coincides with Cervantes's point at the end of *Don Quixote*. On
his deathbed, Cervantes's character (Don Quixote no more) wishes to forestall his own end in order to read more books which might yet instruct him
about the life he is soon to depart: "My judgment is now clear and free from
the misty shadows of ignorance with which my ill-starred and continuous
reading of those detestable books of chivalry had obscured it. Now I know
their absurdities and their deceits, and the only thing that grieves me is that
this discovery has come too late, and leaves me no time to make amends by
reading other books, which might enlighten my soul."[18] The old man's
death provides the narrative closure necessary to complete the series of
adventures which we have read, but leaves the structure of meaning emphatically open to other texts, other truths. In this subversion of a definitive
reading of the literary text, Fuentes links Cervantes to Joyce. Referring to
Joyce's characters, Fuentes writes that they "speak and their words, by
means of poetic association, open up to meaning in many directions, unfolding in vast spirals, in the *corsi e ricorsi* of Vico, translated into the history
of language which is the language of history" (106). Adding a temporal
image from Revelation to the one taken from Vico, Fuentes states that
though the words of Joyce and Cervantes are separated by three centuries,
they "are the initial words of the novel, alpha/omega and omega/alpha.

. . . in their work, the destiny of words is their origin and the origin of their words is their destiny" (97). Joyce's "wake," Fuentes reminds us, is a funeral and a resurrection in a single word.

II.

Terra Nostra also inters and announces, oscillating as it does between the Old World and the New, between medievalism and modernity. The novel begins on July 14, 1999, in Paris. July 14 is Bastille Day, a date which commemorates the beginning of revolutionary destruction and creation, and represents as clearly as any date in European history an end that was simultaneously a beginning. The novel concludes on similarly Janusian dates, the eve of December 31, 1999, and the morning of January 1, 2000. An explicitly apocalyptic ambience pervades both the opening and closing scenes of the novel. The initial scene, on the Quai Voltaire along the Seine in Paris, is filled with "signs of catastrophe" (26). The city is enveloped in smoke, which Pollo Phoibe, the central intelligence of the novel, relates repeatedly to the fog in *Nuit et brouillard,* Alain Renais's powerful film about the Nazis's "final solution." A group of naked flagellants, in the style of the Brethren of the Free Spirit, a medieval heretical group which becomes a crucial symbol in Fuentes's novel, announces the coming of a new kingdom and a new concept of history:

> They are awaiting the millennium that will begin this winter, not as a date, but as an opportunity to remake the world. They quote one of the eremite poets and sing with him that a people without a history is not redeemed from time, for history is a pattern of timeless moments. . . . true history will be to live and to glorify those temporal instants, and not, as until now, to sacrifice them to an illusory, unattainable, and devouring future, for every time the future becomes the present instant we repudiate it in the name of a future we desire but will never have (28).

As the opening scene concludes, Pollo falls into the Seine and, it seems, into the novel's account of the history of Spain and Spanish America. Like the "true history" of the apocalyptic group described above, the novel's history is embodied as a "pattern of timeless moments," a quantity of brief chapters or narrative instants largely unconnected by temporal or causal sequence. The final lines of the first chapter are a palindrome: "This is my story. I want you to hear my story. Listen. Listen. Netsil. Netsil. Yrots ym raeh ot uoy tnaw I. Yrots ym si siht" (31). So the novel immediately proposes a series of emblematic recognitions that retrogression and progression, memory and anticipation are functions of the ongoing present, whether on the level of culture or that of the single text.[19]

Pollo has only one arm, a symbol of his literary relation to Cervantes, who lost an arm in the Battle of Lepanto in 1571, and of his relation to the Spanish literary tradition Fuentes discusses in *Cervantes, or The Critique of Reading*. But it is not only the Spanish tradition to which he is heir: Though set in a specific cultural and historical milieu, *Terra Nostra* transcends the topical even as it embodies it. Pollo is also the literary offspring of Ezra Pound. The character's eponymous literary forebear, Pollo Phoibee, appears in Pound's early poem, "Cino," where he is described as a quester, "Seeking e'er the new-laid rasty-way/To the gardens of the sun. . . ."[20] Celestina, with her gray eyes, is also imaginatively associated with lines from the same poem: "I have sung women in three cities./But it is one./I will sing of the sun." Indeed, Pound himself is integrated into the opening chapter of *Terra Nostra* in the historiographic terms we come to expect in this novel. He is embodied as a "mad old man" who "would not accept a past that had not been nourished in the present or a present that did not comprehend the past . . ."; he also, we are told, "had never learned to distinguish between political treachery and raving humor . . . who confused all symptoms with all causes . . ." (23). Fuentes's fictional use of Pound suggests both utopian optimism – "the gardens of the sun" – and political movements that abuse such optimism; he reminds us not only of Pound's profound uses of past literary texts and traditions, but also of the authoritarian solutions which may be imposed within a utopian philosophical framework.

The title of the final chapter of *Terra Nostra* is "The Last City," and the scene is once again Paris. Although the narrative as a whole has ranged back over two millennia, we find that only six months have elapsed since the opening scene of the novel. Again Pound's poem is invoked, but more important is the invocation of Pound's most influential precursor, Dante. A line from Canto 28 of the *Inferno* is used to describe the climactic androgynous union of Pollo and Celestina: "*ed eran due in uno, ed uno in due*" (777).[21] If until this point in the novel visions of future perfection have been surrounded by disunity and chaos, here for the first time the novel would seem to propose some tenous balance between real history and its idealized projections. The novel ends at a privileged instant between the second and third millennia which is *both* end *and* beginning: "Twelve o'clock did not toll in the church towers of Paris; but the snow ceased and the following day a cold sun shone" (778).

The final androgynous union of Celestina and Pollo has been described by one critic as a "hierogamy – wedding of sky father and earth mother – that reverses time, for its single self-fertilizing being resembles the figure of Uroboros, the undifferentiated wholeness imagined in many ancient mythologies to precede mankind's division into individual creatures of different sexes."[22] Although I would argue that the union does not reverse time but rather advances it to the point where origins are reiterated – or reinstituted – by ends, it is to this basic myth of the medieval hermetic tradition that Fuentes alludes. In this myth, the primordial human being is conceived as a cosmic androgyne who had disintegrated into the material and bisexual world of alien and conflicting parts, yet has retained the capacity for recovering his–her lost integrity. This myth has its most highly developed exposition in the latter thirteenth-century documents collected as *Sefer Ha-Zohar*, "The Book of Splendor," a text explicitly embodied in *Terra Nostra* in the chapter, "The *Zohar*." Meyer H. Abrams discusses the *Zohar* in his study of the philosophical antecedents of the English Romantic poets: "in the *Zohar* sexuality enters into the very nature of God, and the sacred union becomes a central and pervasive symbol which accounts for the origin and sustainment of all life, while the vicissitudes of this union are used to explain the course of history, from the literal genesis through multiform and continued division and dispersion, to the enduring reunion of all things that will occur at the end of time."[23] Abrams relates this tradition to William Blake's central myth of the fall as a splintering of the primordial self; and to the millennial state Blake envisions, where body and spirit, male and female will be reunited. For Blake, and, it would seem, for Fuentes, that androgynous form will exist at the end of time as it did at the beginning.

In Revelation, the final image of unity is Christ's own person: "I am alpha and omega, the first and the last." The striking contrast between the literary metaphor of Revelation and the sexual metaphor of the *Zohar* is placed in its cultural context by Herbert Schneidau, in *Sacred Discontent: The Bible and Western Tradition*. Schneidau contrasts the patriarchal and nomadic world of the ancient Hebrews to the matriarchal and autochthonous world of myth cultures; he observes the Hebrews' insistence that their God had no consort, and their emphasis on fathers and sons rather than on goddesses and what they represent. The final image of the apocalyptic marriage in Revelation is austere and abstractly asexual by comparison to the cultic images of hierogamy, with their associated fertility rites.[24] Although the Bible also uses the imagery of sexual union, as Fuentes well knows, here he wishes to emphasize the patriarchal aspect of Spanish Catholicism which, underlined by the asceticism of Pauline theology, produces the repressive atmosphere dramatized in the sixteenth-century Spain of the novel. It is this repressive atmosphere against which the sexual energy – also abundantly portrayed in the novel – must define itself. In a list of paired opposites in the chapter entitled, "The Thirty-three Steps," Fuentes makes explicit the contrast between the religious cultures and traditions which Schneidau describes. By means of this list, by his choice of a concluding image of androgynous union, and, as we will see, by his use of a heretical sect based on an ethic of sexual egalitarianism, Fuentes comments not only on the historicism of Felipe's Spain, but also on its cultural legacy of the depreciation of women. As he has in many of his novels, Fuentes here asserts the essential procreative and regenerative role of woman.[25] To the extent that *Terra Nostra* can be read as prescriptive, it proposes the radical integration of women into the cultural and political institutions of Spanish America, institutions which have traditionally been monolithically male.

The androgynous union of Pollo and Celestina, with its resonances of mythic finality, would seem to link *Terra Nostra* to the timeless paradisal visions Fuentes criticizes, and to create a closed narrative structure rather than a recuperative Vichian literary structure such as those that he so purposefully integrates into his novel. However, this final *fusion* must be understood in terms of *diffusion,* which is alternately (or simultaneously) transsexual, transnational, transhistoric.[26] If two characters become one at the end of the novel, during the course of the novel the process more often works in the other way. Fuentes has commented that a theme of *Terra Nostra* is the impossibility of encompassing the historical complexity of a single life span, and Celestina tells Ludovico that "several lifetimes are needed to integrate a personality and fulfill a destiny . . ." (774).[27] Furthermore, in the final pages of the novel, set in the Parc Monceau in Paris, Pollo says to Ludovico that everyone dreams of the opportunity to re-live life, "a second opportunity, to choose again, to avoid the mistakes, to repair the omissions, to offer the hand we did not extend the first time . . ." (774). This final phrase performs structurally the function which it describes, extending *Terra Nostra* beyond its own end to Fuentes's subsequent novel, *Distant Relations,* where the extended hand becomes almost a leitmotiv. Thus, the conclusion of *Terra Nostra* calls into question the ultimate cosmic unity which it images, but it does not subvert it. Fuentes balances the image of mythic finality against the empty landscape of the future, waiting to be peopled, much as the new heaven and new earth of Revelation – mythic symbols of historical expectancy – wait silent and empty at the end of the biblical text. The ultimate integration of personality proposed in the androgynous image at the end of *Terra Nostra* coexists with and is counterbalanced by the proliferation of personality which precedes it and which, it seems, will follow it in history. Evidence of closure, in the structure and meaning of the novel, is self-consciously modified by counterevidence of continual historical development and difference.

That the capacity for transformation becomes the dominant value of the historical vision and narrative structure of *Terra Nostra* is epitomized in the lines from W. B. Yeats's poem, "Easter, 1916," which appear at both the beginning and the ending of the novel: "Transformed utterly:/A terrible beauty is born. . . ." This fragment serves as epigraph to *Terra Nostra* and is repeated just before the final union of Pollo and Celestina. Apocalyptic transformation is luminously envisioned in many of Yeats's very best poems, and Fuentes's selection of this particular poem seems calculated to emphasize the political nature of the process. The allusions to Yeats's poem focus and condense what we will see in a more extended way in Fuentes's use of medieval millenarian sects, that is, the thematic insistence upon the relation between revolutionary politics and the ongoing process of historical and literary recuperation.

III.

It is clear by now that the aspect of Fuentes's art which I have been discussing here – the integration of the historical and literary past into the narrative present – implies the rejection of linear, sequential history in favor of a cyclical and synchronic vision of time. It is not, however, simply a pattern of endless repetition which Fuentes envisions. Vico's theory of *corsi e ricorsi* is consonant with Fuentes's historical vision precisely because it combines progression and retrogression in its spiraling form. The image of historical movement presented in Vico's *New Science* is in fact a spiral (despite the frequent misunderstanding of his concept of *ricorsi* as a mere recurrence or repetition of the three stages of culture which he posits). The process of *ricorsi*, the discussion of which occupies the final section of the *New Science*, implies the constant recovery and rendering of the past as present and available in the structure of current and more complex forms. *Ricorsi* is an advance which is made by virtue of a return, the cycle of history widening into a spiral as the historical consciousness looks back upon its finite history and in so doing is simultaneously directed to its ideal term. Hence, there *is* a progressive movement inherent in Vico's spiraling history, but that progress does not imply a depreciation of the present or a dismissal of the past for the sake of a desired future. On the contrary, Vico defines the movement of history as at once actual *and* ideal, and time as the tension between the finite *and* the infinite – that is, between the retrogressive movement of the finite back upon itself and the rectifying force by which the movement is converted in an ideal direction.[28] It is this insistence that history is both finite and infinite, actual and ideal, which provides the philosophic basis for Fuentes's treatment of visionary history in *Terra Nostra*.

A great variety of otherworldly visions are depicted in *Terra Nostra*, the title of which – our earth – suggests Fuentes's skepticism about such visions. Some of these alternative futures do have as their goal *earthly* transformations, and propose precisely the engagement with history that *Terra Nostra* confirms. But to the extent that any of these projections – whether secular or sacred – abuses or displaces the present with visions of an ideal future, to the extent that it separates the actual from the ideal, it is depicted as misguided and potentially dangerous. Indeed, there is throughout *Terra*

Nostra a palpable tension between the linear thrust of future-oriented apocalyptic and utopian temporality on the one hand, and the spiraling temporal
movement of Vico's vision on the other. This tension is also found in the
New Science. Vico, a devout Catholic, excluded the Hebrews from the
historical movement of *recorsi*, drawing a clear distinction between the
Hebrew–Christian people, whose history had been revealed by God, and
the "gentile nations," whose history had been made by humans. Vico's
cyclical theory excluded the Christian teleological view of the Second Coming, which he regarded as the singular culmination of history and the event
toward which all of creation moved. It is of course precisely such a divinely
revealed and teleological conception of history – that of sixteenth-century
Spain – which Fuentes submits to his own historiographic and literary
scrutiny. So we see that Fuentes's Vichian esthetic impels him to return to
and integrate into the "eternal present" of his novel a number of linear
visions which would themselves deny the possibility of such a return, such
an integration.

El Señor is the novel's central example of desperate apocalypticism. His
historical emphasis on the future at the expense of the present is epitomized
in the phrase, *nondum*, "not yet." This is his motto, and it suggests his
otherworldly Catholicism and the wrong-headed utopianism imposed by
Hapsburg Spain on the New World; the chapter of *Terra Nostra* entitled
"Brief Life, Eternal Glory, Unchanging World" dramatizes El Señor's mistaken substitution of the next world for this. He is obsessed by his desire to
arrest time during his life, to create a realm as changeless as that promised
by his medieval Catholic vision of eternity. Like the papal church, which
rested on the Augustinian divorce between *civitas Dei* and *saeculum*, El Señor
denies the significance of secular history, to which he opposes sacred eschatology. This denial of our earth – *terra nostra* – is symbolized in Fuentes's
novel by the Escorial, the royal mausoleum which El Señor builds as a
fortress against time and change, and which he fills with paintings of the
apocalypse. It is in this "necropolis" that he immures himself during his
lifetime and in which he dies his grotesque death, but not before requesting
of the attending priest that the Book of Revelation be read along with the
Requiem Mass and his own will and testament.

Fuentes places El Señor's *nondum* in opposition to the *hic et nunc*, the "here
and now" of the heretical millenarian sects of the time, whose desire for
change on earth underlies their millennial visions and who were doggedly
pursued by Felipe's Inquisition, in part for that reason. Ironically, these
sects are, like Felipe II, impelled by visions of apocalypse, but their vision of
a better realm is focused not on the next world but on this one, and the
means to their end is not divine intervention or death, but social revolution.
Fuentes is interested in the manifestations of the medieval apocalyptic tradition which opposed the institutions of medieval Christianity; that is, the

popular revolutionary movements which were often judged heretical and thus were necessarily subterranean. Norman Cohn terms these movements *millenarian,* a word that suggests a desire for immediate social change, as the word *millennialist* does not.[29] These movements have also been described as *political apocalyptic* in order to emphasize their opposition to the monolithic medieval church. J. G. A. Pocock writes that medieval heretical movements almost invariably had recourse to apocalypticism in order to assert that redemption might be attained through social and historical processes, and not only in the institutional operations of the timelessly based church. Apocalypticism became a powerful instrument of secularization for that reason, undermining the Augustinian dualism of sacred and secular history by depicting redemption as potentially the extension of existing secular processes.[30]

Pocock summarizes the two main streams of political apocalypticism which run through the later Middle Ages and which Fuentes integrates imaginatively in *Terra Nostra:* "the millenarian tradition which relied on the Book of Revelation to expect an overturning of all forms of worldly rule and a reign upon earth of Christ and his saints, located within the end of historic time; and the tradition handed down from Joachim of Fiore through the Spiritual Franciscans, which declared that after an Age of the Father in which God had ruled through the covenant with Israel, and an Age of the Son in which Christ ruled through his mystical body the church, there would come an Age of the Spirit in which God would be manifest in all men so chosen, as now he was incarnate in Christ alone."[31] The revolutionary (and heretical) potential of both of these apocalyptic attitudes is obvious. The word heresy is based on the Greek verb *haireîn,* to choose: These apocalyptic groups are used by Fuentes in *Terra Nostra* to signal the irruption of the modern, multivalent world of relative values and institutions into Felipe's Spain, with its single reigning option of church and crown. For these groups, revelation and revolution were interdependent and, in the most extreme cases, indistinguishable.

The role of "spiritual men" who were to lead the world during Joachim's third age was imputed above all to the Spiritual Franciscans, but it is another self-proclaimed group of spiritual leaders in the Joachimite tradition upon whom Fuentes focuses. That group is the Brethren of the Free Spirit, whose adherents held as their principal tenet the conviction that humanity could regain its original, divine, Adamic state. The Free Spirit, or as they are also called, the Adamites, are identified by Norman Cohn as the most radical of the millenarian groups of the time. Their creed of total emancipation, based on the intrinsic divinity of humanity, represents the most thoroughly revolutionary social doctrine in the late Middle Ages; and from it, according to Cohn, emerges the inspiration for the most ambitious attempt at "total social revolution which medieval Europe was ever to witness."[32] Furthermore, in their unique understanding of human perfection resides a paradigm for the simultaneity of beginnings and ends, of backward and forward historical movement inherent in Fuentes's Vichian vision. The adepts of the Free Spirit aimed to recover the egalitarian state of nature from the past and project it into the future. They insisted that they had found the way back to the purity of Adam before the Fall, and also that they were living in the Last Days, when this world would be replaced by a new order (a vision which Fuentes explicitly invokes in his chapter, "The Free Spirit"). Cohn observes that this mixture of millennialism and primitivism is familiar in modern times in certain strains of romanticism, an observation which recalls my reference to the resemblance between Fuentes's complex historiography and the visionary mythos of William Blake.[33]

For the purpose of achieving Adamic perfection on earth, the Brethren of the Free Spirit included nakedness and sexual freedom as symbolic elements in their ritual practices. Lurid accounts of those practices exist in Inquisition records, though the extent to which they are exaggerated in order to confirm the guilt of their practitioners makes their accuracy questionable. Given their ethic of sexual liberty, it is not surprising that women played a more important role in this group than in other medieval apocalyptic groups. Among the few remaining documents of the Free Spirit (the doctrinal literature that surfaced was for the most part destroyed by the Inquisition) is the German text *Schwester Katrei*. In this text, "Sister Catherine" describes her ecstatic sexual union with God, a description upon which Fuentes bases his chapter of the same name in *Terra Nostra* and from which he takes the exclamation of his character, "Rejoice with me, for I have become God" (572). The mystical union expressed here differs from Catholic mysticism (and foreshadows the final union of Pollo and Celestina) in its insistence on essential transformation: Schwester Katrei is not just momentarily one with God but has become identical to God, and is thus no longer in need of God. In the heresy of the Free Spirit, with its deification of human beings, Fuentes locates a radical intersection of humanistic politics and erotic idealism such as that which characterizes *Terra Nostra* itself.

The chapter entitled "The Rebellion" links the revolutionary attitudes of a number of related millenarian groups – the Free Spirit, the Adamites, the Waldensians, the Cathars, the Beghards and Beguines – to the liberal political factions responsible for the *comunero* uprising at Villalar in 1521. Together these secular and demotic forces oppose Guzmán, Felipe's henchman, to propose "the millennium, the triumph of human grace, God's death, the millennium of man" (636). Spanish novelist Juan Goytisolo singles out this chapter, which contains no paragraph breaks and is twenty-three pages long, as the most successful in Fuentes's "pluridimensional narrative."[34] Clearly this chorus of apocalyptic visionaries represents a culminating point in the novel. Among the seditious voices is that of Celestina, who tells Ludovico to meet her in Paris on July 14, 1999, there to await the millennium. This reference of Celestina's to the opening scene of *Terra Nostra* implies that the novel itself must be included among the visions of apocalypse accumulated here. This self-referential comment is amplified by Fuentes, as we will see, to suggest that it is in art, rather than in utopian ideologies, that the eternal present will be fully realized.

Felipe II and his father before him brought numerous art works from the Netherlands and from southern Italy (both areas part of their empire), and Felipe imported Italian painters who carried out the decoration of the Escorial and left behind enough pupils to lay the foundations for the subsequent flowering of Spanish painting. Fuentes uses one of these imported art works in *Terra Nostra* to represent the opposing historical visions of the Spanish monarchy and the millenarian groups I have been discussing. Felipe's *nondum* and the millenarianists' *hic et nunc* meet on the altar of the Escorial, where sits Hieronymous Bosch's triptych, the work we now know as "The Garden of Earthly Delights" but which Bosch originally titled "The Millennium." In his study of this painting, Wilhelm Franger has argued convincingly that Bosch was a member of the Brethren of the Free Spirit and that his triptych was intended to depict the millennial vision of that group but was immediately misinterpreted by its orthodox Catholic audience.[35] Where Bosch wished to project the earthly paradise of natural humanity in the middle panel of the triptych, contemporary Catholics saw the playful postures of the nude figures as representing human depravity, not innocence. That the middle pannel is misread by Felipe as a scene of earthly debauchery rather than earthly beatitude, and that it confirms for him the fallen nature of humanity rather than – as Bosch intended – the Adamic nature of humanity, is a recurring source of irony in the novel. The centrality of Bosch's triptych in *Terra Nostra* is instructive, for in Bosch's fantastical representation of history, in his simultaneous presentation of past, present, and future, and in his visionary focus on our earth, we see the motivating conceptions of Fuentes's novel – which is, of course, also a highly self-conscious triptych.[36]

Fuentes dramatizes the opposition between the apocalyptic attitudes of Felipe II and Bosch in a number of scenes. In the chapter entitled, "The Seventh Day," Felipe, "petrified before his altar," interrogates the severed head of the artist of the triptych, who explains the painting in terms of the philosophy of the Free Spirit. The left panel, says the head, shows the original paradise, where man and woman, who had previously been united in the image of an androgynous divinity, were separated. Wilhelm Franger notes that the principal motif of Bosch's picture of the Creation, and the basic formula of the entire altarpiece, is the verse from Genesis 2:24: "*Et erunt duo in carne una* – and they shall be one flesh." For the Brethren of the Free Spirit, and presumably for Bosch, this verse was interpreted "not only as the divine command that the human race shall procreate, but also in the sense of a mystic *religio,* a striving to reunite in their original wholeness beings that have become separate in temporal existence."[37] The central panel of Bosch's triptych, the head tells Felipe, depicts paradise restored by the free spirit of humanity, where all flesh is innocent. And the right panel shows the hell which, says the head, Felipe has created. In a grotesque catalogue of images taken from previous scenes in the novel, Fuentes describes the hell which Felipe supposedly sees on Bosch's canvas, thus super-imposing his own apocalyptic narrative art on Bosch's painting. The monarch cannot tolerate so much reality: He hurls the head at the triptych, where a line of blood forms the name of the artist, Bosch, printed in large gothic letters in the novel's text. So blood and paint mix in the letters on the printed page, as if to suggest the complex combination of life and art which *Terra Nostra* proposes.

The scene of Felipe's death, to which I have already referred, concludes by contrasting Bosch's painting – "impenetrable Flemish triptych on the altar, the garden of delights, the millenary kingdom" – to the Escorial – "a harmony of austere lines, mortified simplicity, rejection of all sensual, infidel, and pagan ornament, a convergence of the tumult of the universe into a single center dedicated to the glory of God and the honor of Power" (749). Even after his death, Felipe is made to stare at the triptych and wonder to what age it belongs: "He was unable to place it either in the past or in the future. Perhaps it belonged to an eternal present" (754). Like García Márquez's dictator, who also tries to stop time in *The Autumn of the Patriarch,* Felipe is left "never knowing forever."

It is tempting to argue here that Bosch's triptych is an emblem for Fuentes's three-part novel.[38] However, to insist that a single artwork or esthetic model is the mirror of the novel held up within the novel is to minimize the allusive (hence recapitulative, Vichian) complexity of *Terra Nostra.* In fact, another set of paintings reflecting Fuentes's apocalyptic concerns is also embedded in the novel. These are Luca Signorelli's four monumental frescoes of the end of the world, painted on the walls of the St. Brizio Chapel in the Cathedral of Orvieto, in Italy. Fuentes moves these frescoes imaginatively to the Escorial, where they, like Bosch's work, contrast – no, collide – with the values embodied by Felipe. In the chapter entitled, "All My Sins," paragraphs labeled "The painting" and "The palace" alternate: Thus, our attention oscillates between the expansive vision of the frescoes and the suffocating "Fortress of the Most Holy Sacrament of the Eucharist and the Necropolis of Princes" (93). Later in the novel, in the chapter called "The Restoration," one of the frescoes reappears as a painting, where it is described as moldering behind the altar of a church in Mexico, in the Sierra del Nayar. Fuentes describes a rent in the canvas which, like Bosch's triptych, seems to have bled from its wound; so he superimposes upon Signorelli's art in its fictional Mexican setting his fictional account of the tearing of Bosch's triptych by Felipe. I have said that Fuentes adds his narrative version of hell to Bosch's visual depiction of it; here, too, he adds his own layer of apocalyptic imagery to Signorelli's artistic vision of the end, reinforcing the relation of *Terra Nostra* to previous apocalyptic visions and visionaries.[39]

In Vichian fashion, Fuentes ultimately circles back to the time of Christ and the historical roots of the sixteenth-century apocalyptic movements which his novel dramatizes. In the seven-part chapter entitled, "Manuscript of a Stoic," we are placed in the Roman Empire of the first century, where we see repeated much the same situation as Felipe's sixteenth-century Spain – a tyrannical Caesar, Tiberius, who is desperate to extirpate heresy from his empire. Tiberius's heretics are the Hebrews, who, like Felipe's heretics, urgently expect apocalypse. The Stoic Theodorus, writer of the manuscript, tells Tiberius that he has been to Judea, where peace is threatened by Hebraic messianism, and he refers to the report of the crucification of a self-proclaimed messiah five years earlier. Ironically, Theodorus attempts to reassure Tiberius by minimizing the importance of these seditious elements: "There is a surplus of redeemers, or messiahs, in Judea, Sire; shake any palm tree in the desert, and from it will fall twenty date clusters and ten redeemers" (691). Fuentes designates Theodorus as the source of the three manuscripts in the bottles which are found by the three youths (and as the source of their identifying marks, the crosses on their backs), thus suggesting that the origins of the novel are to be located in the Hebraic apocalypticism described in the Stoic's manuscript, and in the parallel secular utopianism of Greek Stoicism itself.[40]

IV.

When Fuentes labels the history of Spain and Spanish America "the least realized, the most abortive, the most latent and desiring of all histories" (771), he is referring not only to the heretical apocalyptic movements in Spain which I have been discussing, but also to the apocalyptic expectations imposed by Spain upon the New World. In *Terra Nostra,* as in sixteenth-century Spain, the objects of historial longing take various shapes, whether bucolic, as in the terrestrial paradise, or urban, as in the New Jerusalem or El Dorado, the City of the Sun described by Tommaso de Campanella in 1602.[41] It is safe to say that in Spain's imaginative projections of America, all of these idealized loci were contained.

Terra Nostra is separated into three sections, "The Old World," "The New World," and "The Next World," a narrative organization which reiterates structurally Spain's sense of its apocalyptic historical mission, and also the central place of the American territory and inhabitants in fulfilling that mission. In his study, *The Millennial Kingdom of the Franciscans in the New World,* John Leddy Phelan writes that no colonial empire in modern times was built upon so extensive a philosophical and theological foundation as the empire which the Spaniards created in the New World.[42] Phelan says that the Spanish interpreted the conquest as the necessary prerequisite for God's apocalyptic plan. In the virgin territory of America, Spain saw the possibility of the terrestrial paradise promised in the future, and in the American Indians, the lost tribes of Israel who must be converted before the world could end. The urgent policy of the conversion of the Indians was thus conceived and justified by the Spanish clergy not only in terms of the Indians' salvation, but also their own: Conversion was essential to the initiation of God's kingdom on earth. This policy is dramatized in *Terra Nostra,* as are its manifold abuses.

As I have shown in my discussion of the revolutionary millenarian groups in *Terra Nostra,* Fuentes is concerned to portray the historical moment when people were ceasing to think of paradise solely as a divine enterprise, and were beginning to think of it as a political and social one, realizable on this earth by human effort as well as God's will. The author embodies this transition in the Spanish New World in the novel's references to Vasco de Quiroga, a Dominican lawyer who arrived in Mexico less than ten years after the conquest to serve as a member of the second *Audiencia,* the court and executive body established by the Council of the Indies, the Spanish governing body of the Indies.[43] Quiroga came to the New World with a copy, well annotated, of Thomas More's *Utopia.* After fulfilling his term as a Justice, he went to what is now the state of Michoacán, Mexico, where he established hospitals as described by Thomas More, and wrote to the Council of the Indies, proposing the regime of *Utopia* as a model for the organization of the Americas. He apparently received no response.

Quiroga's opposite existed in history, and exists as well in Fuentes's novel, in the figure of Guzmán, Beltrán Nuño de Guzmán, the president of the first *Audiencia,* who became dictator of New Spain from 1524 to 1530.[44] In the short period of Guzmán's rule, the western provinces of Mexico, including the area of Michoacán, were threatened with the same disastrous abuses that had in the preceding generation already destroyed virtually the whole indigenous population of the Antilles. The magnificent film on this earliest colonial period of Latin American history, Werner Herzog's *Aguirre, The Wrath of God,* also contains an odious character called Guzmán. The movie is based on a sixteenth-century Peruvian incident involving a Spanish expedition in search of *El Dorado* – that singularly Latin American version of paradise; the New World is lost in the film, as it is in *Terra Nostra,* because of the greed of individual ownership.[45] The death of a Spanish usurper in Fuentes's novel is explained in these terms by an old sage: "He raised a temple for himself alone. He wished to make himself owner of a piece of the earth. But the earth is divine and cannot be possessed by any man. It is she who possesses us" (387–8). In *Terra Nostra,* Guzmán is the New World extension of Felipe; the history of the Old World seems to cycle disastrously into the New.

I earlier cited the passage where Pollo laments that the abuses of the Old World, symbolized by the dates 1492, 1521, and 1598, have only repeated themselves in the New World. These pairings and repetitions in the novel might seem to say that history is not a spiral but a closed circle in Latin America. There is, however, an allusion here which undermines such fatalism. In the midst of Pollo's catalogue of repeating ills, he says: "History was the same: tragedy then and farce now, farce first and then tragedy . . ." (775). This phrase echoes the opening sentence of Karl Marx's "The Eighteenth Brumaire of Louis Bonaparte," an essay written in late 1851 and early 1852 on class struggle and revolution in France.[46] Marx begins his essay on Louis Bonaparte and the events leading up to his coup d'état on December 2, 1851, by saying, "Hegel remarks somewhere that all great world-historical facts and personages occur, as it were, twice. He has forgotten to add: the first time as tragedy, the second as farce."[47] While Fuentes's quick reversal of the order of tragedy and farce throws Marx's proposed progression into question, his use of the phrase at this point is nonetheless calculated to contradict Pollo's vision of endlessly repeating historical cycles in Latin America, and to suggest instead a dialectical relationship between the Old and New Worlds which may be positive after all.

Underpinning the dialectical relations in *Terra Nostra* between colonialism and independence is the essential dialectic between history and imagination, between reality and its creative embodiment in art. This dialectic brings us back to Vico, whose presence again asserts itself, this time in the very texture of Marx's argument. The second paragraph of "The Eighteenth Brumaire of Louis Bonaparte" begins, "Men make their own history, but they do not make it just as they please; they do not make it under circumstance chosen by themselves, but under circumstances directly found, given and transmitted from the past." This implicit reference to Vico's theory of the human origins of history supports the assertion of a number of scholars that Marx's idea of "making history" is closely connected to Vico's, and that he found some of the seeds of his own theory of class struggle in Vico's study of the developmental stages of civilization.[48] Marx proceeds in this essay to examine the burden of the past upon those engaged in "creating something entirely new." He says that at the outset of this process, "The tradition of all the dead generations weighs like a nightmare on the brain of the living"; the paragraph, and the essay, move on to consider the ways in which the past may nonetheless be assimilated into the revolutionary present.

It is conceivable that Fuentes projects a similar historical progression for

Latin America with regard to its Spanish heritage, and while I think that such an assertion is tentatively borne out in *Terra Nostra,* the allusion to "The Eighteenth Brumaire" at this culminating point in the narration serves a more important function. It shifts the concept of history upon which the novel is based from the theoretical realm, which is Vico's, to the realm of political action, which is Marx's.[49] It is Marx's sense of culture as a struggle, or at least a debate, not only among ideas but also among economic and political and social factions, which is important here. That Fuentes adds Marx to the other historiographic models within the text reinforces what we already know about *Terra Nostra:* The novel does not aim to serve the ends of any single ideological system, but seeks instead to embody in its own structure the debate at the heart of contemporary Latin American culture itself.

Jeffrey Mehlman has called Marx's essay on the Eighteenth Brumaire a "fantasmatics of history," and cites Marx's remarkable description of Louis Bonaparte in *The Class Struggles of France:* "Clumsily cunning, knavishly naive, doltishly sublime, calculated superstition, pathetic burlesque, cleverly stupid anachronism, a world historical piece of buffoonery, an undecipherable hieroglyphic for the understanding of the civilized. . . ."[50] Mehlman notes the Rabelaisian verve of Marx's catalogue and the "proliferating energy [which] generates the motley cast of the Marxian farce" (13). Marx's catalogue recalls Fuentes's descriptions of Felipe and the farcical/fantastical cast which surrounds him. What is interesting in both cases is the narrative energy generated by despotism. Mehlman explains this paradox in terms of Marx's sense of the dialectical movement of history through reversals. Reversals – in this case, the return of a Bonaparte – advance history toward truth. Fuentes's foolish Felipe also embodies this sense that the false is not the opposite of the true but is contained within the true, and plays a necessary part in the fulfillment of history. As Erasmus (to whom Fuentes alludes in *Terra Nostra*) was perhaps the first to recognize, folly is not the opposite of wisdom, but dialectically related to it, and hence essential to its proper definition.

V.

I began this discussion of *Terra Nostra* by suggesting that the complex interaction between historical reality and a variety of visionary historical constructs gives to *Terra Nostra* its structural and thematic coherence.[51] In its portrayal of the conjunction of Edenic, utopian, and apocalyptic traditions, and in its investigation of their historical implications and applications, *Terra Nostra* looks self-consciously backward and forward as do the literary precursors – *Don Quixote, La Celestina, Don Juan* – which are explicitly integrated into its narrative structure. For Fuentes, it is the temporal inclusiveness of narration, not the timelessness of any utopian or apocalyptic future, where historical truth resides. Although he is careful to differentiate among idealized historical visions in *Terra Nostra,* and he certainly does not dismiss the political and philosophical optimism they imply, it is nonetheless clear that for this author, such visions may as easily constitute an eternal nonpresent as an eternal present, as easily a negation of history as its essential aim or end. In the final chapter of the novel, which is filled with references to characters from other works of modern Latin American fiction, Pollo bids farewell to utopia, as Ludovico has just bid farewell to the dying Felipe: "Farewell, Utopia . . . Farewell, City of the Sun . . . Farewell, Vasco de Quiroga . . ." (763). He then enters a library, where he reads in a number of manuscripts the "mute voices of men of other times [which] survive the men of your own time" (764). For Fuentes, it is in these texts, if anywhere, that utopia may be located: Words are their communal property, and the literary tradition their antidote to time's annihilation.

But there is a contradiction in Pollo's phrase. How is he, or are we, to hear or read these "mute voices"? Fuentes's answer lies in creative remembering, in the artistic structures created by the historical imagination. Memory is specifically addressed in these terms by Frances Yates, whose seminal study, *The Art of Memory,* is acknowledged by Fuentes, along with Cohn's *The Pursuit of the Millennium,* in the introduction to *Terra Nostra.* It is the Renaissance memory artist, Guilio Camillo, who is discussed by Yates and given fictional life in *Terra Nostra,* in the chapter entitled "The Theater of Memory." Camillo, in his *L'idea del Teatro* (1550), devised a visual schema in the form of a theater wherein he aimed to represent the totality of human action and thought. Camillo's theater is one of the many *topoi* (objects, rooms, scenes, architectural spaces) where ideas or events were deployed spatially as an aid to memory. Such mnemonic systems were essential in the ages before printing, and later crucial to the hermetic tradition, where truths were not to be written down. In the context of a discussion of Camillo's use of images of creation from the *Zohar,* Yates writes of his theater of memory, "It is because he believes in the divinity of man that the divine Camillo makes his stupendous claim of being able to remember the universe by looking down upon it from above. . . . The microcosm can fully understand and fully remember the macrocosm. . . ."[52]

Fuentes focuses on this universalizing impulse of Camillo's vision, implicitly connecting it to the comprehensive historical perspective of Bosch's millennial vision, and to his own in *Terra Nostra.* Speaking of the Greek poet Simonides, who according to legend originated the art of memory, Fuentes's character Camillo says that it is due to him that memory is no longer merely an inventory of daily tasks. Since memory is exercised in the present, to remember is not only to recall the past but also to integrate the past into the present and the future: Memory must "totally embrace the present so that, in the future, actuality is remembered past" (557). It is creative memory which provides the means to escape from the closed circle of history, the means not only to understand what has been, but also to imagine what has not been, and hence what may yet be.

Vico's *New Science* also has its own particular theory of memory. For Vico, memory is a corrective for the modern mind's tendency toward conceptual abstraction, a means of placing the mind back in touch with the original formative powers of sensation. Memory is not only the ability to recall (*memoria*), but also the ability to reorder what has been recalled (*fantasia*), and combine and integrate past acts with present acts (*ingegno*).[53] Vico insists that great historical writing must combine all three, as Fuentes insists that literature must. Vico's conception of memory is, like Camillo's, connected with place. In fact, Donald Varene has compared Vico's *New Science* to Camillo's theater of memory in that both aim to provide a spatial arena where all of human history is played, where collective cultural memory is made available to the individual. Such a universal structure leads, says Varene, to Vico's collage of topics: "wisdom, giants, sacrifices, poetic logic, monsters, metamorphoses, money, rhythm, song, children, poetic economy, Roman assemblies, the true Homer, heroic aristocracies, natural law, duels, Jean Bodin, legal metaphysic, barbaric history . . . Vico reverses Occam's sense of the economy of thought. We find not Occam's razor, but Vico's magnet."[54] In its similarly creative and comprehensive concept of historical memory, and its strong sense of place, we may also wish to think of *Terra Nostra* as Fuentes's magnet. Or as his theater of memory, an analogy which Fuentes explicitly invites when he lists, in the format of a play at the beginning of the novel, his cast of characters and their roles in his universal drama. It is a drama which is both tragedy *and* farce.

One phrase from a final litany of allusions in *Terra Nostra* seems calculated to epitomize Fuentes's Vichian orientation in this novel: "Time is the relationship between the existent and the non-existent" (773). Fuentes, like Vico, conceives of history as the product of the ceaseless interaction of the actual and the ideal, of desire and its object, of imagination and experience. Neither Vico nor Fuentes, it hardly needs stating, is interested in series of events per se, but in the multitiered realms of the human mind, in coexisting cultures in their various historical stages, and in the social institutions which embody those realms, those stages. Both reject the emphasis of their cultures on rationality and abstract intellectualism – what Vico called the "barbarism of reflection" (¶ 1106) and Fuentes calls the "univocal, frontal space of the rationalist project" – in favor of the imaginative integration of sense and intellect, perception and idea.[55] Fuentes is attracted to Vico because he understands and makes distinctions among cultures in these terms. Both understand and describe historical exhaustion and regeneration in terms of language and imagination.

Though Vico is best known for his theory of historical origins, the *New Science* also contains a highly dramatic description of the end of the historical course of any given society.[56] It is in this passage that Vico outlines the "barbarism of reflection." Of nations "rotting in that ultimate civil disease," Vico writes that their people "have fallen into the custom of each man thinking only of his own private interests and have reached the extreme of delicacy, or better of pride, in which like wild animals they bristle and lash out at the slightest displeasure. Thus no matter how great the throng and press of their bodies, they live like wild beasts in a deep solitude of spirit and will" (¶ 1106). This "deep solitude of spirit and will" results from the loss of a common perspective, a *sensus communis;* when this is gone, all that remains are the overly rational determinations of individuals who have lost touch with the natural forms of imagination. Thus, Vico's "barbarism of reflection" signals an inability to see the gods, that is, to shape the world imaginatively. It is when this condition reaches its fullest extent, according to Vico, that the course of the nation is brought back to the original condition of humanity, who will again establish contact with the world through their senses, and will again develop their powers of memory and imagination.

Vico's description of the dissolution of decadent society and its replacement by a society based on "piety, faith, and truth which are the natural foundations of justice" (¶ 1106), is echoed in the last chapter of *Terra Nostra.* The narrative shifts abruptly from the mob in Paris on New Year's Eve, 1999, to the silent world of New Year's morning, 2000, described in the last sentence of the novel: "Twelve o'clock did not toll in the church towers of Paris: but the snow ceased, and the following day a cold sun shone" (778). The subdued tone and concision of this final sentence are calculated to contrast radically with the two-page sentence that precedes it, and with the syntactic complexity of the novel generally. It is clear that Fuentes conceives of our time as dominated by analytic rationalism (as Vico considered his own to be): The final silent scene of the novel after, and perhaps because of, the androgynous union of Pollo and Celestina, proposes the recuperation of the powers of imagination and memory which Vico describes as inherent in the return to origins, the end and new beginning of a nation's history. It is in this final scene, conclusive yet awaiting completion, that Fuentes's Vichian sense of history as human artifice takes on its fullest significance.

I have argued throughout this book that every concept of narrative ending contains a particular attitude toward the goals of narrative structure, and that every concept of temporal end implies an ideology. Fuentes has denied that his historical fiction is ideological per se. Referring to several Latin American writers, including García Márquez, Cortázar, Paz, and Carpentier, he says, "We're not dealing with ideology. We are dealing with writers who are restoring our civilization, the facts of our civilization, who are creating our cultural identity . . . ."[57] These writers are *reconstructing* the past, Fuentes concludes, in order to *construct* the future. Of course we know, as does Fuentes, that this narrative reconstruction *is* ideological in its purpose of defining and hence directing collective attitudes and actions. In her sociological study of the apocalyptic visions and visionaries, Eleanor Wilner insists that the most original and effective visionaries are precisely those who transvalue the new in terms of the old. All forward movements or radical turns to a different future require an imaginative return to the past. Wilner writes: "The ego, before acting against the established order, must somehow enlist the approval of the inhibiting super-ego, or social conscience, and this can only be done by somehow seeing the new action as approved by the old powers – the parental archetypes, the ancestors, the culture hero, the god or gods of the tribe."[58] Only when a new orientation reformulates and restructures familiar symbols can people begin to take control of the situation in or against which they struggle. Wilner is describing here the necessary syncretism of apocalypse, a point which Fuentes also addresses in an essay on Mexican art. Fuentes writes that only by incorporating the various histories of Mexico – Indian, European, Mestizo – can the "linear simplicity of transposed occidental time" be transformed into the "polyvalent, sculptural space of our indigenous past."[59] *Terra Nostra* is surely an example of this transformative process.

8

INDIVIDUAL AND COMMUNAL
CONCLUSIONS

I considered that we were now, as always, at the end of time. . . .

The priest in "The God's Script," Jorge Luis Borges

MY CRITICAL DISCUSSION of apocalyptic ends and endings would seem to require some definitive final statement, but
there are no last words on the subject. The novels that use the
myth of apocalypse, like the myth itself, are more often than not what
Roland Barthes has called a literature of suspended meaning, of indeterminacy. They propose conclusions but do not provide them; their authors
explore finality while knowing that fiction, if it is good, permits no single
reading – hence, no final one. Furthermore, the increasing number of contemporary novels that entertain visions of apocalypse also seems to defy
conclusion, and I will want at least to mention a few titles. But first I
propose to make some comparative generalizations about the different uses
of the myth of apocalypse in contemporary U.S. and Latin American fiction, and suggest possible reasons for those differences.

In the foregoing chapters, I have discussed a variety of literary uses of the
apocalyptic understanding and narration of history. Apocalyptic texts,
whether biblical or contemporary, respond to temporal and psychic alienation by positing the possibility of eventual integration. It is the apocalyptic
narrators' efforts to understand their present experience that shapes their
vision of the future. Though they see and describe temporal disintegration,
the very fact of their imaginative projection implies their belief in ultimate
temporal coherence. The fiction which seriously employs apocalyptic forms
and themes strives to make connections between past, present, and future,
between the individual and the community, between the real and the ideal.
Yeats said that his apocalyptic system enabled him to hold reality and justice
in a single thought. It is such integration to which the apocalyptic imagination aspires; its object is to overcome the incongruity between the order it
envisions and the world's indifference to that order. This desire underlies
the thematic tensions and narrative momentum of much of the literature I

have discussed here. Apocalyptic narration responds to its historical context by balancing (in various combinations and degrees) description and prescription, accommodation and revision. Apocalyptic texts dramatize the decisive moment when an old world discovers a believable new world and either reacts against the old system or incorporates it into its new design. In contemporary fiction, that new design may be the literary work itself.

Apocalyptic modes of thought and expression increase during times of social disruption and temporal uncertainty. In the fiction of Gabriel García Márquez, Julio Cortázar, and Walker Percy, the myth of apocalypse provides the thematic and narrative means to confront cultural and political corruption. Or it may provide the historical model against which to react, as it does for Thomas Pynchon in his preference for the mechanistic metaphor of entropy, and for Carlos Fuentes in his Vichian vision of a spiraling history. Or again, it may suggest the structural means of avoiding closure and hence of dealing with literary "exhaustion," as it does for John Barth. Though the contemporary authors who use the myth of apocalypse are as varied as contemporary literature itself, uniting their work is the recognition of our crucial moment in history (or, in the case of Barth, the crucial moment in our literary tradition).

It is Jacques Derrida who has recently proposed that the concept of crisis is itself in crisis, an idea which is relevant here.[1] The word is rooted in the Greek word for decision or verdict, and implies a situation in which inheres the necessity, and the means, for critical judgment. In biblical apocalypse, the etymological link between crisis and criticism is thematic: The biblical apocalyptist accepts and intensifies that link in his presentation of the final judgment of history in crisis, and in the constructive outcome of that judgment. However, the relation between crisis and criticism has in our own time become problematic. We are used to the idea of *permanent* crisis, a formulation which immediately undermines the traditional understanding of crisis as an *exceptional* situation or series of events that facilitates judgment. The permanent crisis of nuclear capability – the very idea that the United States alone possesses enough nuclear warheads to destroy the world many times over – has necessarily conditioned our understanding of crisis: We cannot avoid the realization that crisis may no longer catalyze decision or judgment, but paralyze them. Nevertheless, the conception of constructive crisis which the myth of apocalypse proposes gives contemporary writers a means of approaching – both thematically and formally – the conditions of our nuclear age.

It is U.S. writers who, more than Latin American writers, address these technological realities by means of the myth of apocalypse, as Walker Percy's repeated reference to "the bomb" and John Barth's structural use of the fear of nuclear war in *Sabbatical* suggest. Pynchon's *Gravity's Rainbow* is also inevitably understood by contemporary readers at least partially in terms of nuclear war, despite its World War II setting. The extent to which Pynchon encourages his reader to consider the V-2 rockets in this novel as ultimate weapons is the extent to which the metaphor of entropy is conditioned by the metaphor of apocalypse, the author's dismissal of apocalypse notwithstanding. In the final section of my chapter on Pynchon's fiction, I argued that the mechanistic conception of time in his fiction and in much U.S. postmodernist fiction contrasts with the organic conception of time underlying contemporary Latin American fiction. The greater awareness in U.S. fiction of a technological apocalypse serves both to reflect and reinforce this mechanistic vision of time.

There are also a growing number of U.S. novels set beyond the end of the world: "Postapocalyptic" novels, like the early *A Canticle for Leibowitz* (1959), by Walter M. Miller, Jr., and *Alas, Babylon* (1959), by Pat Frank; and, more recently, Russell Hoban's *Riddley Walker* (1980), Denis Johnson's *Fiskadoro* (1985), and Paul Auster's *In the Country of Last Things* (1987) are parables which exploit the ambivalences of apocalypse – fear and wish fulfillment, cultural forgetting and selective cultural re-creation, the dubious self-importance accorded to those few survivors of nuclear holocaust. The collective effect of this literature of postcatastrophe is to create the suspicion that it is not as much concerned with ordering and understanding history – the traditional motivation of apocalyptic texts – as competing with it. As they dramatize the wasted landscape beyond the end, these novels are constructed to convey the urgent sense that history may at any moment overtake their readers with the very events that they describe.

The temporal disruption contemporary apocalyptic fiction addresses is not necessarily (or only) geopolitical. The rapid modernization and technologization of "traditional" or "transitional" societies – terms used by sociologists to describe portions of the populations of a number of Latin American countries – is inevitably accompanied by a process of internal social disintegration and reorientation.[2] With increasing economic expectations in Latin American countries such as Fuentes's Mexico and García Márquez's Colombia, the conception of a future *different* from the past begins to displace the traditional conception of a future which *repeats* the past; the acceptance of an unchanged future based on a stable sense of cultural identity is gradually replaced by the conception of a future open to individual and communal control. However, as poverty and injustice continue, expectations of a future different from the past are accompanied by frustration and ultimately by social and political disequilibrium. Furthermore, as Carlos Fuentes has argued in the case of Mexico, the long coexistence of competing traditions – indigenous and Spanish – has made this historical process of modernization generally more difficult than in the United States. Added to these conditions of change is the question of national identity which has been imposed on Latin America – often inappropriately – by Europe and the United States. We have seen García Márquez's image of cultural and economic imperialism, the banana company hurricane, Fuentes's accumulation of images indicting Spanish colonialism in Mexico, and Cortázar's portrayal of the necessary opposition of socialist revolutions not only to existing regimes in Latin America but also to the countries outside of Latin America which support those regimes.

My point here is that the pressures of national identity and political self-definition in Latin America differ greatly from those in the United States, and, with the exception of the literature of the U.S. South, those pressures have recently served as subjects for literature in Latin America to a far greater extent than in the United States. Hence, the basic difference in the use of the myth of apocalypse in contemporary Latin American and U.S. literature: Whereas visions of apocalypse in U.S. fiction focus primarily on *individual* identity or narrative strategy, they are more often used in Latin American fiction as a means of expressing the *communal* realities of historical identity. This is of course a difference in relative emphasis rather than an absolute dichotomy. What I am proposing is that there is an essentially different proportion of the personal to the political, of the subjective to the political, in contemporary U.S. and Latin American fiction, and that this difference, which is rooted in historical and cultural circumstances, becomes more than usually apparent in texts that invoke the myth of apocalypse.

It is risky to generalize about the ways in which literature chooses to embody (or not to embody) issues of national and communal identity. However, it seems to me fair to say that Latin American writers are currently engaged in a process of cultural and historical self-definition which also engaged the great writers of the last century in U.S. literature – Emerson, Melville, Whitman, James – and the modernist writers in the U.S. South – Faulkner, O'Connor, Wolfe. Indeed, we may regret the absence of historical consciousness in much contemporary U.S. fiction, or its seemingly obsessive focus on the life of the decontextualized self or the verbal structure, even as we recognize that this, too, is the result of a particular historical situation. In much recent U.S. fiction, if historical process is addressed at all, it is often done so ironically, by dramatizing the retreat from communal categories into the hermetic realm of the alienated self. Whereas Latin American novelistic exploration of national identity and purpose has led to expansive projections of mythic regional histories, as did some nineteenth- and early twentieth-century U.S. literature, contemporary U.S. explorations have tended to inspire literary portrayals of the contraction of the single self to a defensive core. Joan Didion, John Updike, Joyce Carol Oates create characters who are haunted by suspicions of apocalypse, and who become isolated from their communal and historical environments as a result. Apocalyptic visions of the future may be individual as well as communal, but when there is only retreat from rather than encounter with a problematic historical reality, then the *critical* potential inherent in *crisis* cannot be maintained.

There are, of course, contemporary U.S. writers whose work does not conform to this generalization. The subject of Robert Coover's novel, *The Origin of the Brunists* (1966), is precisely that area where communal visions of apocalypse still flourish in the United States, fundamentalist Protestantism. Don DeLillo's *White Noise* (1985) creates an explicitly apocalyptic ambience in which to explore the increasing interdependence of the individual and the world community. U.S. minority writers still have a passionate stake in defining, or redefining, communal realities, and often do so in terms of apocalypse. Women writers in the United States are also often trenchant critics of contemporary cultural practice, though I think only of Flannery O'Connor's fiction as consistently engaging apocalyptic devices. Yet another U.S. writer whose fiction is informed by a profoundly historical imagination will serve in a moment to conclude my discussion. In general, however, it is in Latin America that the dissenting potential of the myth of apocalypse, as well as its idealizing vision, are being fully engaged.

The communal emphasis in contemporary Latin American fiction must be understood in terms of cultural and historical tradition. The Spanish New World was colonized on the bases of communal cultural imperatives as North America was not. The earliest European settlers of New Spain aimed to extend the institutions which existed in the Old World – church, crown, social class – an aim dramatized in Fuentes's *Terra Nostra,* as we have seen. The earliest Puritan settlers in New England aimed to do just the opposite, to separate themselves from the institutions which they had left behind for good reason, as did the many indentured servants, convicts, and impoverished immigrants who followed.[3] Thus, whereas the institutions implanted in Latin America were based on assumptions of cultural continuity, U.S. institutions originated in the need to *dis*continue existing European models and create new ones in America. Neither aim was fully achieved, of course, but we may locate in these opposing purposes the roots of our differing U.S. and Latin American cultural attitudes toward community: The "rugged individualism" and the "self-made man" which we have always celebrated in the United States, versus the emphasis placed on family and social relationships in Latin America; the religious pluralism in the United States, versus the shared beliefs and standardized practices of Latin American Catholicism.[4] Indeed, one might argue that the social and political dissent so powerfully expressed in contemporary Latin American fiction is the delayed criticism by New World writers of Old World forms – criticism not only of its political and social forms but of its literary forms as well. Fuentes dramatizes in *Terra Nostra* the apocalyptic visions Europe imposed upon the New World, but it is only now that an apocalyptic perspective is working in the opposite direction.

Individual and Communal Conclusions

The emphasis on communal or national definition in contemporary Latin American fiction coincides with the public involvement in Latin America of intellectuals and artists, who are looked to for political leadership. In his essay, "Revolution and the Intellectual in Latin America," Alan Riding has commented that "intellectuals exercise enormous political influence in Latin America. It is they who provide respectability to governments in power and legitimacy to revolts and revolutionary movements, they who articulate the ideas and contribute the images through which Latin Americans relate to power. . . ."[5] This has in some sense always been the case. The late Angel Rama has reminded us, in his useful study of the history of Latin American literary culture, that the tradition of political literature and literary politicians began with the very first implantation of Spanish culture in the New World.[6] Large numbers of literate functionaries and clerics came from Spain during the sixteenth and seventeenth centuries to impose and maintain the Spanish imperial and ecclesiastical orders in the New World. Those educated emissaries had time not only to rule and convert but also to write literary works, which they did in remarkable quantity. Rama recognizes that the leisure required for such literary productivity was financed by usurped wealth and slave labor, and that the baroque epics and eclogues of the colonizers, like their baroque churches and palaces, attest to the abuses of empire. However, their writings also attest to the early conceptualizing of the social and political function of literature in Latin America; the seventeenth-century writers Sor Juana Inés de la Cruz and Carlos Sigüenza y Góngora provide early examples of the uses of literature to achieve a variety of courtly and Catholic purposes in the Spanish New World. (The visual arts also quickly acquired such public importance, and they have never entirely lost it in Latin America.) The early alliance of language, literature, and politics in the Spanish New World may be understood as an essential historical condition in the development of the tradition of politically powerful universities, and politically involved university students, in Latin America. But if, during the colonial period, this alliance created academic institutions suited to serve the purposes of empire, the current case is obviously to the contrary: Universities, like literature, are now much more likely to oppose imperialism in Latin America than to foster or extend it. The coincidence of intellectual and political leadership continued through the eighteenth and into the nineteenth centuries in Latin America. Examples of writer–statesmen abound: Andrés Bello, Domingo Sarmiento, Justo Sierra, Rómulo Gallegos, José Martí were important political figures who wrote literary works of national and ethical definition, and who actively promoted such literature on the unequivocal assumption that literature could contribute to the construction of a nation's history.

In our own century in Latin America, the offices of politician and writer are less identified than before – indeed, writers are now more likely to be the opponents of official politics than the occupants of public office, more likely to be outside the political establishment than in. Contemporary writers do not, however, feel themselves any less politically responsible than their predecessors. On the contrary, when in recent years official channels – the university, the media – have failed to address (or have been prevented from addressing) actual political and social conditions, literature has often filled the vacuum. Literary and political aims continue to be conceived as complementary, however much the aims and alliances themselves have changed. Vocal participation in politics and dissent against oppressive regimes and influences characterize the Latin American writers whom I have discussed here, and many others besides. Their dissenting stance is well served by apocalyptic narrative strategies and visions of radical transformation: For these writers, literature, insofar as it *is* literature, closely associates revelation and revolution.

The public presence granted Latin American writers is rarely conceded to contemporary U.S. writers. Again, the histories and purposes of European colonization in the New World may provide some insight into this difference. The English Crown did not have Spain's monumental ecclesiastical or economic intentions in the New World; the English never sent, as did the Spanish, large numbers of educated bureaucrats in whom political and intellectual functions were combined. Seventeenth-century Puritan leaders in America did of course write prolifically, and their sermons and theological tracts and histories certainly had social and political functions. But literature (and literacy) were not limited to the colonial leaders, who in any case were selected from the colonizers rather than imposed upon the colonized. (Unlike the philosophical inclusiveness of the Spanish Catholic colonists, the philosophical exclusiveness of the Puritans minimized the impulse to convert the indigenous inhabitants of the New World.) Thus, most Puritan colonists wrote spiritual autobiographies and domestic diaries rather than chronicles or communal histories. The axes and intentions of their writing were vertical rather than horizontal; their texts examined the minutiae of daily life to discover God's plan for their personal salvation.

Imaginative literature was not considered a serious vehicle for the engagement of ethical matters by the Puritans, an idea that continued to haunt writers into the nineteenth-century. Nathaniel Hawthorne, in sketches and stories, repeatedly addresses the inherited suspicion that fiction had no communal function other than that of mere entertainment, which is to say, no proper communal function at all. In his description of the literary imagination as casting a "spell to disclose treasures hidden in some unsuspected cave of Truth," Hawthorne is characteristically compelled to self-justification. (This instance is from his sketch "The Old Manse," where he has just acknowledged the mute presence of an ancestral portrait, an "austere divine," looking down upon him from the library wall.) Here, as elsewhere, Hawthorne's reader senses the anxiety of a great writer who never fully repudiated his Puritan culture's view of the frivolity of his creative enterprise. That such frivolity could also be dangerous – a threat to rational control and hence to the existing order of things – was an intuition that escaped neither Hawthorne nor the austere divines who preceded him. This too may serve to explain the marginal status assigned to imaginative literature in this essentially conservative strain of U.S. literary culture.

I do not mean to say that Puritan conceptions of ethical discourse have prevented U.S. poets and novelists from addressing public issues and assuming public responsibilities. From the beginning of the foment for independence from England until relatively recently, U.S. literature and issues of public policy have often coincided, though never as systematically or continually – or as officially – as in Latin America. Recall the diplomatic careers of Benjamin Franklin, Washington Irving, and James Russell Lowell, the political writings of Harriet Beecher Stowe, and in our own century the complementary political and artistic energies of Upton Sinclair, Theodore Dreiser, James Agee, John Dos Passos. Since World War II, however, we have less and less frequently asked of our writers that they define our public selves, as we did in more formative periods of our national development. In general, our literature has shifted to the more private realms of psychology and ontology, and is less often critical than self-analytical. This is perhaps as it should be. My point here is not to evaluate this shift but to make the comparative observation that, again, we discover a parallel between earlier U.S. literary experience and current Latin American literary attitudes. Literature still matters in the complex political process of national self-definition in Latin America as it has largely ceased to in the United States.

Recent U.S. cultural institutions and attitudes also bear upon this question. Beyond the traditional separation of universities from institutional politics in the United States (as opposed to their traditional involvement in Latin America), the U.S. systems of foreign and civil service are composed of diplomats and government functionaries who have been educated in ways quite apart from the training of literary intellectuals – a degree of specialization not as customary in Latin America as in the United States (though it is gradually becoming more so). Consider, for example, the contrast in U.S. and Latin American legal educations. In Latin America as in the United States lawyers often serve as diplomats and elected officials. But in Latin America law is considered a humanistic subject and taught on the undergraduate level in conjunction with other humanistic subjects, generally over a four- or five-year course of study, whereas in the United States, legal education is treated as a specialized training beyond, and completely separate from, the broader university humanities curriculum.

The current separation of literature and politics in the United States also reflects the fact that over the last forty years or so, following certain strains of European esthetics, we have developed an image of our writers as alienated – a philosophical and narrative stance with inevitable political consequences. If in Latin America the expectation is that writers be committed politically, in the United States the expectation is just the contrary. We have fostered a postromantic conception of artists as separated from the political and social mainstream by their artistic sensibilities and esthetic priorities – as they often are. Even so acute a political and social observer as Norman Mailer writes from an ironically detached perspective, and whatever political indignation he may wish to express is largely subsumed by his own personal flamboyance. The personality of the writer is emphasized rather than the situation; Mailer leaves his readers with only the vestiges of his initial claims to social and political engagement.

The internalization of reality and the structural self-reflection of much postmodern U.S. literature has been supported and encouraged by our literary critical theory and practice. Until about fifteen years ago, prevailing critical thought tended to ignore – or even deny – the significance of the political and social and biographical contexts of literary texts. Though it is never possible to assign clear causal relations between critical theory and literary practice, we may suppose that the New Critical and Structuralist dismissal of extratextual considerations has encouraged a postmodernist literature which only rarely lays claim to political or social influence. Without doubt these critical theories have fostered university curricula composed of contemporary works that highlight esthetic and psychological concerns, rather than historical or social ones; and university courses that study literature rhetorically, rather than socially or politically. Russell Reising's recent study of American literary theory makes clear the ways in which we have systematically, though usually unconsciously, excluded socially and politically engaged writers (often minorities and women) in favor of esthetically innovative writers.[7] More materially minded critics have recently reacted against what Reising calls the *derealization* of U.S. literature, and are now directing attention toward its social subjects and contexts. Deconstructionist, feminist, Marxist, and new historicist modes are profoundly affecting the nature of U.S. literary critical praxis: These theoretical models ask the reader to recognize a variety of competing centers of cultural power, and to recognize the complex cultural environment of which literature is a part. The relevance of these approaches is especially clear to the comparative discussion of American literature in the hemispheric context, which I have delineated in foregoing chapters. But though we may applaud these critical reassessments and the assertion, elegantly argued by Fredric Jameson and others, that literature is by definition a political act, we must nonetheless acknowledge that recent U.S. literature and literary critical practice have often been most political precisely in their rejection of political issues as matters of literary concern.

In fact, Jameson does acknowledge this point. In the following statement, he implies a crucial distinction between the general and the specific uses of the word political, as well as between the attitudes of U.S. literary criticism and criticism in other parts of the world: "That a literary article could be a political act, *with real consequences,* is for most of us little more than a curiosity of the literary history of Czarist Russia or of modern China. . . ."[8] If we look at the U.S. political arena, we see that literary and critical practice have recently had very little to do with actual public definition or political understanding, though this too may be changing as we become increasingly aware of the exclusionary nature of our academic and critical criteria, and as dissident voices – feminist and minority critics, among others – become more powerful. And again, I hasten to add that there are always exceptions to generalizations about something as complex as U.S. literature: Among the exceptions to this one are Joseph Heller's *Catch-22,* which influenced the antiwar movement in the late 1960s, and James Baldwin's fiction and essays, which played a significant role in the 1950s and 1960s in our communal understanding of racial problems and their potential remedies. Of course political content does not automatically give a work of literature urgency or coherence, but in general it is considered critically naive in the United States to look for the actual political engagement of literature – a wrong-headed confusion of journalism with literature.

In Latin America, this is simply not the case, as García Márquez makes clear in his comment on the role of the Latin American writer: "The problems of our societies are mainly political. . . . That is why authors, painters, writers in Latin American get politically involved. I am surprised by the little resonance authors have in the U.S. and in Europe. Politics there is made only by the politicians."[9] Most major Latin American novelists are in fact active journalists; novels about journalists by García Márquez, Vargas Llosa, Cortázar, Allende, and the creative journalism of the Mexican writer Elena Poniatowska suggest that journalism and fiction may be less clearly separated in Latin America than elsewhere. They imply that the novel, like the newspaper, must reflect all levels of society and address current political and social conditions if it is to serve as an instrument of knowledge and, hence, as an instrument of social change. The generic innovations of much contemporary Latin American fiction may be partially understood in these terms. The tendency to integrate into fictional narration the characteristics of nonfictional genres – essays, academic tracts and footnotes, the actual format and/or content of newspaper articles and photojournalism – clearly has as one of its primary motivations the sense that literature must respond not only to imaginative and esthetic imperatives, but also to sociological and political ones.

In referring to their communal sense and political involvement, I do not mean to impute to these Latin American writers an essentialist notion of culture, or to suggest that they necessarily subscribe to some idealized notion of an integrated and homogenous community. My discussion of Cortázar's "We Love Glenda So Much," and Fuentes's *Terra Nostra* makes clear their skepticism about utopian communitarianism, as does the apocalyptic history of Macondo in García Márquez's *One Hundred Years of Solitude*. Rather, my aim here is to point to the historical relations in Latin America between literacy and autocracy, literature and authority, and then to distinguish them from U.S. literary attitudes and practices. Contemporary Latin American writers participate in a tradition that understands literature in terms of communal function, as U.S. writers generally do not. If, as I have said, the literary tradition began in New Spain with the conceptualizing of literature as a tool for European imperial domination and cultural homogenization, it has evolved into a contemporary literary practice responsive to communities that include vast differences in cultures and disparities in educational levels. The Uruguayan novelist, Augusto Roa Bastos, has commented on "the always difficult relations between the reality of history and the unreality of signs, between 'cultured' levels . . . and our populations who do not even have access to [literary] culture."[10] Contemporary Latin American writers may address communal issues even as they recognize their separation from significant segments of that community by language and culture, and by the very fact of the written nature of their literary medium. An awareness of this separation may explain in part the energetic use of nonliterary modes in contemporary Latin American fiction. Beyond the frequent use of indigenous mythic and cultural systems, there is a rich vein of contemporary narrative based on the forms of mass media. As with the fictional uses of nonfictional genres, to which I referred in the preceding paragraph, the self-conscious and sustained use of material from the movies, soap opera, popular music, by Manuel Puig, Guillermo Cabrera Infante, Gustavo Sáinz, Luis Rafael Sánchez, and others, is aimed at bridging the gulf between literary and mass culture, and at indicting the system upon which cultural inequities have traditionally been based in Latin America. These writers use the artifacts of disparate cultures to deconstruct the disparities, and to propose a shared Latin American reality.[11]

While we may celebrate the brilliant narrative art that combined communal and esthetic imperatives have recently produced in Latin America, we should also recognize their inherent dangers, as Mario Vargas Llosa asks us to do in a sensitive essay called "Social Commitment and the Latin American Writer." There are enormous pressures on Latin American writers to be participants in economic, political, and social areas, in both their writing and their actions – pressures which, Vargas Llosa argues, are utterly inescapable. He states that writers in Latin America, unlike their North American and European counterparts, do not have the choice simply to be artists; they are obliged also to be reformers, politicians, revolutionaries, moralists. If a writer should wish to reject these roles, he or she will be considered by his present and potential readers "a deserter and a traitor, and his poems, novels, and plays will be endangered. To be an artist, only an artist, can become, in our countries, a kind of moral crime, a political sin."[12] Vargas Llosa's vehemence, and his tendency to overstatement here, are understandable, for his own work has been impugned in these terms – not for being apolitical but, more insidiously, for being too conservative. Furthermore, we know that there are exceptions to Vargas Llosa's generalization, contemporary Latin American writers who *have* managed to treat subjects other than political ones, and whose work *has* survived the pressures he describes. Borges is the most obvious example, and the one whom Vargas Llosa eventually cites. Nonetheless, Vargas Llosa is right in calling attention to the conditions in Latin America which make demands on artists that they would not be submitted to elsewhere. He is also right in recognizing that those demands may distort or destroy artistic vocations and, further, that the subjects of literature are not limited to, or proscribed by, political and social realities. Vargas Llosa's tragic case in point is the Peruvian novelist José María Arguedas who, unlike Borges, could not withstand the pressures to address himself to social problems, even though he sacrificed his own artistic vision to do so. Vargas Llosa also discusses the related problem of evaluating esthetically a politically committed literature: How can the reader or critic condemn as an artistic failure a novel which protests the oppression of the masses, without himself or herself being identified with the oppressors? This essay makes us poignantly aware of the particular social and political challenges, and the dangers, of being a writer at this time in Latin America.

Of course good literature never consists solely of a political agenda because it necessarily invites interpretations, evades the unambiguous prescriptions necessary to mere calls for social action. Nevertheless, we may observe generally that Latin American literature is currently more engaged by the spectacle of national politics than is U.S. literature, and hence more interested in the *communal* historical vision which apocalypse projects. Though I have cited Percy's and Barth's concern with nuclear war, "the bomb" is more often a metaphor for private concerns than a criticism of contemporary political realities. And if public references are used by Percy and Barth for the development of private concerns in their novels, the reverse is true of the Latin American fiction which I have discussed here. The omnipresent solitude in *One Hundred Years of Solitude* by definition raises the question of the relation between the self and the community.

Though the Buendías initially seem to be characters who result from a complex interplay of personal psychology and social milieu, it is the latter element which eventually outweighs the former. With the possible exception of Ursula and Aureliano Babilonia, García Márquez's characters are not developed as individual personalities but rather as personality types, their repeating names serving to remind us of their lack of individualized psychologies.[13] The Buendías illustrate what their plots dramatize, that human beings are inevitably subject to historical forces. Fuentes's characters in *Terra Nostra* are also closely bound by their historical and cultural roles. The multiplication of Pollo and Celestina, as well as their final union, serve the same narrative purpose as the repeating names of the Buendías, which is to underline their broad historical significance rather than their individualized psychological identity. And though Cortázar's early fiction does contain individualized characters, his later political fiction concentrates on public definition rather than private differentiation. Because of his concern with political and social oppression, Cortázar creates faceless characters such as Glenda's fans, who, like García Márquez's patriarch, wear only the generalized mask of the political oppressor. In this respect, Thomas Pynchon approaches Latin American fiction, for he too suppresses psychological development in favor of historical type: Stencil, Oedipa, Slothrup are not developed as individuals but as reflections of the historical and cultural forces that operate upon them. They, like the Buendías, the Pollos and Celestinas, and Glenda's fans, serve the narrative purpose of making those forces visible.

The characters of García Márquez and Fuentes and Cortázar represent the greater quotient of political and communal concerns in contemporary Latin American fiction when compared to contemporary U.S. fiction, and perhaps even serve as examples of Fredric Jameson's provocative generalizaton that fiction written by postcolonial writers necessarily projects a "national allegory." Jameson argues that psychological and libidinal elements in recent postcolonial fiction must be read primarily in political and social terms, that *"the story of a private individual destiny is always an allegory of the embattled situation of the public third-world culture and society."*[14] While Jameson's argument seems to me too broadly stated, both geographically and generically, and has elicited considerable critical disagreement, it is nonetheless useful in raising the question of the relation of economics to the form of the novel per se. Jameson writes that "One of the determinants of capitalist culture, that is, the culture of the western realist and modernist novel, is a radical split between the private and the public, between the poetic and the political, between what we have come to think of as the domain of sexuality and the unconscious and that of the public world of classes, of the economic, and of secular political power: in other words, Freud versus Marx." Referring to the capitalist culture of the United States, he says, "We have been trained in a deep cultural conviction that the lived experience of our private existences is somehow incommensurable with the abstractions of economic science and political dynamics. Politics in our novels therefore is, according to Stendhal's canonical formulation, a 'pistol shot in the middle of a concert'" (69). Jameson implies that contemporary U.S. culture is based on the same capitalist assumptions which generated the novel as a literary genre, and thus accepts its generic assumptions, including the split between self and society, whereas postcolonial cultures are often based on very different economic assumptions, and hence posit different generic ones.

Though we may question the extent of the "radical split" which Jameson asserts as inherent in the genre of the novel itself (and see behind his assertion Lukács's discussion of the novelistic dualism of inwardness and the outside world), the point is not whether these poles exist – clearly they do. Rather, my interest, and Jameson's, is in the reasons for and the significance of the different proportions and emphases on one pole or the other in different periods and places. This question of proportion (or disproportion) haunted the masters of European modernism – Woolf, Proust, Joyce, Gide – who feared that the novelistic portrayal of public reality would engulf, or already had, the private realms of the self. And they modified those proportions, and the genre, accordingly. The generic innovations of contemporary Latin American writers also stem in part from a dissatisfaction with the prevailing novelistic ratio of the public to the private, and a desire to adjust the relation of the two – their adjustments moving the genre in the opposite direction from their European predecessors, from an emphasis on private narrative realms toward more communal realms of existence.

The narrative strategies which we have come to categorize loosely as magic realism are a part of this complex process of generic innovation in contemporary Latin American fiction, and the myth of apocalypse has played a significant role in that process. The literary devices of biblical apocalypse and magical realism coincide in their hyperbolic narration and in their surreal images of utter chaos and unutterable perfection. And in both cases, their surrealism is not principally conceived for psychological effect, as in earlier European examples of the mode, but is instead grounded in social and political realities and is designed to communicate the writers' objections to those realities. Fantastic literature thus becomes symbolic literature, for in the lurid dreams of unreal beings and events, and in the hyperbolic fervor of their description, are coded the problems of contemporary reality. I have already pointed to the ways in which García Márquez and Fuentes have used the myth of apocalypse to blur fantasy and reality, and ultimately to erase and redraw the lines between fiction and history. Mario Vargas Llosa uses the myth to similar effect in *The War of the End of the World* (1981). This novel is based on a historical event, the Canudos incident, a millenarian uprising in the backlands of Brazil in the late nineteenth century. Vargas Llosa presents an extended consideration of the overlapping areas of myth, history, and fiction, playing the mythic archetypes of apocalypse against historical events of Canudos. The mythologizing of history by the followers of the messianic leader in Canudos parallels the narrativizing of those apocalyptic events, whether by the Brazilian author, Euclides da Cunha, who wrote a famous account of the events, or by Vargas Llosa himself. Other recent Latin American novels (as yet untranslated) which exploit the magical realism inherent in the apocalyptic mode are Ernesto Sábato's *Abaddón el exterminador* (*Abbadon the Avenger,* 1974), a title taken from Rev. 9:7–11; Homero Aridjis's *Espectáculo del año dos mil* (*Spectacle of the Year 2000,* 1981); and Luisa Josefina Hernández's *Apocalipsis cum figuris* (1982), its Latin title taken from another fantastical rendition of apocalyptic history, Albrecht Durer's famous series of woodcut illustrations of Revelation. The pressures of contemporary Latin American reality repeatedly become a communal spiritual possession which finds expression in the fantastic visions of apocalypse.

Although I have emphasized the greater relative engagement of collective history in contemporary Latin American fiction, I nonetheless want to conclude by saying that the best fiction from both the United States and Latin America dramatizes the integral relation between private and social destiny. Because the myth of apocalypse insists on the inevitable link between individual and collective fate, it is precisely those writers prone to apocalyptic visions who are most likely to concern themselves with essential relations between the self and its surroundings, between autonomy and solidarity. Among contemporary U.S. writers who combine a broad historical and cultural perspective with penetrating, intimate portraiture is Saul Bellow. Bellow has persistently addressed the nature and processes of communal history as it operates in the life of the individual, though he does not always do so in terms of apocalypse. Indeed, he recognizes that apocalyptic visions are easily abused, easily turned to the service of simple utopian fantasies or mere descriptions of doom.

Bellow, as much as any American writer, is sensitive to the crises of our century ("Since 1914, war, revolution, fascism, communism, depression, unemployment, devastation, reconstruction . . . have absorbed the imagination of mankind.") and the crisis of our contemporary consumer culture ("This society, like decadent Rome, is an amusement society. That is the grim fact.").[15] In his speech accepting the Nobel Prize for literature in 1976, Bellow observes "in private life, disorder or near-panic; in families – for husbands, wives, parents, children – confusion; in civic behavior, in personal loyalties, in sexual practices (I will not recite the whole list; we are tired of hearing it) – further confusion. And with this private disorder goes public bewilderment. In the papers we read what used to amuse us in science fiction. . . ."[16] Bellow's purpose is not to bring to our attention what he is certain that we already know, but rather to point out the pitch and intensity of the doomsaying: "the terrible predictions we have to live with, the background of disorder, the vision of ruin" (320). He has repeatedly rejected the contemporary rhetoric of catastrophe, what he calls "apocalyptic clichés; . . . violently compact historical judgments; easy formulas about the 'cancellatio of a world'. . . . what a lot of ideological burial-parties the twentieth century has seen."[17] Bellow believes that it is the essence of literature to impugn the moral and ethical abuses of our time, but literature must also transcend the mere cataloguing of evil ("the whole list") to propose a means of continuing to live in our time. He insists that the artist must be a prophet, "not in the sense that he foretells things to come, but that he tells the audience, at risk of their displeasure, the secrets of their own hearts."[18]

Bellow's disparagement of doomsayers might seem to include some of the writers whom I have dealt with here – García Márquez, Pynchon, Percy, Barth. However, Bellow shares with these writers their sense of the potentially positive effects of crisis, whether political or psychological or literary. He continues, in his Nobel speech: "When complications increase, the desire for essentials increases too. The unending cycle of crisis that began with the First World War has formed a kind of person, one who has lived through terrible, strange things, and in whom there is an observable shrinkage of prejudices, a casting off of disappointing ideologies, an ability to live with many kinds of madness, an immense desire for certain durable human goods – truth, for instance, or freedom, or wisdom" (321). This description of the creative potential of crisis closely resembles Walker Percy's statement about the "new breed of person in whom the potential for catastrophe – and hope – has suddenly escalated."[19] And it recalls Percy's contention that the novelist must serve a prophetic function, that is, a communal and historical function. For these novelists, history provides a personal context, and their vision of communal crisis becomes the means of understanding and portraying individual endurance.

Like Faulkner before him and García Márquez after him, Bellow ultimately directs his Nobel Speech to the open question of humanity's survival: "What is at the center now? At the moment, neither art nor science, but mankind determining, in confusion and obscurity, whether it will endure or go under" (324). Bellow's implicit reference to Faulkner in his choice of the word *endure,* and to Yeats in the word *center,* suggests not only his own vision of society but also his self-conscious invocation of the apocalyptic literary tradition. The writers who participate in this tradition are aware of humanity's propensity for communal self-destruction, and they are aware as well of the effects of crisis, for both good and evil, on the individual. This concern with the outcome of our individual and communal histories, coupled with the conviction that literature may yet influence that outcome, has never been more necessary.

NOTES

CHAPTER 1.

1. David Hellholm, ed., *Apocalypticism in the Mediterranean World and the Near East* (Tubingen: Mohr, 1983). This authoritative collection of scholarly essays deals with the question of apocalyptic texts in the canons of various cultural and religious traditions, as well as with the question of genre. In a particularly useful essay on the generic elements of apocalypse, "Survey of the Problem of Apocalyptic Genre," Lars Hartman lists pseudonymity, accounts of visions, pictorial language, interpretation, systematization, history in future form, descriptions of other worlds, visions of a divine throne, and prayers. He notes that apocalyptic narration discloses a transcendent reality which is both temporal, in so far as it envisages eschatological salvation, and spatial, in so far as it involves another, supernatural world.

2. The most comprehensive treatment of the Judeo-Christian myth of apocalypse in the visual arts is by Frederick Van der Meer, *Apocalypse: Visions from the Book of Revelation in Western Art* (New York: Alpine Fine Arts Collection, Ltd., 1978). See also Kathryn Henkel, *The Apocalypse* (College Park, Md.: University of Maryland Department of Art, 1973).

3. Such discussions as Karl Löwith's influential study of "theologies of history," in *Meaning in History* (Chicago: University of Chicago Press, 1949), have popularized the idea that the concept of progress is a secularization of Judeo-Christian eschatological historiography. However, Hannah Arendt argues convincingly against this proposition in her essay, "The Concept of History," in *Between Past and Future* (1961; reprint, New York: Viking Press, 1969). She writes: "Because of the modern emphasis upon time and time sequence, it has often been maintained that the origin of our historical consciousness lies in the Hebrew-Christian tradition, with its rectilinear time-concept and its idea of a divine providence giving to the whole of man's historical time the unity of a plan of salvation . . ." (p. 65). However, Arendt refutes this "doubtful transformation of religious and transcendent categories into immanent earthly aims and standards" by pointing to the decisive element of our calendar system, the eighteenth-century idea of taking the birth of Christ as a turning point from which to count both backward (B.C.) and forward (A.D.):

> The decisive thing in our system is not that the birth of Christ now appears as the turning point of world history, for it had been recognized as such

and with greater force many centuries before without any similar effect on our chronology, but rather that now, for the first time, the history of mankind reaches back into an infinite past to which we can add at will and into which we can inquire further as it stretches ahead into an infinite future. This twofold infinity of past and future eliminates all notion of beginning and end, establishing mankind in a potential earthly immortality. What at first glance looks like the Christianization of world history in fact eliminated all religious time-speculations from secular history. So far as secular history is concerned we live in a process which knows no beginning and no end and which thus does not permit us to entertain eschatological expectations. Nothing could be more alien to Christian thought than this concept of an earthly immortality of mankind (67–8).

Though Arendt compels agreement in her description of our modern conception of infinite history, she does not dismiss what is the basis of my own discussion here, that is, the indirect and intangible ways in which biblical conceptions underlie our secular conceptions of temporal movement. The fact that she feels compelled to argue emphatically *against* Judeo-Christian eschatological expectations in modern secular historiography implies that such expectations still exert their influence in significant ways.

For complete discussions of the form and meaning of apocalypse in general, and of a number of Hebrew and Christian apocalyptic texts in particular, see R. H. Charles, *Eschatology: The Doctrine of a Future Life in Israel, Judaism, and Christianity* (1899; reprint, New York: Schocken Books, 1963); D. S. Russell, *The Method and Message of Jewish Apocalyptic* (Philadelphia: Westminster Press, 1964). Addressing the Book of Revelation are Elizabeth Schussler Fiorenze, "Composition and Structure of the Book of Revelation," *The Catholic Biblical Quarterly*, 39, iii (1977); Austin Farrer, *A Rebirth of Images: The Making of St. John's Apocalypse* (Boston: Beacon Press, 1963).

4. Among the most useful examples of such research are the essays by José María Arguedas and others in *Ideología mesiánica del mundo andino*, ed. Juan M. Ossio A. (Lima: Edición de Ignacio Prado Pastor, 1973). See also Mercedes López-Baralt, "Millenarism as Liminality: An Interpretation of the Andean Myth of Inkarrí," *Punto de Contacto/Point of Contact*, 6 (Spring 1979); Sabine MacCormack, "From the Sun of the Incas to the Virgin of Copacabana," *Representations*, 8 (1984), 30–60; Nathan Wachtel, *The Vision of the Vanquished: The Spanish Conquest of Peru through Indian Eyes 1530–1570*, trans. Ben and Siân Reynolds (New York: Barnes and Noble, 1977), Part III, Chapter I, "Revolts and Millenarianism," pp. 169–87, in which Wachtel discusses the Incan response to the destruction of their society with works of ideological restructuration; Renée Ribeiro, "Brazilian Messianic Movements," in *Millennial Dreams in Action: Essays in Comparative Study*, ed. Sylvia L. Thrupp (The Hague: Mouton, 1962); Ralph Della Cava, "Brazilian Messianism and National Institutions: A Reappraisal of Canudos and Joaseiro," *Hispanic American Historical Review*, 48, iii (1968). These last three are particularly relevant to Mario Vargas Llosa's apocalyptic novel, *La guerra del fin del mundo* (*The War of the End of the World*, 1981), which, of recent Latin American novels, presents perhaps the most specific integration of biblical and indigenous apocalyptic visions.

5. Mikhail Bakhtin, *Esthétique et théorie du roman* (Paris: Gallimard, 1978), p. 384.

The rather lackluster published translation of this phrase is as follows: "the special increase in density and concreteness of time markers – the time of human life, of historical time – that occurs within well-delineated spatial areas." *The Dialogic Imagination,* ed. Michael Holquist, trans. Caryl Emerson and Michael Holquist (Austin: University of Texas, 1981), p. 250.

6. John Barth, "The Literature of Exhaustion," *The Atlantic,* Aug. 1967, 29–34. I cite from the reprinted source: *The American Novel since World War II,* ed. Marcus Klein (New York: Fawcett, 1969), p. 277.

7. Walker Percy, "Notes for a Novel about the End of the World," *Katallagete,* 3 (Fall 1970), 9; reprinted in Percy's collected essays, *The Message in the Bottle* (New York: Farrar, Straus and Giroux, 1979), pp. 101–18.

8. Carlos Fuentes, *Terra Nostra,* trans. Margaret Sayers Peden (1975; New York: Farrar, Straus and Giroux, 1976), p. 771.

9. Christopher Columbus, in his letter to Doña Juana de la Torre, cites passages from Isaiah and Revelation which describe a new heaven and new earth, and the river of paradise: See *The Four Voyages of C. Columbus,* trans. J. M. Cohen (Baltimore: Penguin Books, 1969), pp. 365, 222, 224. In *The Book of Prophecies,* a compendium of excerpts from scripture, the church fathers, and miscellaneous prophets, Columbus interprets his own geographical explorations in the light of the dawn of a more perfect age. See Bernard McGinn, *Visions of the End: Apocalyptic Traditions in the Middle Ages* (New York: Columbia University Press, 1979), pp. 284–5; John Leddy Phelan, *The Millennial Kingdom of the Franciscans in the New World* (1956; rev. ed. Berkeley: University of California Press, 1970), p. 21.

10. Phelan, p. 107. For a discussion of the secular lure of America, see Walker Chapman, *The Golden Dream: Seekers of El Dorado* (New York: Bobbs-Merrill, 1967).

11. John Prest, *The Garden of Eden: The Botanic Garden and the Re-Creation of Paradise* (New Haven; Yale University Press, 1981), p. 42.

12. Phelan, p. 26.

13. There have been a number of studies on the Puritan apocalyptic mentality. See, for example, Michael McGiffert, *God's Plot: The Paradoxes of Puritan Piety* (Amherst, Massachusetts: University of Massachusetts Press, 1972); Sacvan Bercovitch, "The Typology of America's Mission," *American Quarterly,* 32 (Summer 1978), 135–55.

14. Phelan, p. 8. Phelan cites Mendieta's *Historia eclesiastic indiana* (México, D.F.: Editorial Salvadore Chávez Hayhoe, 1945), I, 25–6.

15. I trace the apocalyptic tradition in U.S. literature from the earliest Puritan texts to the contemporary novels of Nathanael West and Robert Coover in my essay, "The Apocalyptic Myth and the American Literary Imagination," in *The Apocalyptic Vision in America: Interdisciplinary Essays on Myth and Culture,* ed. Lois Parkinson Zamora (Bowling Green, Ohio: Bowling Green University Popular Press, 1982), pp. 97–138. R.W.B. Lewis also traces this tradition in his essay, "Days of Wrath and Laughter," in *Trials of the Word* (New Haven: Yale University Press, 1965), as does Douglas Robinson, in *American Apocalypses* (Baltimore: Johns Hopkins Press, 1985).

16. In the United States, this sense of eschatological destiny has at times caused the

mixing of religion and politics for questionable ends; see Ernest Lee Tuveson in *The Redeemer Nation: America's Millennial Role* (Chicago: University of Chicago Press, 1968). See also Ernest Cassara, "The Development of America's Sense of Mission," and Charles H. Lippy, "Waiting for the End: The Social Context of American Apocalyptic Religion," in *The Apocalyptic Vision in America,* ed. Zamora, pp. 64–96, 37–63.

17. The pseudonymity of testamentary apocalypse is a corollary of what I have called the scribal character of apocalypticism; the authority of the text's predictions is increased because it was supposedly written long before, by a respected forefather. When the predictions are attributed to an ancient author, what is really a veiled reference to contemporary events is made to seem like divinely accurate prophecy. An important recent edition of Hebrew apocalyptic writings is *The Old Testament Pseudepigrapha: Apocalyptic Literature and Testaments,* James H. Charlesworth, ed. (Garden City, N.Y.: Doubleday, 1983).

    On the issue of the pseudonymity of apocalyptic texts, G. B. Caird writes, "John's apocalypse is unlike the others. For one thing, Jewish apocalypses are pseudonymous; that is, they purport to have been written by some ancient worthy – Noah, Lemech, Enoch, Baruch, Schealtiel, Daniel, Ezra – who sealed up the message until the time when it should become relevant, the time of the actual author. But John writes openly in his own name for his own contemporaries. . . ." *A Commentary on the Revelation of St. John the Divine, Black's New Testament Commentaries,* ed. Henry Chadwick (London: Adam and Charles Black, 1966), p. 10. J. Massyngberde Ford asserts that Revelation is basically a Hebrew work with Christian redaction, but in spite of this quite plausible possibility, the fact remains that the narrator's identity is handled unconventionally in John's Revelation. *The Anchor Bible,* Revelation, trans., J. Massyngberde Ford, 38 (New York: Doubleday and Company, Inc., 1975), p. xxiii.

18. See H. H. Howley, *The Relevance of Apocalyptic: A Study of Jewish and Christian Apocalypses from Daniel to Revelation* (New York: Association Press, 1963), pp. 1–65; Paul D. Hanson, *The Dawn of Apocalyptic* (Philadelphia: Fortress Press, 1975).

19. See, for example, the collection of essays on the sociology of apocalypse in Sylvia L. Thrupp, ed., *Millennial Dreams in Action: Studies in Revolutionary Religious Movements* (New York: Schocken Books, 1980).

20. See Christopher Butler, *Number Symbolism* (New York: Barnes and Noble, 1970), especially Chapter 2, "The Early Medieval Period: Biblical Exegesis and World Schemes," pp. 22–46.

21. Northrop Frye, *Anatomy of Criticism: Four Essays* (Princeton: Princeton University Press, 1957), p. 136.

22. Roland Barthes, *Mythologies,* trans. Annette Lavers (1957; New York: Hill and Wang, 1972), p. 110.

23. Peter Brooks discusses narrative plot in ways which are suggestive for the apocalyptic narrations I will analyze here, referring to the beginning of plot as the prompting of desire. See *Reading for the Plot: Design and Intention in Narrative* (New York: Knopf, 1984).

24. In Revelation, the opprobrium of apostasy is often cast in sexual terms, the

most explicit image being the Whore of Babylon. Herbert N. Schneidau discusses the patriarchal orientation of biblical sexual imagery in terms of the Hebraic rejection of the polytheistic fertility cults. See Chapter 4, "The Paradigms of History and Paternity," in *Sacred Discontent; The Bible and Western Tradition* (Baton Rouge: Louisiana State University Press, 1977). Susan M. Bachmann provides an illuminating pyschological reading of Revelation from a feminist perspective in "Narrative Strategy in The Book of Revelation and D. H. Lawrence's *Apocalypse*," Dissertation, SUNY Buffalo, 1985.

25. Northrop Frye, *The Great Code: The Bible and Literature* (New York: Harcourt Brace Jovanovich, 1982), p. 138.

26. See E. M. Cioran, *Historia y utopía,* trans. Esther Seligson (1960; México, D.F.: Artífice Ediciones, 1981), pp. 80–101.

27. For a discussion of the specific historical events addressed in Revelation, see John M. Court, *Myth and History in the Book of Revelation* (Atlanta: John Knox Press, 1979).

28. See Claude Lévi-Strauss, "The Structural Study of Myth," in *Myth: A Symposium,* ed. Thomas A. Sebeok (Bloomington: Indiana University Press, 1955), pp. 81–106.

29. Henri Bergson, *Creative Evolution* (1907), trans. Arthur Mitchell (1911; reprint, New York: Modern Library, 1944), pp. 45–52.

30. See in particular Hayden White, "The Value of Narrativity in the Representation of Reality," *Critical Inquiry,* 7, i (1980), pp. 5–27.

31. This discussion has been intelligently carried forward by such theoretical studies as D.A. Miller's *Narrative and Its Discontents: Problems of Closure in the Traditional Novel* (1981), Marianna Torgovnick's *Closure in the Novel* (1981), and David H. Richter's *Fable's End: Completeness and Closure in Rhetorical Fiction* (1974). The works to which I have already referred by Robert Alter, Herbert N. Schneidau, and Northrop Frye are indispensable to any literary critical consideration of the contemporary fictional uses of biblical narrative. Gerald Hammond's two-part article, "The Bible and Literary Criticism," in *Critical Quarterly* (Summer and Fall, 1983), has also been provocative in suggesting the far-reaching implications and applications of current critical approaches to biblical literature.

Besides these studies, there have been a number of literary critical investigations of apocalyptic narration which are less generally theoretical than specifically textual. In the last ten years or so, we have had *Apocalyptic Visions Past and Present* (1988), edited by William Cloonan and Jo Ann James, a collection of essays on apocalyptic disclosure in literature and film; Thomas J. J. Altizer's *History as Apocalypse* (1985), a study of the classical and biblical foundations of the Christian epic; Douglas Robinson's discussion of nineteenth- and twentieth-century U.S. literature, *American Apocalypses: The Image of the End of the World in American Literature* (1985); Forrest S. Smith's *Secular and Sacred Visionaries in the Late Middle Ages* (1984), a study of works by such writers as Rutebeuf, Brunetto Latini, and Dante; *The Apocalypse in English Renaissance Thought and Literature* (1984), edited by C. A. Patrides and Joseph A. Wittreich, Jr.; Zbigniew Lewicki's survey of U. S. writers from Melville to Updike, *The Bang and the Whimper: Apocalypse and Entropy in American Literature* (1984);

Sarah Urang's *Kindled in the Flame: The Apocalyptic Scene in D. H. Lawrence* (1984); David G. Roskies's *Against the Apocalypse: Responses to Catastrophe in Modern Jewish Culture* (1984), a discussion of Jewish writers, intellectuals, and artists from the late nineteenth century to the present; Arthur Edward Salmon's *Poets of the Apocalypse* (1983), a study of selected twentieth-century British poetry; W. Warren Wagar's *Terminal Visions: The Literature of Last Things* (1982), a discussion of "public endtimes" in speculative literature; Lakshmi Mani's *The Apocalyptic Vision in Nineteenth-Century Fiction: A Study of Cooper, Hawthorne and Melville* (1981). Preceding these studies are Bernard McGinn's "textual history," *Visions of the End: Apocalyptic Traditions in the Middle Ages* (1979); John R. May's *Toward a New Earth: Apocalypse in the American Novel* (Notre Dame, 1972); and David Ketterer's study of the apocalyptic vision in science fiction, *New Worlds for Old: The Apocalyptic Imagination, Science Fiction, and American Literature* (Doubleday, 1974).

32. Useful inter-American comparative studies do of course exist. Of general interest are the comparative essays collected in the *Proceedings of the Xth Congress of the International Comparative Literature Association*, Vol. III, "Inter-American Literary Relations," ed. M. J. Valdés (New York, Garland Publishing, Inc., 1985); and *Actes du VIIe Congrès de l'Association International de Littérature Comparée: Littératures Américaines: Dépendance, indépendance, interdépendance*, eds. Milan V. Dimić and Juan Ferraté (Stuttgart: Bieber, 1979). See also Alfred J. MacAdam, *Textual Confrontations: Comparative Readings in Latin American Literature* (Chicago: University of Chicago Press, 1987); *Reinventing the Americas: Comparative Studies of Literature of the United States and Spanish America*, eds. Bell Gale Chevigny and Gari Laguardia (Cambridge: Cambridge University Press, 1986); and *Do the Americas Have a Common Literature?*, ed. Gustavo Pérez Firmat (Durham, NC: Duke University Press, forthcoming).

33. Angel Rama has discussed the history and difficulties of treating Latin American literature as an entity in "Un proceso autonómico: De las literaturas nacionales a la literatura latinoamericana," in *Homenaje a Angel Rosenblat en sus 70 años: Estudios filológicos y lingüísticos* (Caracas: Instituto Pedagógico, 1974), pp. 445–58; and "Autonomía literaria americana," *Sin nombre*, 12, 4 (1982), 7–24.

34. Carlos Fuentes, "A Harvard Commencement," in *Myself with Others: Selected Essays* (New York: Farrar, Straus and Giroux, 1988), p. 199.

García Márquez has commented in an interview, "I think my books have had political impact in Latin America because they help to create a Latin American identity; they help Latin Americans to become more aware of their own culture. . . . People often think that politics are elections, that politics are what governments do. But literature, cinema, painting and music are all essential to forging Latin America's identity. And that is what I mean by politics." Marlise Simmons, "García Márquez on Love, Plagues, and Politics," *New York Times Book Review*, 21 Feb. 1988, p. 23. In my conclusion, I will explicitly return to this question of the role of contemporary fiction in the creation of a Latin American communal identity.

35. "Every time I hear my leftist friends complain about North American penetration in Latin America I laugh into my coat lapels because the real cultural

penetration is that of Latin America into the United States." Interview with García Márquez by Enrique Fernández, *Village Voice,* 3 Jul. 1984.

36. Octavio Paz, "The Mexican Intelligentsia," in *The Labyrinth of Solitude: Life and Thought in Mexico,* trans. Lysander Kemp (1950; New York, Grove Press, 1962), pp. 172–3.

CHAPTER 2.

1. Alfred J. MacAdam, *Modern Latin American Narratives: The Dreams of Reason* (Chicago: University of Chicago Press, 1977), p. 87.
2. Frank Kermode, *The Sense of an Ending: Studies in the Theory of Fiction* (New York: Oxford University Press, 1967), p. 167. See my reference to Arendt's discussion in Note 3 of Chapter 1.
3. By this assertion, I do not mean to minimize the extent to which García Márquez's fiction is grounded in, and specifically addresses, Colombian history and politics. In this regard, see Stephen Minta, *García Márquez: Writer of Colombia* (New York: Harper and Row, 1987), and Lucila Inés Mena, "*Cien años de soledad:* Novela de 'La violencia,'" *Hispamérica,* V, No. 1 (1976), 3–23.
4. Gregory Rabassa, "Beyond Magic Realism: Thoughts on the Art of Gabriel García Márquez," *Books America,* 47 (1973), p. 450.
5. Gabriel García Márquez, *One Hundred Years of Solitude,* trans. Gregory Rabassa (1967; New York: Avon Books, 1971), pp. 382–3. Subsequent references are cited parenthetically in the text.
6. Discussions of the cyclical elements of *One Hundred Years of Solitude* abound. See, for example, Carmen Arnau, *El mundo mítico de Gabriel García Márquez* (Barcelona: Editorial Península, 1971), pp. 129, 131–2; Ricardo Gullón, *García Márquez o el olvidado arte de contar* (Madrid: Editorial Taurus, 1979), p. 27; G. D. Carillo, "Lo cíclico en *Cien años de soledad,*" *Razón y Fábula,* 23 (1973), 18–32; Roberto Paoli, "Carnavalesco y tiempo cíclico en *Cien años de soledad,*" *Revista Iberoamericana,* Nos. 128–9 (1984), 979–98. Michael Palencia-Roth discusses the apocalyptic archetypes in the novel, contrasting, as I do, the linear to the cyclical, in *Gabriel García Márquez: La línea, el círculo y las metamórphoses del mito* (Madrid: Gredos, 1983).
7. Mikhail Bakhtin, *The Dialogic Imagination,* ed. Michael Holquist, trans. Caryl Emerson and Michael Holquist (1975; Austin: University of Texas Press, 1981), p. 248.
8. Georges Poulet, *Studies in Human Time,* trans. Elliott Coleman (1949; Baltimore: Johns Hopkins Press, 1956), p. 29. Poulet says that the modern time sense, as opposed to the romantic time sense which characterizes the Buendías, is based on the feeling that "any moment can be realized as a new moment, and that time can always be freely created from the present moment forward. . . . Each instant appears as the instant of a choice."

   The Buendías's temporal dilemma has been submitted to psychoanalytic investigation by Josefina Ludmer, *Cien años de soledad: Una interpretación* (Buenos Aires: Editorial Tiempo Contemporáneo, 1972).
9. The short story "One Day after Saturday" is, like "Big Mama's Funeral," a

comic treatment of apocalyptic expectation. Father Antonio Isabel de Santísimo Sacramento del Altar, the ninety-four-year-old priest of Macondo, experiences another kind of rain, this time of dead birds, and he tries in vain to remember if there was such a plague described in Revelation. He locates the agent of the catastrophe: A peasant boy, in Macondo because he has missed his train, whom the befuddled priest labels The Wandering Jew. The plague of the dead birds reappears in *One Hundred Years of Solitude,* as does Padre Antonio Isabel, who again gives his "apocalyptic chat," inspired by The Wandering Jew (this time an old man with wings). In another early work, however, García Márquez's treatment of apocalyptic concerns is hardly comic: The epigraph of *Leaf Storm* (1955) is from *Antigone,* and its short italicized prologue describes the "whirlwind" of the U.S. banana company and the leaf storm which follows it into Macondo. (The word *hojarasca,* which is translated as leaf storm, has the connotation of a collection of useless and insubstantial items and elements – trash, rubbish, waste.) The entire novel is written in the same cataclysmic register as the final pages of *One Hundred Years of Solitude:* Whereas the biblical hurricane which ultimately sweeps Macondo away arrives only at the end of the later novel, the metaphoric leaf storm pervades the earlier novel from its opening paragraph.

10. Otto Plöger, *Theocracy and Eschatology,* trans. S. Rudman (Richmond: John Knox Press, 1964), pp. 9–10, 65.

   It is this apocalyptic policy that leads Martin Buber to argue that the biblical apocalyptist fails to engage the factual immediacy of human history; and it leads Robert Alter to suggest that apocalyptic thinking produces literature which withdraws from the "complexities and threats of history." The assertions would seem to ignore the radical political evolution of post-Joachimite apocalyptic thought, which I will discuss in the context of the fiction of Walker Percy and Carlos Fuentes. And though Alter's statement is no doubt partially tenable in its suggestion that visions of apocalypse may lead to literary and political resignation, it ignores a good deal of contemporary literature that does not. We will see that contemporary visions of apocalypse in Latin America are more likely to result in fiction that is formally and thematically critical and even subversive than passively tolerant or escapist in its attitude toward historical reality. Martin Buber, "Prophecy, Apocalyptic, and the Historical Hour," in *Pointing the Way: Collected Essays,* trans. and ed. Maurice Friedman (New York: Harper, 1957), pp. 192–207; Robert Alter, "The Apocalyptic Temper," in *After the Tradition* (New York: E. P. Dutton, 1969), p. 57; see also "The New American Novel," *Commentary* 60, no. 5 (November 1975), pp. 44–51.

11. Plöger, pp. 47–50, 108–12.

12. Earl Rovit, "American Literature and the American Experience," *American Quarterly,* 13 (Summer 1961), pp. 118–19.

13. Octavio Paz, *The Labyrinth of Solitude,* trans. Lysander Kemp (1950; New York: Grove Press, 1961), p. 208.

14. Gabriel García Márquez and Mario Vargas Llosa, *La Novela en América Latina: Diálogo* (Lima: Carlos Milla Batres/Ediciones Universidad Nacional de Ingeniería, 1968), p. 53.

In Luis Harss and Barbara Dohmann, *Into the Mainstream* (1966; New York: Harper Colophon, 1969), García Márquez says, "When I first read Faulkner, I thought: 'I must become a writer.'" Harss and Dohman conclude: "The chaotic materials that went into Faulknerian art, he says, were much like the raw stuff of life in Colombia. Faulkner showed him how this elemental turbulence could be manipulated and transformed" (pp. 322–3); in *La Novela en América Latina: Diálogo,* cited above, García Márquez says, "I believe that the greatest debt that we Latin American novelists have is to Faulkner . . . Faulkner is present in all Latin American fiction; I believe that . . . the great difference between our grandfathers . . . and us is Faulkner; he was the only thing that happened between the two generations" (p. 52, my translation); see also Mario Vargas Llosa, "García Márquez: De Aracataca a Macondo," in *Nueve Asedios a García Márquez* (Santiago de Chile: Editorial Universitaria, 1972), p. 140; Armando Durán, "Conversaciones con Gabriel García Márquez," in *Sobre García Márquez,* ed. Pedro Simón Martínez (Montevideo: Biblioteca de Marca, 1971), p. 34.

15. Roberto González Echevarría argues that, among Latin American writers, it is Carpentier who has had the greatest influence on contemporary Latin American fiction; he names García Márquez and Fuentes as among those most influenced by Carpentier. "Historia y alegoría en la narrativa de Carpentier," *Cuadernos Americanos,* No. 228 (1980), 200–20.

16. Carlos Fuentes to Christopher Sharp in *W,* a supplement to *Women's Wear Daily,* 29 October 1976, p. 9.

17. Jonathan Tittler, "Interview with Carlos Fuentes," *Diacritics,* 10, iii (1980), 52.

18. For a more general treatment of the reception of Faulkner in Latin America, see Arnold Chapman, *The Spanish American Reception of United States Fiction, 1920–1940* (Berkeley: University of California Press, 1966).

19. García Márquez has said that *Absalom, Absalom!* is the novel by Faulkner that has most interested him. See William Kennedy, "The Yellow Trolley Car in Barcelona and Other Visions," *The Atlantic Monthly,* Jan. 1973, p. 57.

20. Hayden White, "The Value of Narrativity in the Representation of Reality," *Critical Inquiry,* 7, i (1980), p. 5. See also by Hayden White, *Metahistory: The Historical Imagination in Nineteenth-Century Europe* (Baltimore: Johns Hopkins University Press, 1973), and *Tropics of Discourse: Essays in Cultural Criticism* (Baltimore: Johns Hopkins University Press, 1978).

21. Peter Brooks, "Fictions of the Wolfman: Freud and Narrative Understanding," *Diacritics,* 9, i (1979), 72–81. See also Brooks's article, "Incredulous Narration: *Absalom, Absalom!,*" *Comparative Literature,* 34, iii (1982), 247–68, in which Quentin's narrative attempts to connect past to present are seen in psychological terms as his need to establish his relationship to his father(s), terms suggestive of another similarity between *Absalom, Absalom!* and *One Hundred Years of Solitude.*

22. William Faulkner, *Absalom, Absalom!* (New York: Modern Library, 1936), pp. 8, 38. Subsequent quotations from this novel are cited parenthetically in the text.

Yoknapatawpha is not, of course, unsettled territory when Sutpen arrives; in *The Bear,* Faulkner looks back further to a time when the land was yet undefiled by European usurpers, when the primitive world of nature and its Chickasaw inhabitants existed in a state of equilibrium.

23. The Puritan uses of the myth of apocalypse have been much commented upon: See, for example, Sacvan Bercovitch, *The American Jeremiad* (Madison, Wisconsin: University of Wisconsin Press, 1978); James W. Davidson, *The Logic of Millennial Thought: Eighteenth-Century New England* (New Haven: Yale University Press, 1977); Ernest R. Sandeen, *The Roots of Fundamentalism: British and American Millenarianism, 1800–1930* (Chicago: University of Chicago Press, 1970). See also the chapter, "A Puritan Tragedy: *Absalom, Absalom!*," in Peter Swiggart, *The Art of Faulkner's Novels* (Austin, Texas: University of Texas Press, 1962).

24. There have been numerous critical examinations of *Absalom, Absalom!* in terms of tragedy. See Cleanth Brooks, "*Absalom, Absalom!* The Definition of Innocence," *Sewanee Review*, 59 (Autumn, 1951), 543–58; Walter L. Sullivan, "The Tragic Design of *Absalom, Absalom!*," *South Atlantic Quarterly*, 50 (October, 1954), 552–66.

    John Paterson denies the tragic nature of the novel in "Hardy, Faulkner, and the Prosaics of Tragedy," *Centennial Review*, V (1961), 160–75. Comparing *Absalom, Absalom!* to *The Mayor of Casterbridge*, Paterson writes, "With the grisly death of Thomas Sutpen, however, the light goes out as if forever. Succeeded not by the Farfraes and Elizabeths, those pledges of a peaceful and pious future, but by a totally demoralized Quentin Compson, Sutpen passes on not a new and better world born out of the violence and ashes of the old, but a ruined universe incapable of regeneration."

    See Kermode, pp. 25*ff.*, for a discussion of the relative natures of tragedy and apocalypse.

25. Shreve participates, of course, in Quentin's narrativizing of history, but he is beyond the scope of my discussion because he is not exiled from the world he describes, nor does he have any real moral stake in it. He is not, in short, an apocalyptic narrator in the way that Quentin, Miss Rosa, and Mr. Compson decidedly are.

    For specific treatments of Shreve's narration, see Terence Doody, *Confession and Community in the Novel* (Baton Rouge: Louisiana State University Press, 1980), pp. 173–84, and Lynn G. Levins, "The Four Narrative Perspectives in Faulkner's *Absalom, Absalom!*," *PMLA*, 86 (January 1970), 35–47.

26. Several critics have dwelt on Sutpen's history as a paradigm for the history of the South: Examples are Donald M. Kartiganer, "Faulkner's *Absalom, Absalom!:* The Discovery of Values," *American Literature*, 37 (November, 1965), 291; F. Garvin Davenport, Jr., *The Myth of Southern History: Historical Consciousness in Twentieth-Century Literature* (Nashville: Vanderbilt University Press, 1970).

27. In Marta Gallo, "El futuro perfecto de Macondo," *Revista Hispánica Moderna*, 38 (1974–1975), 115–35, the author analyzes the grammatical structure of the first sentence of *One Hundred Years of Solitude* and finds its future perfect tense to contain a paradigm of the novel.

28. During Melquíades's days of feverish scribbling, we are told that the only words distinguishable in the "rocky paragraphs" are "equinox" and the name

of Alexander von Humboldt. The first may suggest the temporal balance implied by Aureliano Babilonia's assertion that Melquíades has concentrated a century of daily episodes in one instant. The second, a German naturalist and traveller (1769–1859), was a great observer and namer of the South American New World. His *Kosmos* is not only a graphic description but also an imaginative conception of the physical world that prefigures Melquíades's narrative intention (and García Márquez's achievement).

For an exhaustive treatment of the implications of Melquíades's Sanskrit parchments, see Victor Farías, *Los manuscritos de Melquíades: Cien años de soledad, burguesía latinoamericana y dialéctica de la reproducción ampliada de negación* (Frankfurt/Main: Verlag Klaus Dieter Vervuert, 1981).

29. Roland Barthes, *Mythologies,* trans. Annette Lavers (1957; New York: Hill and Wang, 1972), p. 125.

30. It has been suggested that Aureliano Babilonia is Melquíades's alter ego or perhaps García Márquez's ideal reader. See George R. McMurray, *Gabriel García Márquez* (New York: Frederick Ungar Publishing Co., 1977), p. 87: "the 'speaking mirror,' into which [Aureliano] gazes upon reaching the last page, implies his perfect communication with his double, Melquíades."

31. I have discussed this novel in detail in "Ends and Endings in García Márquez's *Crónica de una muerte anunciada,*" *Latin American Literary Review,* 13, No. 25 (1985), 104–16.

32. Quoted in *Writers at Work: The Paris Review Interviews* (New York: The Viking Press, 1958), p. 141.

33. Hershel Parker and Henry Binder, "Exigencies of Composition and Publication: *Billy Budd, Sailor* and *Pudd'nhead Wilson,*" *Nineteenth-Century Fiction,* 30, i (1978), 131–43.

34. Marlise Simmons, "A Talk with Gabriel García Márquez," *New York Times Book Review,* 5 Dec. 1982, p. 7.

35. Kermode, p. 12. Kermode discusses in detail the defining of the myth of transition by Joachim of Fiore in the twelfth century; the Sibylline emperor cults enlarged the concept of the transitional period with their belief that the period would see not only the coming of the Antichrist but also the coming of a "knight faithful and true," the last emperor of the earth. I will return to Joachim and the Sibylline cults in my discussion of Walker Percy and Carlos Fuentes.

36. Two beasts appear during the period of transition described in Revelation. The first reigns for forty-two months – three and a half years; the second, the duration of whose reign is not stated, probably represents the priesthood of the imperial cult. John describes the second beast: "And I beheld another beast coming up out of the earth; and he had two horns like a lamb, and he spake as a dragon. And he exerciseth all the power of the first beast before him, and causeth the earth and them which dwell therein to worship the first beast . . ." (Rev. 13:11–12). *The Interpreter's Bible* (New York: Abingdon Press, 1957), pp. 12, 460–4.

37. García Márquez, *The Autumn of the Patriarch,* trans. Gregory Rabassa (New York: Harper and Row, 1975), p. 86. Subsequent references are cited in the text.

38. Kermode, pp. 101–2.
39. Marlise Simmons, "A Talk with García Márquez," p. 7.
40. García Márquez, Nobel Prize Acceptance Speech, *Proceso*, No. 319 (13 diciembre de 1982), p. 46. Translated by Marina Castañeda, *The New York Times*, 6 Feb. 1983, sec. 4, p. 17.

CHAPTER 3.

1. Octavio Paz, *The Labyrinth of Solitude: Life and Thought in Mexico,* trans. Lysander Kemp (1950; New York: Grove Press, 1962), p. 211.
2. Bertrand Russell, in *Religion and Science* (London: Oxford University Press, 1949), p. 81, writes: "There is no law of cosmic progress, but only an oscillation upward and downward, with a slow trend downward on the balance owing to the diffusion of energy." The more direct philosophical precursor of contemporary North American novelists of entropy is Henry Adams, as is clear in Chapter 25 of *The Education of Henry Adams* (1907) and in his posthumously published essays, *The Degradation of Democratic Dogma* (New York: Capricorn Books, 1958).

   See Tony Tanner, "The American Novelist as Entropologist," *The London Magazine,* 10:7 (October 1970), 5–18, for a general discussion of entropy as a novelistic metaphor in North American fiction. Zbigniew Lewicki discusses entropy as a literary concept in *The Bang and the Whimper: Apocalypse and Entropy in American Literature* (Westport, Connecticut: Greenwood Press, 1984), which includes a chapter on Thomas Pynchon.
3. Irving Howe, "Mass Society and Post-Modern Fiction," *Partisan Review* (Summer, 1959), 420–36. Reprinted in *The American Novel since World War II,* ed. Marcus Klein (New York: Fawcett Publications, 1969), p. 130. Citations from the reprinted source.
4. In "The Crisis in Culture," Hannah Arendt writes, "Mass culture comes into being when mass society seizes upon cultural objects, and its danger is that the life process of society (which like all biological processes insatiably draws everything available into the cycle of its metabolism) will literally consume the cultural objects, eat them up and destroy them. Of course I am not referring to mass distribution. . . . This does not mean that culture spreads to the masses, but that culture is being destroyed in order to yield entertainment. The result of this is not disintegration but decay. . . ." *Between Past and Future: Eight Exercises in Political Thought* (1961; reprint, New York: Viking, 1969), p. 207.
5. Thomas Pynchon, *Slow Learner* (Boston: Little, Brown and Co., 1984), p. 5.
6. For several discussions of the concept of entropy, see Norbert Wiener, *The Human Use of Human Beings: Cybernetics and Society,* 2nd ed. (Garden City, New York: Doubleday, 1969); P.C.W. Davies, *Space and Time in the Modern Universe* (Cambridge: Cambridge University Press, 1977), Chapter 3, "The Asymmetry of Past and Future." A study consonant with Pynchon's pessimistic use of entropy as a metaphor for social disintegration is Jeremy Rifkin, *Entropy* (New York: Viking Press, 1980).

   For a useful treatment of a variety of mythological structures in Pynchon's fiction, see Kathryn Hume, *Pynchon's Mythography: An Approach to Gravity's Rainbow* (Carbondale: Southern Illinois University Press, 1987).

7. Pynchon, "Entropy," *Kenyon Review,* 23 (Winter, 1960), 281. Subsequent page references are cited in the text. Pynchon's early stories, including this one, have been collected in *Slow Learner;* I cite, however, from the original sources.

8. Pynchon, "Under the Rose," *Noble Savage,* 3 (1961), 224. Subsequent page references are cited in the text.

9. Pynchon, *V.* (1963; New York: Bantam Books, 1964), p. 431. This comment is made by Stencil, Sr., who continues, "Ten million dead. Gas. Passchendaele. Let that be now a large figure, now a chemical formula, now an historical account. But dear lord, not the *Nameless Horror,* the sudden prodigy sprung on a world unaware" (431). Stencil's "Nameless Horror" resembles the "Force" which Propentine recognizes: Both refer to the entropic disintegration they perceive so acutely.

10. William Burroughs, *Naked Lunch* (New York: Grove Press, 1959), pp. 223–4.

11. Pynchon, *The Crying of Lot 49* (1966; New York: Bantam Books, 1967), p. 5.
    For a useful discussion of paranoia in Pynchon's historical fictions, see Thomas H. Schaub, *Pynchon: The Voice of Ambiguity* (Urbana: University of Illinois Press, 1981), Chapter 4, pp. 76–102.

12. Henry Adams, "A Letter to American Teachers of History," in *The Degradation of Democratic Dogma,* p. 138. In this essay, Adams outlines the development and implications of the idea of entropy, starting with the publication of William Thompson's article, "On a Universal Tendency in Nature to the Dissipation of Mechanical Energy," in October, 1852, in which "this young man of twenty-eight . . . tossed the universe into the ash-heap . . ." (pp. 137–8). Adams explains that physicists soon gave their support to Thompson's theory, "but to the vulgar and ignorant historian it meant only that the ash-heap was constantly increasing in size; while the public understood little and cared less about Entropy, and the literary class know only that the Newtonian universe, in which they had been cradled, admitted no loss of energy in the solar system, where the planets, at the end of their planetary years, returned exactly to their positions at the beginning" (p. 138).

13. Pynchon, "Mortality and Mercy in Vienna," *Epoch,* 9 (Spring 1959), 199.
    To take the names of Pynchon's characters too seriously can be misleading. Nevertheless, the name Lupescu resembles and suggests the name of Stephane Lupasco, whose book *Logic and Contradiction* (1947) proposes radical changes in traditional methods of reasoning. In particular he introduces into bipolar logic, where everything was either true or false and thus subject to objective proof, the possibilities of accident, chance, and feeling. Because feelings are discontinuous and illogical and nonsequential, they are excluded from the old system of logic. Lupasco insists that logic no longer can deal exclusively in rational certainties: Thus, his name, and the name of Pynchon's character, "the man . . . possessed by the heart of a darkness . . ." (212).

14. Callisto's name derives from the Latin verb, to stand still, and, it has been argued, from the Spanish masterpiece by Fernando de Rojas, *La Celestina* (1499), a work to which I will return in my chapter on Carlos Fuentes. See Peter L. Lays and Robert Redfield, "Pynchon's Spanish Source for 'Entropy'," *Studies*

in Short Fiction, 16, *iv* (1979), 327–34. Another allusion relevant in my comparative context is to Remedios Varo, the Spanish-born Mexican painter. See David Cowart, "Pynchon's *The Crying of Lot 49* and the Painting of Remedios Varo," *Critique*, 18, *iii* (1977), 19–26.

15. Earl Rovit, "On the Contemporary Apocalyptic Imagination," *The American Scholar*, 37, *iii* (1968), 454.

16. R. W. B. Lewis suggests that the term, the "whole sick crew," is perhaps adapted from the Puritan tract *The Day of Doom* (1662), by the New Englander Michael Wigglesworth, who refers to the "sinful crew." This suggestion is supported by the fact that at the end of the novel, Benny Profane runs hand in hand into the Mediterranean with one Brenda *Wigglesworth*. See Lewis, "Days of Wrath and Laughter," in *Trials of the Word* (New Haven: Yale University Press, 1965), p. 204.

17. The equations for the statistical probability of information transmission and for increasing entropy are identical. This fact is mentioned in *The Crying of Lot 49* in the context of a discussion of a nineteenth-century experiment devised by the Scottish scientist, James Clerk Maxwell (62), and again as Oedipa contemplates the replica of Maxwell's Demon, produced by a Berkeley inventor, John Nefastis: "For John Nefastis (to take a recent example) two kinds of entropy, thermodynamic and informational, happened, say by coincidence, to look alike, when you wrote them down as equations" (80). For a detailed discussion of Maxwell's Demon, see Anne Mangel, "Maxwell's Demon, Entropy, Information: *The Crying of Lot 49*," *Tri-Quarterly*, 20 (1971), 194–208.

18. Richard Pearce calls the end of this novel a "climax if not a conclusion." Similarly, in his discussion of the endings of Pynchon's other novels, he can make no assertion without qualification, concluding that "Each ending, then, may be read in diametrically opposing ways. . . ." Mr. Pearce finds this indeterminancy to be rooted in a parodic impulse; I would agree, but add that, on a more basic level, it is attributable to the entropic ethic and esthetic under discussion here. "Pynchon's Endings," *Novel*, 18, *ii* (1985), pp 145–53.

19. Rudolph Arnheim, *Entropy and Art: An Essay on Disorder and Order* (Berkeley: University of California Press, 1971), p. 26.

20. Pynchon, *Gravity's Rainbow* (New York: The Viking Press, 1973), p. 105. Subsequent page references are cited in the text.

21. David Riesman, "The Themes of Work and Play in the Structure of Freud's Thought," in *Individualism Reconsidered* (Glencoe: Free Press, 1954), p. 325.

22. Rovit, p. 462.

23. I have contrasted Pynchon's attitude toward popular language to the attitudes of several contemporary Latin American novelists in "Clichés and Defamiliarization in the Fiction of Manuel Puig and Luis Rafael Sánchez," *Journal of Aesthetics and Art Criticism*, 44, *iv* (1983), 421–36.

24. The Argentine novelist Ernesto Sábato, who earned a doctorate in theoretical physics, specifically repudiates entropy as a useful metaphor for human activity. Instead, he uses apocalyptic metaphors liberally in his fiction, and his novel, *Abaddón, el exterminador* (1974), takes its title from the avenging angel in Revelation 9:11. See Joaquin Neyre, *Ernesto Sábato* (Buenos Aires: Ediciones Culturales Argentinas, 1973), pp. 105–23.

25. José Lezama Lima, *Algunos tratados en La Habana* (Barcelona: Editorial Anagrama, 1971), p. 102.
26. "Interview with Loic Bouvard," in *Lion in the Garden: Interviews with William Faulkner 1926–1962*, eds. James B. Meriweather and Michael Millgate (New York: Random House, 1968), p. 72. I am grateful to Dan Garver for his observations on Adams and Bergson in his unpublished paper, "Creative Evolution in Faulkner's Modernism versus Entropy in Pynchon's Postmodernism."
27. Hugh Kenner, *A Homemade World: The American Modernist Writers* (New York: William Morrow and Company, 1975), p. 212.
28. Henri Bergson, *Creative Evolution* (1907), trans. Arthur Mitchell (1911; reprint, New York: Modern Library, 1944), p. 45. Subsequent page references are cited in the text.
29. William Faulkner, *The Sound and the Fury* (New York: Random House, 1946), pp. 102, 105.

CHAPTER 4.

1. In this respect, Cortázar is in the modern tradition that begins with William Blake. The importance of the metaphor of apocalypse for the Romantic poets has been discussed by M. H. Abrams in *Natural Supernaturalism: Tradition and Revolution in Romantic Literature* (New York: W. W. Norton, 1975), and by Mario Praz in *The Romantic Agony* (London: Oxford University Press, 1951). See also Eleanor Wilner, *Gathering the Winds: Visionary Imagination and Radical Transformation of Self and Society* (Baltimore: Johns Hopkins University Press, 1975), a study of William Blake, Thomas Lovell Beddoes, and Karl Marx.
2. Austin Farrer, *A Rebirth of Images: The Making of St. John's Apocalypse* (1949; reprint, Boston: Beacon Press, 1963), pp. 17–18.
3. D. H. Lawrence, "Apocalypse," in *Phoenix: The Posthumous Papers of D. H. Lawrence,* ed. Edward D. McDonald (1931; New York: The Viking Press, 1964). The complete writings of Lawrence on apocalypse are contained in *Apocalypse and the Writings on Revelation,* ed. Mara Kalnins (Cambridge: Cambridge University Press, 1980).
4. Earl Rovit discusses apocalyptic myth in terms of its spatial nature, arguing, as does Lawrence, that it "is most revolutionary in that it provides a fully 'open-ended' form, circumferential without being what we normally think of as circular and spherical." "On the Contemporary Apocalyptic Imagination," *The American Scholar*, 37, iii (1968), 464–5.
5. Cortázar's narrative structures are organized according to techniques of juxtaposition, montage, interpolation, rather than linear progression, creating structures that have been termed *spatial* after an influential essay by Joseph Frank; more recently, literary analysis based on semiotic theory has focused attention on the text as a spatial model in which time is a function of space, event a function of the spatial perspectives from which it is perceived and rendered. See Joseph Frank, "Spatial Form in Modern Literature," *Sewanee Review*, 53 (Spring, Summer, Fall, 1945), 221–40, 433–56, 643–53; reprinted in condensed form in *The Widening Gyre: Crisis and Mastery in Modern Literature* (New Brunswick, New Jersey: Rutgers University Press, 1963); and Jurij M.

Lotman's discussion of spatial modeling in "On the Metalanguage of a Typological Description of Culture," *Semiotica,* 14, *ii* (1975), 97–123.

6. Carlos Fuentes, "Julio Cortázar, 1914–1984: The Simón Bolivar of the Novel," *New York Times Book Review,* 4 March 1984, p. 10.

7. Interview with Antonio Marimon and Braulio Peralta in the Mexico City newspaper, *Uno más uno,* 3 marzo 1983, p. 15.

8. Using spatial metaphors, Cortázar describes the artist's responsibility – and compulsion – to cause "an explosion that opens wide a much larger reality," to find the "opening" through which to project his or her dynamic vision. See Cortázar's essay, "Algunos aspectos del cuento," *Cuadernos Hispanoamericanos,* 255 (1973), 406–7.

9. Julio Cortázar, "The Pursuer," in *End of the Game,* trans. Paul Blackburn (1964; New York: Pantheon Books, 1967), p. 199. Subsequent references to "Blow-up" and "The Pursuer" are from this edition.

10. Cortázar's use of this phrase may be construed ironically, because John in the Book of Revelation exhorts his contemporaries to be faithful to Christ in that time of persecution, even if they must suffer martyrdom. Johnny Carter is not faithful to a religious ideal but to his art, and to death itself, hoping to find answers in death that he has found only incompletely in life. The full passage from Revelation 2:10 is: "Fear none of those things which thou shalt suffer: behold, the devil shall cast some of you into prison, that ye may be tried; and ye shall have tribulation ten days: be thou faithful unto death, and I will give thee a crown of life."

11. Claude Lévi-Strauss, *The Raw and the Cooked,* trans. John and Doreen Weightman (1964; New York: Harper & Row, 1969), pp. 15–16.

12. The comparative connection between Dylan Thomas and Cortázar has been explored by Hugo J. Verani, "Las máscaras de la nada: *Apocalipsis* de Dylan Thomas y 'El perseguidor' de Julio Cortázar," *Cuadernos Americanos,* 227 (1979), 234–47.

13. See Susan M. Bachmann, "Narrative Strategy in the Book of Revelation and D. H. Lawrence's *Apocalypse,*" Dissertation, SUNY Buffalo, 1984.

14. Octavio Paz, *The Bow and the Lyre: The Poem. The Poetic Revelation. Poetry and History,* trans. Ruth L. C. Simms (1956; New York: McGraw-Hill, 1975), p. 121. Subsequent references are noted in the text.

15. I have discussed a number of Cortázar's artist/protagonists in "Voyeur/Voyant: Julio Cortázar's Spatial Esthetic," *Mosaic,* 14, *iv* (1981), 45–68.

16. Cortázar, *Hopscotch,* trans. Gregory Rabassa (1963; New York: Avon Books, 1966), p. 489. Subsequent page references are noted in the text.

17. Fuentes, "Julio Cortázar, 1914–1984: The Simón Bolivar of the Novel," p. 10.

18. Cortázar, *Territorios* (México, D.F.: Siglo Veintiuno Editores, 1978), p. 96, my translation.

19. Cortázar states, "You know well that in *Hopscotch* there are very few, or practically no allusions of a historical or political sort. . . . I was completely consumed by literary and esthetic concerns, and my interest in historical process did not go beyond a theoretical sympathy or a knowledge which came from reading the classics. . . . I had absolutely no personal commitment. . . .

The change which would necessarily be reflected in my writing occurred when I became aware of the Cuban revolution." *Uno más uno,* 3 marzo 1983, p. 15, my translation.

20. Paz, "Revolt, Revolution, Rebellion," in *Alternating Current,* trans. Helen R. Lane (1967; New York: Seaver Books, 1967), p. 142.

21. Cortázar, "Reunión," in *Todos los fuegos el fuego* (Buenos Aires: Editorial Sudamericana, 1974), pp. 74–5. Some of the stories from this collection were published in *End of the Game,* but this one has not been published in English. The translations in the text are mine.

22. I do not mean to suggest that the structure of the story is itself closed off or circumscribed by that ideal end: The "design" to which the narrator refers may be considered a Cortázarian *figura,* conditioning the text's openness to multiple and shifting perspectives. Cortázar's growing commitment to Marxist socialism never implied a shift to the techniques of social realism. He rejected writing that was dictated by revolutionary theory, saying that he wished to be among the revolutionaries of literature, not the literary men of the revolution. Steven Boldy addresses the tension between political commitment and serious literary experimentation in Cortázar's fiction and in his statements about his fiction: *The Novels of Julio Cortázar* (Cambridge: Cambridge University Press, 1980), pp. 161–5.

   For Cortázar's discussion of socialism and literature, see, "La literatura en la revolución y revolución en la literature," in a collection of related articles under that title by Oscar Collazos, Julio Cortázar, and Mario Vargas Llosa (México, D. F.: Siglo Veintiuno Editores, 1971), and *Viaje alrededor de una mesa* (Buenos Aires: Editorial Rayuela, 1970).

23. Georg Lukács, *History and Class Consciousness: Studies in Marxist Dialectics,* trans. Rodney Livingston (1923; Cambridge: MIT Press, 1971), p. xxxv. The "Preface to the New Edition," from which I cite, was written in 1967 to introduce the reprinted German edition.

24. This connection between Judeo-Christian eschatology and Marxism has been influentially asserted by Karl Löwith in *Meaning in History* (Chicago: University of Chicago Press, 1949), Chapter 2, "Marx," pp. 33–51; and by Walter Schmithals, *The Apocalyptic Movement, Introduction and Interpretation,* trans. John E. Steely (Nashville: Abingdon Press, 1975), who asserts: "Marx himself occupied the position of apocalyptist. His missionary consciousness has a prophetic format, his vision the character of revelation, which, to be sure, in harmony with the secular point of view, is worked out as a science" (p. 238).

25. Cortázar, "Apocalypse at Solentiname," in *A Change of Light and Other Stories,* trans. Gregory Rabassa (New York: Knopf, 1980), p. 121. The stories in this collection were originally published in two separate collections, *Alguien que anda por ahí* (1977) and *Octaedro* (1974). "Apocalypse at Solentiname" is from the former.

26. Saul Sosnowski compares "Blow-up" to "Apocalypse at Solentiname" in "Imágenes del deseo: El testigo ante su mutación," *INTI,* Nos. 9–10 (1980), pp. 93–7.

27. This biographical information is taken from Jose Promis Ojeda et al., *Ernesto*

Cardenal: Poeta de la liberación latinoamericana (Buenos Aires: Fernando Garcia Cambeiro, 1975).

28. Ernesto Cardenal, *Nueva antología poética: Ernesto Cardenal* (México, D.F.: Siglo Veintiuno Editores, 1978), p. 94, my translation.

29. Cardenal, "Apocalypse," in *Apocalypse and Other Poems,* eds. Robert Pring-Mill and Donald D. Walsh, trans. Thomas Merton, Kenneth Rexroth, et al. (New York: New Directions, 1977), pp. 33–7. "Apocalypse" is translated by Robert Pring-Mill; it was originally published in *Oración por Marilyn Monroe y otros poemas* (1965).

30. Eric Nepomunceno, *Uno más uno,* 3 Marzo 1983, p. 7. An anthology of Cortázar's "denunciatory literature" has been collected under the title *Textos políticos* (Barcelona: Plaza & Janés, 1984).

The volumes published in 1980 and 1983 are Cortázar's final collections of short stories, but a collection of miscellaneous writings, primarily poems and short nonfiction prose pieces, has been published posthumously under the title of *Salvo el crepúsculo* (México, D.F.: Editorial Nueva Imagen, 1984). One of the poems, "Los vitrales de Bourges," takes its epigraph from Revelation.

31. The violations of human rights by the military government in Argentina in the late 1970s are being fully exposed. See, for example, John Simpson and Jana Bennett, *The Disappeared: Voices from a Secret War* (London: Robson Books, 1985).

32. Cortázar, "We Love Glenda So Much," in *We Love Glenda So Much,* trans. Gregory Rabassa (1980; New York: Knopf, 1983), p. 10. Subsequent page references are noted in the text.

33. Milan Kundera, *The Book of Laughter and Forgetting,* trans. Michael Henry Heim (1979; New York: Knopf, 1980), p. 22.

34. Cortázar, "Epílogo a un cuento," in *Deshoras* (México, D.F.: Siglo Veintiuno Editores, 1983), p. 14, my translation.

35. See, for example, Norman O. Brown, "Apocalypse: The Place of Mystery in the Life of the Mind," *Harpers,* May 1961, 46–9; this essay is translated into Spanish in a collection which includes translations of Eric Fromm, Herbert Marcuse, Daniel and Gabriel Cohn-Bendit, entitled *Ensayos sobre el apocalipsis,* ed. Luis Racionero (Barcelona: Editorial Karios, 1973). See also Brown's *Life against Death: The Psychoanalytic Meaning of History* (Middletown, Connecticut: Wesleyan University Press, 1959).

36. Cortázar, *A Manual for Manuel,* trans. Gregory Rabassa (1974; New York: Pantheon, 1978), p. 389.

37. Paz, "Revolt, Revolution, Rebellion," in *Alternating Current,* pp. 143–4, Paz's emphasis.

38. Henry James, "Preface to *Roderick Hudson,*" in *The Art of the Novel,* ed. R. P. Blackmur (1907; reprint, New York: Charles Scribner's Sons, 1962), p. 6.

CHAPTER 5.

1. John Barth, "The Literature of Exhaustion," *The Atlantic,* Aug., 1967, pp. 29–34. Reprinted in *The American Novel since World War II,* ed. Marcus Klein

(New York: Fawcett Publications, 1969), p. 274. Citations are from the reprinted source.

2. Barth, "Muse, Spare Me," *Book Week,* 26 September, 1965, pp. 28–9. Reprinted in *The Sense of the Sixties,* ed. Edward Quinn and Paul J. Dolan (New York: Free Press, 1968), p. 440. Citations are from the reprinted source.

3. For my comments on Scheherazade here as elsewhere in this chapter, I am indebted to Wendy B. Faris, "1001 Words: Fiction against Death," *The Georgia Review,* 36, iv(1982), 811–30, in which Faris discusses the uses of the figure of Scheherazade in the fiction of Barth, Borges, Proust, and Nabokov.

4. Earl E. Fitz has pointed to a particular Latin American literary influence on Barth's own work, in "The Influence of Machado de Assis on John Barth's *The Floating Opera,*" *The Comparatist,* 10 (May 1986), 56–66.

5. José Ortega y Gasset, "Notes on the Novel," in *The Dehumanization of Art and Other Writings on Art and Culture,* trans. Willard A. Trask (Garden City, N.Y.: Doubleday, 1956), p. 56. The essay was originally published in 1925 under the title, "Ideas sobre la novela." See *Obras completas* (Madrid: Revista de Occidente, 1955), III, pp. 387–419.

6. Borges refers to Ortega's theory of literary exhaustion and takes partial exception to it in a prologue to a novel by Bioy-Casares, written in 1940. Borges's reference to *The Dehumanization of Art* at the outset of the prologue, even to refute it, suggests its importance at the time. See "Prologue to *The Invention of Morel,*" in *Borges: A Reader,* eds. Emir Rodríguez Monegal and Alastair Reid (New York: E.P. Dutton, 1981), pp. 122–4.

   See also Peter G. Earle, "Ortega y Gasset in Argentina: The Exasperating Colony," *Hispania,* 70, iii (1987), 476–86, and Roberto González Echevarría, "Borges, Carpentier, y Ortega: Dos textos olvidados," *Revista Iberomericana,* 43 (1977), 697–704. González Echevarría cites texts by Borges and Carpentier on the occasion of Ortega's death in 1955 which are revealing in this question of Ortega's influence on the esthetics of that generation of Latin American writers. González Echevarría notes that Borges's objections to Ortega may have been based as much on political grounds as on the stylistic ground which Borges himself proposes in his note of eulogy. This seems likely, for Borges's assertion that he was hardly familiar with the work of Ortega is dubious, as his discussion of Ortega in his 1941 prologue to *The Invention of Morel* shows.

7. Barth, *The Floating Opera* (1956; rev. ed., Garden City, N.Y.: Doubleday and Company, Inc., 1967), p. 3. Subsequent page references are noted in the text.

8. Barth, *LETTERS* (New York: G. P. Putnam's Sons, 1979), p. 279.

9. Barth, *The End of the Road* (1958; New York: Bantam Books, 1967), p. 196. Subsequent page references are noted in the text.

10. G. E. Lessing, *Laökoon,* trans. Dorothy Reich (1766; London: Oxford University Press, 1965).

11. Frank Kermode, *The Sense of an Ending: Studies in the Theory of Fiction* (New York: Oxford University Press, 1967), p. 133.

12. John Enck, "John Barth: An Interview," *Wisconsin Studies in Contemporary Literature,* 6 (1965), 11.

13. José Ortega y Gasset, "The Dehumanization of Art," in *The Dehumanization of Art and Other Writings on Art and Culture,* pp. 3–54.

14. Seminal discussions of Barth's "self-consuming" fiction are by Tony Tanner, "The Hoax that Joke Bilked," *Partisan Review* 34 (Winter 1967), 102–9; Beverly Gross, "The Anti-Novels of John Barth," *Chicago Review* 20 (November 1968), 95–109; Richard Poirier, "The Politics of Self-Parody," *Partisan Review* 35 (Summer 1968), 339–53; and John Stark, *The Literature of Exhaustion: Borges, Nabokov, Barth* (Durham, N.C.: Duke University Press, 1974). In *American Apocalypses: The Image of the End of the World in American Literature* (Baltimore: Johns Hopkins University Press, 1985), Douglas Robinson opposes the idea of the "self-decreation" of *Giles Goat-Boy*, arguing that a community is in fact ultimately established and affirmed by the novel (pp. 222–32). More convincing is Walter L. Reed's argument that the self-consuming nature of Barth's fiction, especially in *The Sot-Weed Factor*, results from the author's subversion of certain traditional myths about American history: See *An Exemplary History of the Novel: The Quixotic versus the Picaresque* (Chicago: University of Chicago Press, 1981), pp. 252–61.

15. Julio Cortázar, *We Love Glenda So Much*, trans. Gregory Rabassa (1980; New York: Knopf, 1983), pp. 129–45.

16. Barth, *Lost in the Funhouse* (1968; New York: Bantam Books, 1969), p. 90, emphasis Barth's. Subsequent page references are noted in the text.

17. Hugh Kenner, *A Homemade World: The American Modernist Writers* (New York: William Morrow and Co., Inc., 1975), p. 211.

18. Barth, "A Gift of Books," *Holiday* 40 (December, 1966), 171.

19. Joe David Bellamy, "Algebra and Fire: An Interview with John Barth," *Writer's Yearbook* (1972), 70–2, 120–1.

20. Barth, *Chimera* (1972; Greenwich, Connecticut: Fawcett Publications, 1973), p. 215. Subsequent page references are noted in the text.

21. David Morrell discusses the central place of Scheherazade in Barth's thinking about narration in *John Barth: An Introduction* (University Park and London: The Pennsylvania State University Press, 1976), pp. 135–6.

22. See Bruno Bettelheim, "The Frame Story of the Thousand and One Nights," in *The Uses of Enchantment: The Meaning and Importance of Fairy Tales* (New York: Knopf, 1976), p. 87. Bettelheim explains that translators and compilers who worked on the tales often took the figure of 1,001 literally, adding tales to make up the requisite 1,001.

23. *Chimera*, p. 32 (emphasis Barth's). See pages 12, 42, 46, 52, 55 for references to series of seven; see pages 35, 44, 59 for instances where temporal progression, potentially infinite, is carefully controlled by elaborate numerical patterns.

24. *The Arabian Nights' Entertainment, or, The Thousand and One Nights*, trans. Edward William Lane (New York: Tudor Publishing Co., 1927), p. 962.

25. Borges, "Commentary on 'The Aleph,'" in *The Aleph and Other Stories: 1933–1969*, ed. and trans. Norman Thomas di Giovanni (New York: E. P. Dutton, 1970), p. 264.

26. Borges, "The Other Death," in *The Aleph and Other Stories: 1933–1969*, p. 111.

27. For this reference to Beverley and for the observations which follow, I am indebted to James Rother, "Parafiction: The Adjacent Universe of Barth, Barthelme, Pynchon, and Nabokov," *Boundary 2, 5, i* (1976), 21–43. Rother finds a modern analogue to Beverley in Bertrand Russell who, Rother asserts,

proposed the notion that the earth was created a few minutes ago and furnished
with inhabitants able to remember only a fictitious past.

28. Rother, p. 32.

29. Barth, "The Literature of Replenishment," *The Atlantic* (Jan. 1980), p. 68.
    Subsequent page references are noted in the text.

30. Barth, "Welcome to College – and My Books," *New York Times Book Review*,
    16 Sept. 1984, p. 37.

31. Barth, *Sabbatical: A Romance* (New York: G. P. Putnam's Sons, 1982), p. 365.

CHAPTER 6.

1. Walker Percy, "Notes for a Novel about the End of the World," *Katallagete*, 3
   (Fall 1970), 9: Reprinted in Percy's collected essays, *The Message in the Bottle*
   (New York: Farrar, Straus and Giroux, 1979), pp. 101–18. Pages cited are
   from the original source.

   For general discussions of Percy's eschatological vision, see Thomas
   LeClair, "The Eschatological Vision of Walker Percy," *Renascence*, 26 (Spring
   1974), 115–22; Cecil L. Eubanks, "Walker Percy: Eschatology and the Politics
   of Grace," *The Southern Quarterly*, 28, iii (1980), 121–36, reprinted in *Walker
   Percy: Art and Ethics,* ed. Jac Tharpe (Jackson, Mississippi: University of Mississippi Press, 1980). For Percy's eschatological cultural and family context, see
   Lewis A. Lawson, "William Alexander Percy, Walker Percy, and the Apocalypse," *Modern Age,* 24, iv (1980), 396–406.

   As the titles of the articles cited above suggest, both *eschatological* and *apocalyptic* are applied by critics to Percy's work, a practice Percy himself encourages by using the terms interchangeably, and by using the term *prophetic* as
   well. Bernard McGinn writes that strictly speaking the eschatological author
   differs from the apocalyptic author more in degree than in kind: The first
   understands events in terms of the end of history, the second is convinced that
   the age is itself about to end and that he or she is witnessing the last events
   themselves. In any case, writes McGinn, "Every Christian view of history is in
   some sense eschatological insofar as it sees history as a teleological process and
   believes that Scripture reveals truths about its End." *Visions of the End,* p. 4.

2. Carlos Fuentes, "La novela como tragedia: William Faulkner," and "William
   Styron en México," in *Casa con dos puertas* (México, D. F.: Joaquín Mortiz,
   1970), pp. 52–78, 144–50. The essay on Styron has been translated by Margaret Sayers Peden in *Review 76* (Spring 1976), 67–70.

3. Fuentes, "William Styron in Mexico," p. 69. Fuentes states that Styron's South
   in *Lie Down in Darkness* (1951) is far from the idealized image of *Gone with the
   Wind* (1936) or the mythic image of *Absalom, Absalom!*. It is rather a South
   inhabited by a prosperous bourgeoisie with memories, however fictionalized,
   of an aristocratic past. This is also Percy's South, though Percy's Christian
   apocalypticism is not as pessimistic as that implied in Styron's allusive title,
   which comes from Thomas Browne's *Urn Burial*. The passage from which the
   title comes serves as epigraph to the novel, and reads, in part: ". . . our longest
   sun sets at right descensions, and makes but winter arches, and therefore it
   cannot be long before we lie down in darkness, and have our light in ashes;
   since the brother of death daily hunts us with dying mementos, and time that

grows old in itself, bids us hope no long duration; diuturnity is a drama and folly of expectation." *Lie Down in Darkness* (New York: The Bobbs-Merrill Co., 1951).

4. For a general discussion of the rapid process of modernization in the South, see Daniel Joseph Singal, *The War Within: From Victorian to Modernist Thought in the South, 1919–1945* (Chapel Hill, N.C.: University of North Carolina Press, 1982), especially Chapter 7, "The Agrarian Response to Modernism."

5. The connection between Percy's existentialism and French existentialist fiction has often been made. Percy himself describes his debt to the French existentialists primarily in terms of narrative procedures rather than philosophical affinity. He says that he admires Sartre because he translated philosophy into fiction: "Sartre's version of existentialism was peculiarly suited to novel writing. So to me it was a very happy example of how a philosopher can work successfully in fiction." Bradley R. Dewey, "Walker Percy Talks about Kierkegaard: An Annotated Interview," *The Journal of Religion*, 54 (1974), 296. Percy comments more specifically in another interview: "A novel like Sartre's *La Nausée* for instance, is a revolution in its technique for rendering a concrete situation, and it has certainly influenced me." Ashley Brown, "An Interview with Walker Percy," *Shenandoah*, 18, iii (1967), 9. See also Zoltan Abadi-Nagy, "A Talk with Walker Percy," *The Southern Literary Journal*, 6, i (1973), 5; Phillip H. Rhein, "Camus and Percy: An Acknowledged Influence," in *Albert Camus,* ed. Raymond Gay-Crosier (Gainesville: University Presses of Florida, 1980), pp. 257–64.

6. Hayden White, "The Burden of History," in *Tropics of Discourse* (Baltimore: Johns Hopkins University Press, 1978), pp. 25–50. White writes, "Both Spengler, in so many ways the progenitor of Nazism, and Malraux, the recognized father of French Existentialism, taught that history was valuable only insofar as it destroyed, rather than established, responsibility toward the past," p. 37. White comments on the ahistoricism of *The Stranger* and *The Rebel,* by Camus, and links Sartre to the "current rebellion against the past," to the sense that art is opposed to history rather than participating in it.

Percy is perhaps the contemporary U.S. writer most influenced by Christian existentialist philosophy and philosophical narration such as Kierkegaard's parables and his *Diary of a Seducer,* but there is a great distance between the Christian and the French existentialist concepts of time, as will become clear in my discussion of Percy's sources. For now, the French existentialist sense of the present may be understood – and implicitly contrasted to Percy's – in the following passage from *La Nausée*. The character Roquentin thinks:

> The true nature of the present revealed itself: it was what exists, and all that was not present did not exist. The past did not exist. Not at all. Not in things, not even in my thoughts. It is true that I had realized a long time ago that mine had escaped me. But until then I believed that it had simply gone out of my range. For me, the past was only a pensioning off: it was another way of existing, a state of vacation and inaction; each event, when it had played its part, put itself politely into a box and became an honorary event: we have so much difficulty imagining nothingness. Now I know; things are entirely what they appear to be – and behind them . . . there is nothing.

Jean-Paul Sartre, *Nausea,* trans. Lloyd Alexander (1938; New York: New Directions, 1964), pp. 95–6. Edith Kern notes that Roquentin begins to see the past "as non-existent and as being retained only by means of words emptied of their content." *Existential Thought and Fictional Technique* (New Haven: Yale University Press, 1970), p. 11.

7. See also Percy's review of Walter M. Miller, Jr.'s *A Canticle for Leibowitz,* in which Percy states that we live "at the end of an age and the beginning of another, at a time when ages overlap. . . ." *The Southern Review,* 7 (April 1971), p. 574.

8. Ihab Hassan, *Radical Innocence: The Contemporary American Novel* (Princeton: Princeton University Press, 1961), p. 79. Allen Tate, in *The Forelorn Demon,* also addresses this opposition, using an image – "the angelic imagination" – which combines with his title to describe the moral dialectic characteristic of the South. Tom More's "chronic angelism–bestialism" in *Love in the Ruins* is an obvious example of this aspect of Southern apocalypticism in Percy's fiction.

9. Interview with William Goyen, in *Had I a Hundred Mouths: New and Selected Stories 1947–1983* (New York: Clarkson N. Potter, 1985), p. 270.

10. Percy, *The Last Gentleman* (New York: Farrar, Straus and Giroux, 1966), p. 23.

11. The term wayfarer points to Percy's sense of the inherent relation between existential alienation and the Christian concept of fallen human nature: "By the very cogent anthropology of Judeo-Christianity, whether or not one agreed with it, human existence was by no means to be understood as the transaction of a higher organism satisfying this or that need from its environment, by being 'creative' or enjoying 'meaningful relationships,' but as the journey of a wayfarer along life's way. . . . human alienation was first and last the homelessness of a man who is not in fact at home." See "The Delta Factor," in *The Message in the Bottle,* p. 24.

Relevant here is J. Gerald Kennedy's discussion of Tom More's vision of social disintegration in terms of Arnold Toynbee's *A Study of History:* "The Sundered Self and the Riven World," in *The Art of Walker Percy,* ed. Panthea Reid Broughton (Baton Rouge: Louisiana State University Press, 1979), pp. 128–36.

12. Percy, *Lancelot* (1977; New York: Avon Books, 1978), p. 272.

13. Percy, *The Moviegoer* (New York: Farrar, Straus and Giroux, 1960), p. 228.

14. In addition to "Notes for a Novel about the End of the World," see in *The Message in the Bottle:* "The Man on the Train," p. 84, and "The Delta Factor," pp. 22*ff,* in which Percy begins section after section with "At the end of an age . . ." or, "The modern age began to come to an end when. . . ."

15. Lewis A. Lawson, "The Gnostic Vision," *Renascence* 32 (Fall 1979), 55.

16. Percy, "Notes for a Novel about the End of the World," p. 6. Percy compares his strategy to Flannery O'Connor's: "How can one possibly write of baptism as an event of immense significance, when baptism is already accepted but accepted by and large as a minor tribal rite somewhat secondary in importance to taking the kids to see Santa at the department store? Flannery O'Connor conveyed baptism through its exaggeration in one novel as a violent death by drowning. In answer to a question about why she created such bizarre charac-

ters, she replied that for the near-blind you have to draw very large simple caricatures. . . . Perhaps it is only through the conjuring up of catastrophe . . . that the novelist can make vicarious use of catastrophe in order that he and his reader may come to themselves." "Notes for a Novel about the End of the World," p. 12.

17. Several of the essays in *The Message in the Bottle* are relevant on this point: "Semiotic and Theory of Knowledge," "The Mystery of Language," and "Symbol as Need"; see also "A Semiotic Primer of the Self" in *Lost in the Cosmos: The Last Self-Help Book* (New York: Farrar, Straus and Giroux, 1983). My essay is also relevant here: "The Reader at the Movies: Semiotic Systems in Walker Percy's *The Moviegoer* and Manual Puig's *La traición de Rita Hayworth*," *The American Journal of Semiotics*, 3, i (1984), 49–67.

18. Percy, "The Delta Factor," in *The Message in the Bottle*, p. 45.

19. J. P. Telotte's suggestion, in "A Symbolic Structure for Walker Percy's Fiction," *Modern Fiction Studies*, 26, ii (1980), p. 232, that Lancelot's development of a language with Anna while in prison is sufficient indication of his potential success in establishing a new world, ignores Lancelot's moral hubris, his arrogation to himself of God's power to impose ends on others, his utter lack of contrition at the murders he has committed in the past, and his plans for violence in the future. All of these moral errors must subvert his vision of a new world in virgin territory.

20. See, for example, Lynn Haims, "Apocalyptic Vision in Three Late Plays by Yeats," *The Southern Review*, 14 (Winter, 1978), 46–65.

21. Kermode writes, "Yeats is certainly an apocalyptic poet, but he does not take it literally, and this, I think, is characteristic of the attitude not only of modern poets but of the modern literary public to the apocalyptic elements. All the same, like us, he believed them in some fashion, and associated apocalypse with war. At the turning point of time he filled his poems with images of decadence, and praised war because he saw in it, ignorantly we may think, the means of renewal. 'The danger is that there will be no war. . . . Love war because of its horror, that belief may be changed, civilization renewed'. " *The Sense of an Ending: Studies in the Theory of Fiction* (New York: Oxford University Press, 1967), p. 98.

22. See the discussion of O'Connor's novel in John R. May, *Toward a New Earth: Apocalypse in the American Novel* (Notre Dame: University of Notre Dame Press, 1972). The title of the novel is taken from the apocalyptic vision in the gospel of Matthew (11:12).

23. Cleanth Brooks, "Walker Percy and Modern Gnosticism," *Southern Review*, 13 (Autumn 1977), 667–87; Lewis A. Lawson, "The Gnostic Vision in Lancelot," *Renascence*, 32 (Autumn 1979), 52–64.

24. Gregor Sebba, "Prelude and Variations on the Theme of Eric Voegelin," *Southern Review*, 13 (Autumn 1977), 655, 652.

25. Voegelin labels these abuses "modern gnosticism." See *The New Science of Politics* (Chicago: University of Chicago Press, 1952), pp. 107–89, and Voegelin's *Science, Politics, and Gnosticism* (Chicago: Henry Regnery Co., 1968).

26. Norman Cohn makes this assertion at the beginning of Chapter 6 of *The*

Pursuit of the Millennium (1957; rev. ed., New York: Oxford University Press, 1970), p. 108.

27. Lewis A. Lawson, "William Alexander Percy, Walker Percy, and the Apocalypse," *Modern Age,* 24, iv (1980), 396–406.

28. Bernard McGinn, in his study of medieval apocalyptic, asserts that Joachim sought to give ultimate historical validation to the institutions of monasticism, in particular to the Spiritual Franciscans. *Visions of the End: Apocalyptic Traditions in the Middle Ages* (New York: Columbia University Press, 1979), p. 129. Norman Cohn explores the medieval millenarian movements engendered by Joachim's vision of the earthly leader who would usher the world into its third and final stage of history. See Chapter 6, *The Pursuit of the Millennium* (1957; rev. ed. New York: Oxford University Press, 1970).

29. Marjorie Reeves, *Joachim of Fiore and the Prophetic Future* (London: S.P.C.K., 1976), pp. 10–11; see also Reeves, *The Influence of Prophecy in the Later Middle Ages* (Oxford: Clarendon Press, 1969), and Reeves and Beatrice Hirsch-Reich, *The Figurae of Joachim of Fiore* (Oxford: Oxford University Press, 1972).

30. Cecil L. Eubanks, "Walker Percy: Eschatology and the Politics of Grace," in *Walker Percy: Art and Ethics,* ed. Jac Tharpe (Jackson, Mississippi: University of Mississippi Press, 1980) p. 134.

31. Reeves, *Joachim of Fiore and the Prophetic Future,* p. 172.

32. Frank Kermode, *The Sense of an Ending,* p. 47.

33. Frank Kermode provides a succinct comparative definition of the two concepts in their historical, biblical sense: "*Chronos* is 'passing time' or 'waiting time' – that which, according to Revelation, 'shall be no more' – and *kairos* is the season, a point in time filled with significance, charged with a meaning derived from its relation to the end." *The Sense of an Ending,* p. 47.

In this context, Kermode cites the two most notable theorists of these temporal concepts; they are Oscar Cullmann, *Christ and Time: The Primitive Christian Conception of Time and History* (New York: Harper, 1952); and John Marsh, *The Fullness of Time* (New York: Harper, 1952). For a rather different discussion of this subject, see James Barr, *Biblical Words for Time* (Naperville: A. R. Allenson, 1962).

34. Romano Guardini, *The End of the Modern World,* trans. Joseph Theman and Herbert Burke (New York: Sheed and Ward, 1956), p. 124.

35. Guardini writes, "The mind of today attempts continually to lock man into categories when he will not fit. Mechanical, biological, psychological or sociological abstractions . . . [ignore] man's very act of being which constitutes a man in the primitive, absolute sense. . . . *The End of the Modern World,* p. 100.

Percy's skepticism about science as a source of ultimate understanding is well known. On this point, see Lewis A. Lawson, "Walker Percy's Indirect Communications," 867–900, and Percy's own assertions on the subject in his essay, "The Loss of Creature," in *The Message in the Bottle,* pp. 46–63, and in "The Coming Crisis in Psychiatry," *America* (5 Jan. 1957), p. 391.

36. Octavio Paz, "Mexico and the United States," trans. Rachel Phillips, *The New Yorker,* 17 Sept. 1979, p. 152. Subsequent references are cited in the text.

37. Guardini argues that the absolute beginning and end affirmed for history by Scripture gave humanity a sense of its own position in the realm of being. The

modern sense of time as limitless, which results from the loss of belief in that beginning and end – the loss, in other words, of an eschatological sense of time – deprives the single historical event of its unique significance. Furthermore, Guardini argues, humanity is deprived of its sense of the uniqueness of its own existence and experience, and hence, of the ability to understand the world in symbolic terms. *The End of the Modern World*, pp. 44ff.

In the context of this kind of ethical critique of modern culture, Thomas J. J. Altizer's book, *Total Presence* (New York: The Seabury Press, 1980), is also relevant. In the final chapter, called "The Solitude of the End," Altizer writes:

> Ever increasingly, as modernization proceeds, authority and legitimacy in all their forms become totally objectified or fully exterior and external, thereby they are wholly divorced from internal assent or meaning, and thereby they also wholly transcend all symbolic or imaginable identity. Objectification now realizes itself as a total presence throughout the whole domain of our public consciousness and life, an objectification which, Kierkegaard was the first to realize, is finally identical with the public realm. But as Kierkegaard so clearly and so prophetically foresaw, the dominance of a public and objective consciousness is only possible by way of the negation and dissolution of an individual and subjective consciousness. . . . We do not need the imagery of "black holes" or thermonuclear explosion to envision an apocalyptic end, we only have to acknowledge the advent of a totally alien and totally present objectivity, an objectivity which brings a real and historical end to all actual or individual subjectivity, and does so with a total and irreversible finality (94–5).

Though I find much to disagree with here, I cite this passage as epitomizing the attitude toward technology and mass society of Guardini and, to a large extent, of Percy.

38. Ashley Brown, "An Interview with Walker Percy," *Shenandoah*, 18 (Spring, 1967), 6.

39. Voegelin, *Israel and Revelation*, Vol. I of *Order and History* (Baton Rouge: Louisiana State University Press, 1956), pp. 1–11. See also Eugene Webb, *Eric Voegelin: Philosopher of History* (Seattle: University of Washington Press, 1981), especially Chapters 2, 3, and 4.

40. I am indebted to my colleague, Ted L. Estess, for making available to me his unpublished manuscript, "Ending and Beginning: Walker Percy's Eschatological Fiction," which includes a detailed discussion of the temporal orientations of Will and Allie in *The Second Coming*.

41. Percy, "Stoicism in the South," *Commonwealth*, 6 July 1956, 343. Though I have concentrated on the political implications of Voegelin's discussion in my treatment of *Lancelot*, Voegelin also addresses the passive subjectivism which Percy refers to as Southern Stoicism. See Voegelin's discussion of gnosticism as cultural archetype in "On Hegel – A Study in Sorcery," *Studium Generale*, 24 (1971), 335–68.

42. Percy, "The Man on the Train," in *The Message in the Bottle*, p. 84.

43. Percy, *The Moviegoer*, p. 171. Of primary interest in this regard is Ortega's *Meditaciones del Quijote* (*Meditations on the Quixote*, 1914). Ortega was, of course, also greatly interested in German romanticism and in twentieth-century German philosophy. He explicitly combines these interests in relevant ways in an essay discussing Goethe's temporal context, where he writes an

extended footnote arguing for the affinity of his own work to Heidegger's *Being and Time*. Although not religious, Ortega was interested in religious questions, and in an essay entitled "Un diálogo" (1927), he expressed his approval of certain German Catholic writers, including Romano Guardini. These connections and others suggest provocative comparative links between Percy and Ortega which have not, to my knowledge, been pursued at all.

44. Martin Heidegger, *Being and Time*, trans. John Macquarrie and Edward Robinson (1927; New York: Harper and Brothers, 1962), Chapter 4, "Temporality and Everydayness." Subsequent references to this work are cited in the text by section number and page.

45. Karl Löwith, in *Meaning in History* (Chicago: University of Chicago Press, 1949), objects to the existentialist minimizing of the essential futurity of the Christian eschaton. Löwith refers to Kierkegaard's emphasis on the "ever *present* situation of being challenged by Christ, here and now, to a final commitment," and to "Rudolph Bultmann's existential interpretation of the Christian eschatology [which] minimizes the fact that *Christian* 'decision' depends on the hope in a *future* fulfillment. . . . Both Heidegger and Bultmann insist that the 'true' futurity of the human and divine *eschaton,* respectively, lies in the instant of our decision. . . . Following Kierkegaard's thesis of 'appropriation' of the objective truth by an existing individual concerned with that truth, Heidegger and Bultmann go so far in appropriating the imminence of death and the Kingdom of God, respectively, as to annul their essential remoteness and givenness" (emphasis Löwith's, pp. 252–3, n. 21). Percy's characters coincide with Heidegger and Bultmann's eschatology, as described by Löwith. In this context, see also Rudolph Bultmann's *History and Eschatology* (Edinburgh: The University Press, 1957).

CHAPTER 7.

1. Jonathan Tittler, "Interview with Carlos Fuentes," *Diacritics,* 10, iii (1980), 49.
2. Carlos Fuentes "La violenta identidad de José Luis Cuevas," in *Casa con dos puertas* (México, D. F.: Joaquín Mortiz, 1970), pp. 239–79; I cite from the bilingual edition, *El mundo de José Luis Cuevas,* trans. Consuelo de Aerenlund (New York: Tudor Publishing Co., 1969), p. 8.
    For a discussion of the specific uses of indigenous myths in a number of Fuentes's novels, see Malva E. Filer, "Los mitos indígenas en la obra de Carlos Fuentes," *Revista Iberoamericana,* No. 127 (1984), 475–89.
3. Alfred MacAdam and Charles Ruas, "Interview with Carlos Fuentes," *The Paris Review,* 20, No. 82 (1981), 169. Fuentes's novel, *Cristóbal Nonato* (1987), is narrated by an unborn fetus on the 500th anniversary of Columbus's landing in the New World, October 12, 1992; this novel would thus seem to push Fuentes's concern with the origins of the individual and the Americas back to their very conception.
4. Fuentes, *El mundo de José Luis Cuevas,* p. 26.
5. Mircea Eliade, *Myth and Reality,* trans. Willard R. Trask (1963; reprint, New York: Harper Colophon Books, 1975), especially Chapter 5, "Time Can Be Overcome," pp. 75–91.

6. Fuentes, "El tiempo de Octavio Paz," in *Casa con dos puertas* (México, D. F.: Joaquín Mortiz, 1970), p. 156, my translation.
7. See Fuentes's comments in Emir Rodríquez Monegal, *El arte de narrar: Diálogos* (Caracas: Monte Ávila Editores, 1968), pp. 113–46.
8. Fuentes, "El otro K," *Vuelta*, 28 (marzo 1979); also published as the prologue to Milan Kundera's *La vida está en otra parte*.; and in English translation as, "The Other K," *Tri-Quarterly*, 51 (Spring 1981), 256–75.
   The second English edition of *Terra Nostra* is published with an afterword by Milan Kundera in which Kundera stresses the apocalyptic character of Fuentes's novel.
9. Fuentes, "La reconquista de utopía," a section of the longer essay, "De Quetzalcoatl a Pepsicoatl," in *Tiempo mexicano* (México, D.F.: Joaquín Mortiz, 1971), p. 39, my translation.
10. Norman Cohn, *The Pursuit of the Millennium* (1957; rev. ed. New York: Oxford University Press, 1970).
11. Jason Weiss, "An Interview with Carlos Fuentes," *The Kenyon Review*, New Series, 5, *iv* (1983), 105, 106.
12. *The New Science of Giambattista Vico,* trans. and eds. Thomas Goddard Bergin and Max Harold Fisch (Ithaca: Cornell University Press, 1970), see especially paragraph 331. The first edition of the *New Science* was published in 1725, the second edition in 1730, and the third, which I use here, in 1744. Further references to paragraphs of the *New Science* are cited in the text.
   The following works have been particularly useful for the purposes of this discussion: A. Robert Caponigri, *Time and Idea: The Theory of History in Giambattista Vico* (Chicago: Henry Regnery Company, 1953); Donald Phillip Varene, *Vico's Science of Imagination* (Ithaca: Cornell University Press, 1981); Isaiah Berlin, *Vico and Herder: Two Studies in the History of Ideas* (New York: The Viking Press, 1976); Hayden White, "The Tropics of History: The Deep Structure of the *New Science*," in *Tropics of Discourse; Essays in Cultural Criticism* (Baltimore: Johns Hopkins University Press, 1978), pp. 197–229.
13. There have been objections to Fuentes's "explanation" of his novel on the grounds that it imposes a singular reading on a multivocal text and that it oversimplifies the historical issues contained in the novel. In this regard, see Fernando García Nuñez, "Herejías cristianas y superposición en *Terra Nostra*," *Cuadernos americanos*, No. 232 (1980), 94–110, and Roberto González Echevarría, *The Voice of the Masters: Writing and Authority in Modern Latin American Literature* (Austin: University of Texas Press, 1985), pp. 86–97.
14. Fuentes, *Cervantes o la crítica de la lectura* (México, D. F.: Joaquín Mortiz, 1976), p. 103, my translation. A slightly different version of this work has been published in English under the title, *Cervantes, or The Critique of Reading* (Austin: University of Texas Press, 1976), and a shortened version in Fuentes's collection of essays, *Myself with Others* (New York: Farrar, Straus and Giroux, 1988), pp. 49–71. I will, however, use my own translations throughout.
15. Fuentes, *Terra Nostra,* trans. Margaret Sayers Peden (1975; New York: Farrar, Straus and Giroux, 1976), pp. 774–5. Subsequent references to this novel are cited in the text.

16. Norman Cohn, *The Pursuit of the Millennium*, pp. 32–3. Bernard McGinn, *Visions of the End: Apocalyptic Traditions in the Middle Ages*, pp. 18–21, 122–3. McGinn reminds us that Virgil also used a Sibylline go-between, the Cumaean Sibyl, to guide Aeneas through the underworld, and to predict the return of the Golden Age. "Now is the last age of the song of Cumae/The great line of the centuries begins anew." Eclogue 4:4–5. See also William L. Siemens, "Celestina as *Terra Nostra*," *Mester*, 11, i (1982), 57–66.

17. Fuentes has commented that he read *The New Science of Politics* shortly after it appeared and that it is one of the most important books he has ever read. My conversation with the author, July 7, 1984, Mexico City.

18. Miguel de Cervantes, *Don Quixote*, trans. J. M. Cohen (Baltimore: Penguin Books, 1950), p. 935. Walter L. Reed places *Terra Nostra* in the Cervantine tradition in *An Exemplary History of the Novel: The Quixotic versus the Picaresque* (Chicago: University of Chicago Press, 1981), pp. 277–80.

19. See Wendy B. Faris, "The Return of the Past: Chiasmus in the Texts of Carlos Fuentes," *World Literature Today*, 57, iv (1983), 578–84.

20. Ezra Pound, *Collected Early Poems of Ezra Pound*, ed. Michael John King (New York: New Directions, 1965), pp. 10–12.

21. Fuentes mis-cites the number of Dante's Canto in the text of *Terra Nostra* as Canto 25. In this and the multitude of other mis-citations and invented facts, *Terra Nostra* can be compared to the texts of Borges's character, Pierre Menard, which, we are told, have enriched the art of reading by a new technique, that of "deliberate anachronism and erroneous attribution." Fuentes has recognized the connection of Dante's line to Ezra Pound's poem, "Near Perigord," which uses it as its epigraph. See Allen Josephs, "The End of *Terra Nostra*," *World Literature Today*, 57, iv (1983), 565.

22. Wendy B. Faris, *Carlos Fuentes* (New York: Frederick Ungar Publishing Co., 1983), pp. 157–8.

23. M. H. Abrams, *Natural Supernaturalism: Tradition and Revolution in Romantic Literature* (New York: W. W. Norton and Co., 1971), pp. 155–6. Abrams writes that for several centuries, the *Zohar* was for many Jews a canonical text, on the level with the Bible and the Talmud. See also Allen Josephs, "The End of *Terra Nostra*," pp. 563–7.

24. Herbert Schneidau, *Sacred Discontent: The Bible and Western Tradition* (Baton Rouge: Louisiana State University Press, 1977), p. 239. Susan M. Bachmann discusses the male-dominant point of view in the Revelation of St. John in "Narrative Strategy in The Book of Revelation and D. H. Lawrence's Apocalypse," Dissertation, SUNY Buffalo, 1984. Also relevant is the sexual identity of the gods in Aztec mythology: See Malva E. Filer, "Los mitos indígenas en la obra de Carlos Fuentes," *Revista Iberoamericana*, No. 127 (1984), pp. 485–6.

25. See Gloria Durán, *La magia y las brujas en la obra de Carlos Fuentes* (México, D. F.: Universidad Nacional Autónoma de México, 1976), translated and augmented as *The Archetypes of Carlos Fuentes: From Witch to Androgyne* (Hamden, Conn.: The Shoe String Press, 1980).

26. For a discussion of this process of fusion and diffusion, see Margaret Sayers Peden, "A Reader's Guide to *Terra Nostra*," *Review*, 31 (1982), 46. Peden

points out that the changing and changeable characters in the novel may be placed in four basic categories: a female character, a power figure, a young adventurer, and a storyteller.

27. See the interview with Carlos Fuentes in *Hispania,* 63 (May 1980), 415.

28. Isaiah Berlin, p. 110; A. Robert Caponigi, p. 144.

29. In the revised edition of *The Pursuit of the Millennium,* Cohn acknowledges his emphasis on the most violent segments of medieval millenarianism. Bernard McGinn points out that though medieval millenarian movements were often proto-revolutionary, some of the movements also served to maintain the political, social, and economic order. See McGinn, *Visions of the End,* pp. 29–35.

30. J. G. A. Pocock, *The Machiavellian Moment* (Princeton: Princeton University Press, 1975), pp. 45–6. Pocock, like McGinn, notes that millenarian groups were not always agents of political instability: "Princes and heretics were, with limits, natural allies; they shared a disposition to undermine the Augustinian monolith by displacing the *nunc-stans* in favor of the eschaton, the *civitas Dei* in favor of Christ's return to his saints at the end of history" (p. 45).

31. Pocock, p. 45. Bernard McGinn describes Joachim's "Third Status" or Age of Spirit, as a "distinctive form of utopianism that sought . . . to give ultimate historical validation to the institutions to which Joachim was most devoted, especially monasticism" (p. 129). Despite Joachim's intentions, however, a variety of groups arrogated to themselves the role of *viri spirituales:* "Although the Spiritual Franciscans are the most noteworthy example, many other religious bands identified themselves at one time or another with the hoped for remnant of spiritual men who would form the seed of the rulers of the age to come." McGinn concludes that Joachim's prophecies have been so constantly influential because "almost from the moment of his death, various groups found in this image a transcendental justification for their own historical importance" (pp. 146–7). Eric Voegelin discusses the extent of Joachim's influence in twentieth-century totalitarian movements in *The New Science of Politics.*

32. Cohn, p. 149. Thomas J. J. Altizer extends the revolutionary significance of medieval millenarianism generally: "The rebirth of apocalypticism in medieval Europe initiated or gave expression to a historical process that was to culminate with the social, political, and cultural revolutions of the modern world." *Total Presence* (New York: The Seabury Press, 1980), p. 55.

33. See Cohn, pp. 180–1, 197.

34. Juan Goytisolo, "Our Old New World," *Review 76,* No. 19 (Winter 1976), 18–19.

35. Wilhelm Franger, *The Millennium of Hieronymus Bosch,* trans. Eithne Wilkins and Ernst Kaiser (London: Faber and Faber, 1952). Franger argues that the misreading of Bosch's work originated in 1599 in the error of Fray José e Sigüenza, a member of the Spanish Order of St. Jerome who wrote a contemporary chronicle of the building of the Escorial. Sigüenza's "misinterpretaton has prevailed unanimously, so that a work unique in the history of art and religion has become petrified into a monument of prejudice" (p. 8).

During Felipe's lifetime, Bosch's triptych hung in his study, a room which connected to the throne room. The work, which apparently meant much to

Felipe, is an odd and intriguing choice for the pious and normally conservative king. Mary Cable, *The Escorial* (New York: Newsweek Book Division, 1971), p. 63.

36. Beyond its three-part structure, *Terra Nostra* abounds in threes, from Joachim's tripartite vision of history to Vico's, who not only conceived of history as having three ages, but also almost everything else as divisible by three, a fact which Fuentes acknowledges in his chapters "Number 3" and "Two Speak of Three." See the introduction to *The Autobiography of Giambattista Vico* (1731), trans. Max Harold Fisch and Thomas Goddard Bergin (1944; rev. ed. Ithaca: Cornell University Press, 1962), pp. 58–9.

The number three becomes for Fuentes an essential "arithmythic" link between Vico, Joachim, and his own multivocal narration. He notes specifically the "eschatological dynamic" associated with trinitarian patterns in *Ulysses* and *Finnegans Wake* (*Cervantes o la crítica de la lectura*, pp. 104–5). Walter L. Reed notes that *Terra Nostra* expresses symbolically the conflict between monolithic imperialism and anarchic pluralism in unitary, binary, and ternary groupings: "Earth emerges as the third, creative term between Heaven and Hell; on earth, between life and death, in the creative medium of memory" (p. 276).

37. Franger, p. 46.

38. An earlier, and no doubt influential, use of an apocalyptic painting to represent a fictional apocalyptic history is Alejo Carpentier's *El siglo de las luces* (México, D. F.: Companía General de Ediciones, 1962). The novel is given the title of the painting by Monsù Desiderio in its English translation: *Explosion in a Cathedral*, trans. John Sturrock (Boston: Little, Brown and Company, 1963). Carpentier describes the emblematic painting:

> the painting was a huge canvas by an unknown Neopolitan master which confounded all the laws of plastic art by representing the apocalyptic immobilization of a catastrophe. It was called "Explosion in a Cathedral," this vision of a great colonnade shattering into fragments in mid-air – pausing a moment as its lines broke, floating so as to fall better – before it dashed its tons of stone down onto the terrified people beneath. ("I don't know how you can look at it," his cousin used to say, though she was strangely fascinated herself in reality by the terrible suspense of this static earthquake, this silent cataclysm, this illustration of the End of Time, hanging there within reach of their hands . . .) (pp. 18–19).

The novel has as its epigraph a phrase from the *Zohar,* and contains a scene in which the canvas is torn, as is the canvas of Bosch's painting in Fuentes's novel.

Roberto González Echevarría notes that Spengler's philosophy is replaced by Vico's as the historiographic basis of Carpentier's later work: "If Spengler posited a circular history whose cycles were repeated throughout the universe, Vico offers an idea of return that does not deny historicity but affirms it." *Alejo Carpentier: The Pilgrim at Home* (Ithaca: Cornell University Press, 1977), p. 259. This connection between Fuentes and Carpentier remains to be explored.

39. In *Cervantes o la crítica de la lectura,* Fuentes contrasts Signorelli's frescoes to medieval icons: "Signorelli's figures and spaces spin, flow, change, dilate. . . . In Signorelli's frescoes, there is only time, or rather, an uncontainable time which battles with space, expanding like the universe itself" (27). Sig-

norelli's use of the nude body as an expressive instrument, not only in his portrayal of the apocalypse but also in his murals and paintings of flagellants, suggests a possible biographical connection with the millenarian group that I have been discussing here.

Fuentes also refers to Signorelli's Orvieto frescoes in his novel *Zona sagrada* (1967) for another purpose, that of suggesting the deeply disturbed state of his narrator: "All those men have their backs to us. There is an impenetrable sodomy – you say – in the murals of the Creation and the Apocalypse; all turn their backs on the ancient terror of dying and being born, but Signorelli turns fear into sensuality, the same as us." Translated by Suzane Jill Levine as *Holy Place* in the collection *Triple Cross* (New York: E. P. Dutton, 1972), p. 125.

40. Norman Cohn discusses two works written "under strong Stoic influence . . . [that] illustrate most vividly the kind of egalitarian phantasy which the ancient world was to bequeath to the Middle Ages" (p. 189). One of these manuscripts, which dates from second-century B.C. Greece and was edited and translated many times during the Renaissance, describes Heliopolis, the City of the Sun. The Stoics derived the sun as a symbol of justice and equality from Chaldean astrology, in which the sun god, like the sun itself, is impartially beneficent.

41. Fuentes chooses to invoke Campanella's utopia, rather than the book which gives its name to the tradition (or Bacon's or Machiavelli's prescriptive utopias, for that matter), because Campanella's *The City of the Sun* is based upon the vision of a world unified under Spanish rule. If the discovery of America provided Thomas More with his fictional device – a narrator just returned from the New World, exotic fauna and flora drawn from the explorers' fantastical accounts, etc. – it provided Campanella with the confirmation of his vision of a single, universal system of governance under Spain. Whereas More's *Utopia* is an intellectual exploration and critique of political and social institutions, Campanella's *The City of the Sun* was part of a practical political campaign. (Campanella was a native of Calabria, Italy, which was then under Spanish rule.) Campanella is, of course, consciously extending the classical tradition to which I have referred in the preceding note, as was Pound in his poem, "Cino " (and as is Fuentes in *Terra Nostra*). Campanella's utopia is thus a complete fusion of nationalism and universalism, and of egalitarian fantasies, both classical and modern.

If Thomas More's intellectual utopia is based on Christian ethics, Campanella's political utopia is based on philosophical principles provided by science and astrology. In Campanella's city, almost all of the social and political activities are determined by astrologers. A section on the measurement of time is particularly interesting for our purposes. Campanella suggests that the raison d'être of the astrologers is to predict the date of the world's end. He explains that they give absolute credence to the coming of the apocalypse; from astronomical anomalies as well as from Christ's word, they know that the world is not eternal and they do not wish to be surprised (like thieves in the night, says Campanella, taking his image from Rev. 16:15) when it happens. Tommaso Campanella, *The City of the Sun: A Poetical Dialogue,* trans. Daniel J. Donno (Berkeley: University of California Press, 1981), p. 109.

42. John Leddy Phelan, *The Millennial Kingdom of the Franciscans in the New World* (1956; rev. ed. Berkeley: University of California Press, 1970), especially Part I, "Eschatology of the Discovery and Conquest of the New World," pp. 1–40. See also Robert Richard, *The Spiritual Conquest of Mexico: An Essay on the Apostolate and the Evangelizing Methods of the Mendicant Orders in New Spain, 1523–1572*, trans. Lesley Byrd Simpson (1933; reprint, Berkeley: University of California Press, 1966).

43. Eugenio Imaz, "Topía y utopía," in *Utopías del renacimiento,* ed. Eugenio Imaz (México, D.F.: Fondo de Cultura Económica, 1982), pp. 15–17; Lesley Byrd Simpson, *Many Mexicos* (1941; rev. ed. Berkeley: University of California Press, 1974), p. 446. See, for a general discussion of the subject, Gastón García Cantú, *Utopías mexicanas* (México, D.F.: Fondo de Cultura Económica, 1978).

44. Simpson, p. 38.

45. See Gregory A. Waller, *"Aguirre, The Wrath of God:* History, Theater, and the Camera," *South Atlantic Review,* 46, ii (1981), 55–69.

46. Fuentes explicitly distinguishes between Marxist dialectics and contemporary communist regimes which have misused Marx's eschatological vision to justify totalitarianism: "La reconquista de utopía," *Tiempo mexicano,* p. 41. In his essay, "The Other K," Fuentes again cites Marx's phrase in the context of considering the totalitarian abuse of utopian thinking: "History, Marx said, first appears as tragedy; its repetition is a farce. Kundera draws us into a history that denies all right to tragedy and to farce in order to consecrate itself perpetually in the idyll" (p. 270).

47. Karl Marx, *The Eighteenth Brumaire of Louis Bonaparte* (Moscow: Foreign Languages Publishing House, 1953), p. 15.

48. See Giorgio Tagliacozzo, ed., *Vico and Marx: Affinities and Contrasts* (Atlantic Highlands, N.J.: The Humanities Press, 1983), especially the essays by Terence Ball, "On 'Making' History in Vico and Marx," pp. 78–93, and Alain Pons, "Vico, Marx, Utopia, and History," pp. 20–37. Benedetto Croce refers to the connection between Vico and Marx in *The Philosophy of Giambattista Vico* (1913), as does Marx's son-in-law, Paul La Fargue, in his *Economic Determinism: The Historical Method of Karl Marx* (1907). Trotsky quotes Vico on the first page of *History of the Russian Revolution* (1932–1933), and Edmund Wilson begins *To the Finland Station* (1940) with Michelet's discovery of Vico.

49. For a discussion of the contrast between Vico and Marx in this regard, see Hannah Arendt, "The Concept of History," in *Between Past and Future* (1961; reprint, New York: Viking Press, 1967), pp. 77–82.

50. Cited by Jeffrey Mehlman, *Revolution and Repetition: Marx/Hugo/Balzac* (Berkeley: University of California Press, 1977), p. 8. Further references are cited in the text.

51. Even Fuentes's playful remark in an interview, that *Terra Nostra* is narrated by a character from *Aura* who wants to write a factual history of the conquest and colonization of the Americas but writes instead a surreal account of a magical world, points in this direction. Jason Weiss, "An Interview with Carlos Fuentes," *The Kenyon Review,* New Series 5, iv (1983), 105.

52. Frances A. Yates, *The Art of Memory* (Chicago: The University of Chicago

Press, 1966), pp. 147–8; See especially Chapter 6, "Renaissance Memory: The Memory Theatre of Giulio Camillo," and Chapter 7, "Camillo's Theatre and the Venetian Renaissance."

53. See Varene, Chapter 4, "Memory." Varene discusses the frontispiece of the *New Science,* which Vico says in his opening sentence is to serve as a conception of the work before it is read, and as an aid to the imagination and memory after it is read. The engraving is a complex collection of symbols which would have been immediately recognized by Vico's contempories: Perhaps because we have lost the ability to "read" such a language, the frontispiece is not considered an integral part of Vico's text. At least we may speculate that this is why it is not published in the standard English translation of the *New Science.*

   Interestingly, in its original Spanish edition, *Terra Nostra* also contains a frontispiece, as well as a drawing on the final page of the novel. The initial pen and ink drawing contains a number of images suggestive of the contents of the novel; the final drawing is based on a most Mexican image, José Guadalupe Posada's smiling skull in a woman's hat. Again, neither of these images is included in the English translation of the work.

54. Varene, p. 106; see also pp. 187–92.
55. Fuentes, *El mundo de José Luis Cuevas,* p. 9.
56. Vico is the *point de départ* of Edward W. Said's *Beginnings: Intention and Method* (New York: Basic Books, 1975).
57. Jason Wiess, "An Interview with Carlos Fuentes," *The Kenyon Review,* 113.
58. Eleanor Wilner, *Gathering the Winds: Visionary Imagination and Radical Transformation of Self and Society* (Baltimore: Johns Hopkins University Press, 1975), pp. 21–2.
59. Fuentes, *El mundo de José Luis Cuevas,* p. 9.

CHAPTER 8.

1. Jacques Derrida, "Economies de la crise," *La Quinzaine littéraire,* octobre 1984, pp. 6–7.
2. Thomas J. Cottle and Stephen L. Klineberg, *The Present of Things Future: Exploration of Time in Human Experience* (New York: The Free Press, 1974), pp. 180–2.
3. See Perry Miller's discussion of the apocalyptic expectations of the early Puritan settlers in *Errand into the Wilderness* (Cambridge: Harvard University Press, 1956), "The End of the World," pp. 217–39. See also John van der Zee's *Bound Over: Indentured Servitude and American Conscience* (New York: Simon and Schuster, 1985), in which it is asserted that as many as half of the early white settlers in North America came as indentured servants.
4. Octavio Paz provides a detailed discussion of these contrasting original attitudes in his essay, "Mexico and the United States," *The New Yorker,* 17 September 1979, 137–53.
5. Alan Riding, "Revolution and the Intellectual in Latin America," *New York Times Magazine,* 13 March 1983, p. 31. See also Octavio Paz's comparative discussion of this point in his collection of essays, *Tiempo nublado* (Barcelona: Seix Barral, 1983), pp. 139–60.

6. Angel Rama, *La ciudad letrada* (Hanover, N.H.: Ediciones del Norte, 1984), pp. 26–7, 33.

7. Russell Reising, *The Unusable Past: Theory and the Study of American Literature* (New York and London: Methuen, 1986).

8. Fredric Jameson, "Third-World Literature in the Era of Multinational Capitalism," *Social Text*, 15 (Fall 1986), 76–7, my italics.

9. Marlise Simmons, "A Talk with Gabriel García Márquez," *New York Times Book Review*, 5 Dec. 1982, p. 7.

10. Augusto Roa Bastos, "Les debía carta. . . ." *Prismal/Cabral*, 12/13 (1984), 139, my translation. Roa Bastos's comments are in the form of a letter addressed to the late Angel Rama, whose important work on the sociology of literature in Latin America I have already cited. See also Frantz Fanon's study of literacy and literary culture in the Caribbean and Africa in the 1950s and early 1960s, *Les Damnés de la terre* (Paris: F. Maspero, 1960), translated into English as *The Wretched of the Earth* (1963); and more recently, Ariel Dorfman's *Hacia la liberación del lector latinoamericano* (Hanover, N.H.: Ediciones de Norte, 1984).

11. Of course there is a separation between literary and mass culture in the United States too, but as I have argued elsewhere, the contemporary response of U.S. writers such as Thomas Pynchon to this separation differs significantly from that of contemporary Latin American writers. See my "Clichés and Defamiliarization in the Fiction of Manuel Puig and Luis Rafael Sánchez," *Journal of Aesthetics and Art Criticism*, 41, iv (1983), 421–36.

12. Mario Vargas Llosa, "Social Commitment and the Latin American Writer," *The Modern Experience*, Vol. 2 of *Readings in Latin American History*, ed. John J. Johnson, Peter J. Bakewell, and Meredith D. Dodge (Durham: Duke University Press, 1985), pp. 455–64.

13. Saul Karsz makes a similar point in relation to the visual arts in Latin America, using the generalized human types in the murals of Mexican artists Rivera, Siqueiros, and Orozco as examples. "Time and Its Secret in Latin America," in *Time and the Philosophies*, ed. H. Aguessy (Paris: UNESCO Press, 1977), pp. 158–62.

14. Jameson, "Third-World Literature in the Era of Multinational Capitalism," p. 69, the author's italics.

15. Saul Bellow, "Culture Now: Some Animadversions, Some Laughs," *Modern Occasions*, 1 (Winter, 1971), 164, 178.

16. Bellow, "The Nobel Lecture," *The American Scholar*, 46 (Summer 1977), 319–20.

17. Bellow, "Culture Now," 163, 171.

18. Bellow, "Culture Now," 178.

19. Walker Percy, "Notes for a Novel about the End of the World," *Katallagete*, 3 (Fall 1970), 9; this essay is reprinted in Percy's collected essays, *The Message in the Bottle* (New York: Farrar, Straus and Giroux, 1979), pp. 101–18.

INDEX

Index